Divided We Sta

Divided We Stand

The 2020 Elections and American Politics

Andrew E. Busch and
John J. Pitney Jr.

ROWMAN & LITTLEFIELD
Lanham • Boulder • New York • London

Published by Rowman & Littlefield
An imprint of The Rowman & Littlefield Publishing Group, Inc.
4501 Forbes Boulevard, Suite 200, Lanham, Maryland 20706
www.rowman.com

6 Tinworth Street, London SE11 5AL, United Kingdom

British Library Cataloguing in Publication Information Available

Library of Congress Cataloging-in-Publication Data

Library of Congress Control Number: 2021931577

ISBN: 9781538141526 (cloth)
ISBN: 9781538141533 (paper)
ISBN: 9781538141540 (electronic)

Dedicated to our mothers,
Mary Katherine Furey Pitney and Maxine Busch

Contents

Preface   ix

Acknowledgments   xv

1 Disrupter, Disrupted: The Trump Presidency   1

2 The Epic Journey of Joseph Robinette Biden:
   The Democratic Nomination   33

3 Disease, Disorder, Downturn: The Interregnum   69

4 Blue over Red: The General Election   109

5 The Imperfect Tie: Congressional and State Elections   147

6 A Republic, If You Can Keep It: Election Aftermath and
   the Future   181

Index   217

Preface

Divided We Stand: We chose this title before the events of January 6, 2021. That day drove home how fitting those words are. A mob of insurrectionists, some armed, stormed the United States Capitol, trashing offices and threatening the people inside. They built a makeshift gallows, shouting, "Hang Mike Pence!" Rioters reportedly came within one hundred feet of Pence and his family.[1] Five people died, including a Capitol Police officer. The mob's actions demonstrated the depth of the nation's political divisions and the virulence of the passions that gushed out. And yet the government stood. That evening, the House and the Senate continued the business that the insurrectionists had tried to stop: the official counting of electoral votes. When it was over, Congress had confirmed the results—by a vote of 306–232, Joseph Biden would be the next president of the United States.

Though legal experts debated the technicalities of the term "incite," it was clear that President Trump's words and actions led to the attack on the Capitol. Repeating the ill-founded charge that Democrats had cheated him out of reelection, he had invited protesters to Washington, tweeting, "Big protest in D.C. on January 6th. Be there, will be wild!"[2] At a rally just before the attack, he told the crowd that they had to fight or they would not have a country anymore. What followed was the first breach of the Capitol by a horde of invaders since the War of 1812.[3] Some attackers waved the Confederate battle flag inside the building, which never happened during the Civil War. And during the bloody siege, terrorized lawmakers reportedly begged for help, but Trump was too busy watching television coverage to respond quickly.[4]

Despite surely knowing the potential for violence, Trump encouraged the gathering, and his political allies promoted it.[5] Just as important, his failure to head off the bloodshed was arguably a violation of his oath of office. Unique among all federal officials, the president has a constitutional duty to take care that the laws be faithfully executed. It would be hard to contend that the president met that duty on that day. One week later, the House impeached him.

In this book, we establish context for these events by analyzing the elections of 2020 and the social fissures that came to light. In that awful pandemic year, police shootings led to mass protests. A September survey found that two-thirds of African Americans supported the protests, compared with one-third of whites and less than half of Hispanics. Three out of four Democrats backed the protests, compared with fewer than one in ten Republicans.[6] A number of the protests turned violent, leading to two dozen deaths, massive property damage, and the injury of hundreds of law enforcement personnel, including an estimated 472 in New York City alone.[7] Some political leaders embraced the extreme rhetoric that often thundered during the protests, and many others rationalized it or looked the other way. We discuss how this protest and violence, and the rhetoric surrounding them, shaped the presidential and congressional races.

The nation was divided on the pandemic. In an international study, the Pew Research Center asked people in twenty developed countries about their trust in scientists. It found that the United States was the most ideologically polarized.[8] Democrats and Republicans split over issues such as masking, contact tracing, and vaccine acceptance.[9] They were also deeply divided over state and local lockdowns and the question of how quickly to end them. There were unruly demonstrations against pandemic restrictions and vaccination, and, in Michigan, the protests degenerated into an alleged plot to kidnap the governor and overthrow the state government.

Democrats and Republicans both became more certain that the other party's stands posed a clear and present danger to the nation. A survey taken in August found that three-fourths of Republicans said that Democratic policies pose a threat, while nearly two-thirds of Democrats said the same of GOP positions. Just 30 percent of Democrats said that GOP policies were mistaken but not dangerous, while 19 percent of Republicans said that of the Democratic agenda.[10] They differed not just on policy preferences but also on basic facts. The insurrectionists believed that there was massive fraud in the 2020 elections. It did no good to show them news accounts, court decisions, and government reports that disproved such claims, because they did not believe such sources. Similarly, the summer rioters were convinced that the police intentionally engaged in the planned murder of Black suspects as a matter of course, though the data do not bear this allegation out. And whether it was the danger of vaccines or the efficacy of lockdowns, those on different sides of the pandemic debate could find an echo chamber to confirm their dubious assumptions. As many have observed, the media technology of the twenty-first century served to harden the knowledge silos. It was easy for partisans to get all of their information from cable television networks and websites that reinforced their views.

Set aside questions of vote fraud and other disputed facts. Americans differed on how to interpret the results of the 2020 elections. Democrats could make these points:

- Biden's raw popular vote total was the largest in history.
- Biden's percentage of the aggregated popular vote was the highest for a challenger since FDR in 1932.
- Biden won a larger share of the popular vote than Trump in 2016, Bush in 2004 or 2000, Clinton in 1996 or 1992, Reagan in 1980, Carter in 1976, Nixon in 1968, Kennedy in 1960, or Truman in 1948.
- Biden was the first challenger to defeat an incumbent since Bill Clinton beat George H. W. Bush in 1992.
- Trump was the first president since Benjamin Harrison in 1892 to lose the popular vote twice in a row.

But, with equal accuracy, Republicans could make these points:

- About 49 percent of the electorate voted against Biden.
- Biden's support was tightly concentrated. He carried only about one out of every six counties in the United States, fewer than any other winning candidate in history.[11] As we discuss in chapter 4, California alone accounted for nearly three-fourths of Biden's popular-vote margin.
- Aside from the 1930s and 1940s, Biden's party has never enjoyed a broad, stable base in presidential elections. In the entire history of the United States, only two non-Southern Democrats have ever won 52 percent or more of the aggregated popular vote: Franklin Roosevelt (all four times) and Barack Obama in 2008.
- Biden's party lost seats in the House of Representatives. As the new session of Congress began, the Senate was split 50–50 and Democrats had the third-smallest House majority in ninety years.[12]

Republicans and Democrats differed over ideologies, facts, and interpretations. These differences, in turn, stemmed from who they were and where they lived. Whites without college degrees made up 57 percent of Republican voters but only 30 percent of Democratic voters. Religiously unaffiliated voters accounted for 38 percent of Democrats but only 15 percent of Republicans.[13] Nearly two-thirds of Republicans told survey researchers that they would prefer to live where houses are larger and farther apart but schools, stores, and restaurants are several miles away. By contrast, most Democrats would rather live in a denser community where schools, stores, and restaurants are within walking distance.[14] These findings seem to bear some relationship to the distribution of the vote. Although the nationally aggregated popular vote gave Biden an edge of just over four percentage points, the picture was different at the local level. In 2020, 58 percent of voters lived in a county where either Biden or Trump won by twenty points or more. In 1976, by contrast, just 26 percent lived in such "landslide counties."[15]

Donald Trump was both a creature and a creator of these divisions in American society. Although his religious affiliation was nominal at most, he enjoyed intense support from white evangelical Christians. This most urban of American presidents won overwhelming margins in rural communities. In both 2016 and 2020, he pledged to be the champion of an America that he did not inhabit, and he warned his followers that the other side posed a mortal threat to their religion, their economy, and their way of life. In August, he said of Joe Biden, "He's going to do things that nobody ever would ever think even possible. Because he's following the radical left agenda. Take away your guns. Destroy your Second Amendment. No religion, no anything. Hurt the Bible, hurt God. He's against God. He's against guns. He's against energy, our kind of energy."[16]

For their part, Democrats had moved far enough to the left that many Americans found Trump's warning to contain more than an inkling of plausibility. Whatever Biden himself wanted to do—and that was not always clear—progressives indicated their agenda included further restricting gun rights, narrowing the constitutional and legal understanding of freedom of religion, and eliminating fossil fuels. To be sure, Trump poured gasoline on the fire, but he was not the only one. And the fire itself has been slowly burning, if not since the world was turning, then at least since the 1960s.

America divided was not America inert. The 2020 election had record voter turnout and record contributions to political campaigns. Despite the limits of the pandemic, people participated in a wide variety of ways. As political analyst Harry Enten writes, "Love him or hate him, President Donald Trump made most Americans feel strongly about politics in a way no politician has in our lifetimes."[17] Only time would tell how this division-driven activity would shape the country's future.

NOTES

1. Ashley Parker, Carol D. Leonnig, Paul Kane and Emma Brown, "How the Rioters Who Stormed the Capitol Came Dangerously Close to Pence," *Washington Post*, January 15, 2021, https://www.washingtonpost.com/politics/pence-rioters-capitol-attack/2021/01/15/ab62e434-567c-11eb-a08b-f1381ef3d207_story.html.

2. Donald J. Trump, Twitter post, December 19, 2020, https://twitter.com/real donaldtrump/status/1340185773220515840.

3. There have been smaller but significant intrusions, including a bomb set off in 1983 by a left-wing terrorist organization and a 1954 invasion by a small group of Puerto Rican nationalists who opened fire in the House chamber and wounded five members of Congress.

4. Ashley Parker, Josh Dawsey and Philip Rucker, "Six Hours of Paralysis: Inside Trump's Failure to Act After a Mob Stormed the Capitol," *Washington Post*, January 11, 2021, https://www.washingtonpost.com/politics/trump-mob -failure/2021/01/11/36a46e2e-542e-11eb-a817-e5e7f8a406d6_story.html.

5. Andrea Salcedo, "Republican AGs Group Sent Robocalls Urging Protesters to the Capitol. GOP Officials Now Insist They Didn't Know about It," *Washington Post*, January 11, 2021, https://www.washingtonpost.com/nation/2021/01/11/gop-robocalls -trump-rally-capitol.

6. Joel Rose, "Americans Increasingly Polarized When It Comes to Racial Justice Protests, Poll Finds," National Public Radio, September 3, 2020, https://www .npr.org/2020/09/03/908878610/americans-increasingly-polarized-when-it-comes-to -racial-justice-protests-poll-f.

7. Don Babwin, "With Anger at Police High, Officers Face Greater Danger," Associated Press, September 27, 2020, https://abcnews.go.com/US/wireStory/anger -police-high-officers-face-greater-danger-73277330.

8. Cary Funk, Alec Tyson, Brian Kennedy and Courtney Johnson, "Science and Scientists Held in High Esteem across Global Publics," Pew Research Center, September 29, 2020, https://www.pewresearch.org/science/2020/09/29/science-and -scientists-held-in-high-esteem-across-global-publics.

9. Michael Dimock and Richard Wike, "America Is Exceptional in the Nature of Its Political Divide," Pew Research Center, November 13, 2020, https://www.pew research.org/fact-tank/2020/11/13/america-is-exceptional-in-the-nature-of-its-political -divide.

10. David A. Cox, "Democrats and Republicans Believe Their Opponents' Policies Threaten the National Interest," Survey Center on American Life, September 30, 2020, https://www.americansurveycenter.org/2020/09/democrats-and-republicans -believe-their-opponents-policies-threaten-the-national-interest.

11. Alan Greenblatt, "It Took Decades for America to Become This Divided," *Governing*, January 5, 2021, https://www.governing.com/now/It-Took-Decades-for -America-to-Become-This-Divided.html.

12. Democrats started with 222 seats; only Republicans after 2000 and 1952 had a smaller majority contingent, with 221. Democrats after 1942 also had 222. https:// history.house.gov/Institution/Party-Divisions/Party-Divisions/.

13. Carroll Doherty, "In Changing U.S. Electorate, Race and Education Remain Stark Dividing Lines," Pew Research Center, June 2, 2020, https://www.pewresearch .org/politics/2020/06/02/in-changing-u-s-electorate-race-and-education-remain-stark -dividing-lines/.

14. Bradley Jones, "Big Houses, Small Houses: Partisans Continue to Want Different Things in a Community," Pew Research Center, February 18, 2020, https://

www.pewresearch.org/fact-tank/2020/02/18/big-houses-small-houses-partisans-continue-to-want-different-things-in-a-community.

15. Bill Bishop, "For Most Americans, the Local Presidential Vote Was a Landslide," *Daily Yonder*, December 17, 2020, https://dailyyonder.com/for-most-americans-the-local-presidential-vote-was-a-landslide/2020/12/17.

16. Donald Trump Speech Transcript at Ohio Airport August 6: Says Joe Biden "Against God," August 6, 2020, https://www.rev.com/blog/transcripts/donald-trump-speaks-at-ohio-airport-transcript-august-6-says-joe-biden-against-god.

17. Harry Enten, "How Trump Made People Care About Politics Again," CNN, January 2, 2021, https://www.cnn.com/2021/01/02/politics/trump-politics-analysis/index.html.

Acknowledgments

We want to thank Jessy Nesbit for her invaluable work as a research assistant. We also want to thank Jim Ceaser for the many years he devoted to this election series. We missed him enormously, but he couldn't have picked a smarter time to decide he had seen enough.

Chapter One

Disrupter, Disrupted

The Trump Presidency

One cannot write a story of the 2020 election without starting with Donald Trump and his administration. Attempting to summarize the Trump presidency from 2017 to 2020 in a coherent way, however, is not an easy task.

Is the story one of key events, issues, or policy departures? Held together by scandals, semi-scandals, and pseudo-scandals? Made sensible by reference to public opinion? Defined by the relationship between Trump and the media, or between Trump and Democrats? Was the key theme of the Trump years the institutional question of Trump's handling of, and effect on, the presidency? Or was it the growing partisan and social polarization that became an increasingly worrisome feature of American politics? There were so many cross-cutting stories that it was hard to make sense of them all. One thing was certain: Donald Trump promised to be the Great Disrupter, and there was little doubt that he had accomplished that, for better or worse.[1] And that was before the wild ride of the year 2020 made what came before look tame by comparison.

Amid the multitudinous storylines that formed the overall arc of Trump's presidency, two broad narratives emerged. His opponents would say that he was a narcissistic proto-authoritarian, a vicious demagogue, and an incompetent administrator who was dismantling many of the norms of civility and self-control that American democracy requires to flourish (and possibly to survive). His supporters would counter that Trump was trying to drain an arrogant, corrupt, and self-serving Washington swamp and to restore much-needed balance after the progressive excesses of the Obama years, but he was fought every step of the way by a national media that had given up even the pretense of neutrality and by Democrats who were driven to madness, embracing the far left as if Henry Wallace had returned from the grave to avenge himself.

1

What neither supporters nor opponents could admit was that they might both be right. The election might be, as many argued, a "binary choice," but a realistic description of American politics was not an either/or proposition. The forces arrayed against each other were locked in a symbiotic spiral of conflict, each convinced that the other represented an existential threat.

DISRUPTION FROM THE GOLDEN ESCALATOR TO INAUGURATION

From January 2017 to January 2020, a succession of events created a veritable roller coaster of national politics. Some were engineered by Trump and others were thrust upon him, but he wound up at the center of them all.

Of course, the story began with the election of 2016, a contest that Trump won despite the fact that almost no analysts expected him to.[2] (The two most notable exceptions were the film-maker Michael Moore and creator of the *Dilbert* comic strip Scott Adams, neither of whom were expert political prognosticators.) Already a well-known business personality and reality television star, Trump had burst into the political world in July 2015 when he descended the golden escalator at Trump Tower in New York to announce his candidacy for the presidency after having held no prior political offices. He immediately began offending people, saying, "When Mexico sends its people, they're not sending their best. . . . They're sending people that have lots of problems, and they're bringing those problems with us. They're bringing drugs. They're bringing crime. They're rapists. And some, I assume, are good people."[3] Almost as quickly, he took the lead in the polls from the putative frontrunner, Jeb Bush. Facing a crowded field of sixteen other Republican contenders, Trump broke through with brash (and often obnoxious) tweets, packed rallies, and a message of frustration with the nation's political elite of both parties. Though Trump lost the first-in-the-nation Iowa caucuses to Senator Ted Cruz, he bounced back in New Hampshire and never really looked back. In the process, he insulted all of his major primary opponents (each of whom received a degrading nickname fashioned by Trump), numerous media personalities, John McCain, a Hispanic federal judge, the Muslim family of a U.S. Marine killed in action, and many others. He also generated more energy than any candidate in the field and benefited from an estimated $2 billion in free media by mid-March.[4]

On Labor Day, Trump trailed Hillary Clinton by a solid (though not insurmountable) margin. He fell further behind in early October, when a long-buried tape of a Trump interview with Billy Bush on *Access Hollywood* surfaced. In the tape, Trump bragged about varying sexual exploits, some of which seemed to meet the definition of assault. Trump's support cratered, as dozens of Republicans withdrew their endorsements; even House Speaker Paul Ryan stopped campaigning with him.[5] However, the crisis happened just long enough before Election Day that Trump had time to recoup.

He was also lucky in his opponent. If Trump was the most disliked presidential nominee since polling began, Hillary Clinton came in a close second. She also had scandals of her own hanging around her neck, including the State Department's conduct and subsequent obfuscation when U.S. ambassador to Libya J. Christopher Stevens was killed by terrorists during Clinton's watch and her use of an unsecure email server while secretary of state, which was the subject of an FBI investigation. In late October, Republican voters began "coming home" to Trump in large numbers, and he shocked the nation by winning a series of key swing states in the Rust Belt—Ohio, Iowa, Pennsylvania, Michigan, and Wisconsin, the last three by the skin of his teeth. Trump also benefited from certain fundamentals in place in 2016. A slow and uneven recovery from the "Great Recession" had left most Americans dissatisfied with the economy and the overall state of the nation; roughly three in five said the country was on the "wrong track."[6] Clinton was also trying to win a third consecutive term in the White House for her party, a feat that has been performed successfully only one other time in seven tries since 1960. Not least, though media accounts of Trump were overwhelmingly negative, his tweets and rallies garnered more attention and enthusiasm than Clinton's more cautious, traditional campaign.

In the end, the Electoral College vote was not close—Trump won states with 306 electoral votes, Clinton states with 232. In the nationally aggregated popular vote, however, Trump trailed Clinton by three million votes, or about 46 percent to 48 percent, after having lost California by about 4.3 million votes. Though Clinton held a plurality of popular votes, neither candidate won the support of a majority of Americans, and the tidal wave of Latino and women's votes for Clinton, widely predicted by analysts, did not materialize. In exit polls, majorities held that both Trump and Clinton were not honest and trustworthy. Additionally, 63 percent of voters said that Trump did not have the temperament to be president; one in five of them voted for him anyway.[7]

Civil unrest began in the streets late on election night, leading to sometimes violent protests in New York, San Francisco, Portland, Denver, Cleveland, Minneapolis, and Columbus, Ohio, among other places, in the following days.[8] Some universities set up special counseling services for students and staff who were traumatized by Trump's victory.[9] A national network of demonstrations were held in state capitals on the December day when electors met to cast their votes, protesting Trump's probable victory and encouraging electors of both parties to disregard their pledges and form a bipartisan coalition to elect someone else (though the prominent figures who were mentioned as possible beneficiaries of such votes rejected the effort).[10] Ultimately, two electors pledged to Trump and five pledged to Clinton defected to vote for someone else, the largest number of "faithless electors" for president since 1872 but far fewer than needed to elect an alternate candidate or throw the election into the House.[11]

DISRUPTION ARRIVES IN THE WHITE HOUSE

When Donald Trump took office on January 20, 2017, it was clear that he had his work cut out for him. He had not become a less divisive figure since Election Day. Protests dogged Trump's inauguration on January 20 and recurred in force at numerous points over the next four years, especially in October 2018 and the late spring and summer of 2020.

His inaugural address emphasized his campaign themes. The new president began by thanking President and Michelle Obama for their "gracious" and "magnificent" aid in the transition; then he proceeded to indict the entire political establishment without regard to party: "For too long, a small group in our Nation's Capital reaped the rewards of government, but the people have borne the cost. Washington flourished, but the people did not share in its wealth."[12] He represented the solution, Trump argued, which was that the people must reassert control over the government. Borrowing a New Deal term, "The forgotten men and women of our country will be forgotten no longer." Trump then pointed to inner-city poverty, rusted-out factories, a failed education system, and crime, drugs, and gangs that defied the dreams of ordinary Americans. "This American carnage," he declared, "stops right here and stops right now."

Turning to the world, Trump indicted the establishment for enriching foreign countries at the expense of Americans, and promised that "From this day forward, it's going to be only America first, America first . . . America will start winning again, winning like never before." Breaking from prior notions of "nation-building" and humanitarian intervention, Trump announced that "we do not seek to impose our way of life on anyone, but rather to let it shine as an example." He did not completely eschew cooperation with other countries, though, as he promised to reinforce old alliances and create new ones in the fight against radical Islamic terrorism.

The speech was longer on a recitation of troubles, and shorter on lofty rhetoric, than many inaugural addresses, and it received a mixed reaction from analysts. Some saw it as dark, divisive, accusatory, and perhaps impolite; after all, the living presidents sitting behind Trump as he spoke were responsible for the trade deals and the nation-building exercises he condemned.[13] Others celebrated his assertion of popular control over the apparatus of government, a theme embraced by storied American leaders from Jefferson to Jackson to Reagan, and noted his nods to national unity. "[W]hether we are Black or Brown or White, we all bleed the same red blood of patriots," Trump had concluded. Like the analysts, the people seemed divided. The first Gallup poll to come out after the inauguration, taken from January 22–24, showed that 46 percent of Americans approved of Trump's job performance, while 45 percent disapproved.[14] For the next three years, through a steady stream of notable events, nothing much changed.

The disruptive moments began on January 27, 2017, when Trump signed Executive Order 13769 (Protecting the Nation from Foreign Terrorist Entry into the United States), suspending for 90 days the entry of certain aliens from seven countries: Iran, Iraq, Libya, Somalia, Sudan, Syria, and Yemen.[15] At one point during the campaign, he had pledged to block immigration of Muslims to the United States before moderating his position. This executive order was an even more limited attempt to appeal to the spirit of his initial pledge. It provoked immediate outrage from critics who equated it with (and sometimes incorrectly called it) a "Muslim ban," and was haphazardly implemented, leading travelers to be stranded unexpectedly.[16] Federal courts blocked the first two versions of the order. After extended legal wrangling, the Supreme Court upheld the third version of the ban, Presidential Proclamation 9645, which included the countries of Chad, Iran, Iraq, Libya, North Korea, Syria, Venezuela, and Yemen. Trump deemed these countries either friendly to terrorism or suffering from "failed states" that generated internal anarchy.[17] Trump had chosen to lead with a divisive issue that stirred his base rather than an issue such as infrastructure that might have crossed party lines. In this choice, he followed the footsteps of Bill Clinton (who advanced health care reform ahead of welfare reform) and George W. Bush (who led his second term with Social Security reform over tax reform). Whatever the wisdom of their selections, though, Clinton and Bush had led with ambitious structural reforms. Trump's first weeks were dominated by a largely symbolic issue.

Trump then pivoted into a bigger issue, and a bigger campaign promise: the attempted repeal of Barack Obama's Patient Protection and Affordable Care Act (ACA). Since 2010, Republicans had made it a priority to repeal the ACA, which they saw as a big-government takeover of the health care system. Though Mitt Romney had made such a pledge and lost in 2012, the GOP had gained control first of the House in 2010 and then of the Senate in 2014, largely on the basis of opposition to Obamacare. And now Trump had run and won on a promise to repeal and replace the ACA. For the first time, the president and both houses of Congress were on the same page—or seemed to be. Moreover, there were good reasons to revisit the act. Significantly fewer people than expected had signed up, insurance costs were an estimated 25 percent higher than they would have been without the ACA, and Obama's promise that people could keep the insurance they had if they liked it had long ago been exposed as hollow, earning him the "Lie of the Year" award from *Politifact*.[18]

Nevertheless, with a narrow 51–49 majority in the Senate (if one counted as Democrats two Independent senators who caucused with them), Republicans bogged down in the details of what to replace the ACA with. There was no consensus among Republicans favoring one of the many approaches on offer, and public opinion, which had narrowly favored repeal as recently as the 2016 election, turned supportive of the ACA in early 2017, a textbook example of the effect of "loss aversion" in public opinion.[19] People, in this theory, are more afraid of the negative potential of change than they are hopeful that good consequences will materialize. When Obamacare passed, most Americans were worried about what might result. Now that it was the entrenched status quo, they were worried about what might happen if it went away. When it came to health care, regardless of the flaws of the status quo, disruption was not desirable. Perhaps decisive was the fact that Trump knew little about health care policy, did not seem interested in learning, and was unable or unwilling to provide any sustained leadership on the issue, which would have required him to become an educator and a persuader.

Despite the obstacles, after one false start, the Republican House passed a repeal-and-replace bill in April. The Senate worked on one approach but pulled up short of the fifty-one votes needed under reconciliation rules. Senate Republicans came back later with a different approach, handing most authority back to the states, but again came up just short in July when John McCain held out to the last minute and then dramatically signaled thumbs down. The seven-year-long Republican effort to bring down the ACA legislatively was at an end. Americans on the left were angry they had tried; those on the right were angry they had failed.

In the meantime, even more raw anger seized the day in Charlottesville, Virginia. Extreme right forces including the Ku Klux Klan, neo-Nazis, and the "Alt-Right" leader Richard Spencer sponsored a "Unite the Right" rally protesting the city's plans to remove Confederate statues. The nation endured the bizarre spectacle of neo-Nazis holding a tiki torch assembly on the grounds of Thomas Jefferson's university. Far left forces, including Antifa, converged on Charlottesville to do battle. Caught in the crossfire were more ordinary demonstrators protesting the neo-Nazis. On August 12, a neo-Nazi drove a car into the crowd of protestors, killing a woman. For a moment, one could imagine Charlottesville as the streets of Berlin in 1931.

Initially, Trump unequivocally condemned the neo-Nazis, saying, "Racism is evil, and those who cause violence in its name are criminals and thugs, including the KKK, neo-Nazis, white supremacists, and other hate groups that are repugnant to everything we hold dear as Americans."[20] At a press conference the next day, he said, "Well, I think the driver of the car is a disgrace to himself, his family, and this country." At the same press conference, however, he seemed to water down his comments, saying, "You had some very bad people in that group, but you also had people that were very fine people, on both sides."[21] His defenders would long maintain that he was referring to both ordinary protestors (simply supporting the statues) and ordinary counterprotestors (who objected to the KKK and neo-Nazis) and was equally critical of the white supremacists and the violent left.[22] His critics accused him of asserting a moral equivalency between pro- and anti-Nazi demonstrators.[23] Whether he was blowing a white supremacist dog whistle or was taken out of context, he paid a heavy political price. By a 2–1 margin, Americans disapproved of Trump's response to Charlottesville; a year later, a small plurality agreed that he was a racist.[24] Three years later, Trump was still paying a price for Charlottesville.

While focus was heavily on the violent "Unite the Right" elements seen in Charlottesville, their violent counterparts in Antifa on the left were flexing their muscles as well, and not just in Charlottesville. Trump's victory had mobilized and activated Antifa, though it was not new. In multiple episodes in Portland, Berkeley, Charlottesville, and elsewhere, so-called "black bloc" militants, frequently armed with simple weapons, intimidated and assaulted a growing list of enemies.[25] Though Antifa stood for "anti-fascist," by the summer of 2017, it made clear that it considered as "fascist" all conservatives, Trump supporters, capitalists, and law enforcement personnel. Others on the far left went solo. In June, Bernie Sanders volunteer and Occupy Wall Street supporter James T. Hodgkinson shot House Majority Whip Steve Scalise and four others at a House Republican baseball practice.[26]

Throughout 2017, Trump was buffeted by the Russia investigation. Weeks before the inauguration, the intelligence community issued a report concluding that Russia had provided some assistance to the Trump campaign, with the probable goal of disrupting the American political system. (This conclusion was bolstered by subsequent information revealing that Bernie Sanders and Green Party candidate Jill Stein had also been beneficiaries of Russian aid, as had both pro- and anti-police groups engaged in demonstrations.[27]) The FBI was already engaged in a counterintelligence investigation trying to ascertain whether the Trump campaign had been complicit. Attorney General Jeff Sessions recused himself overseeing the investigation, leaving that task to deputy attorney general Rod Rosenstein. On May 9, Trump fired FBI director James Comey, and a week later former FBI director Robert Mueller was named independent counsel.

Trump had left himself open to suspicions. He had praised Russian strongman Vladimir Putin, had benefited from Facebook ads and social media posts paid for by Russia, and had seemingly invited Russian intervention during the campaign when he said that maybe Russia could find the estimated 30,000 emails missing from Hillary Clinton's private server. His campaign also benefited from what seemed to be Russian hacking of the Democratic National Committee and Clinton campaign. More substantively, he seemed to harbor hopes for a rapprochement with Russia that might restore the de facto alliance against Islamic radicalism that had been helpful in the early days after 9/11. Shortly after taking office, Trump's National Security advisor, General Michael Flynn (ret.), had resigned when it became known he had undisclosed contacts with Russian officials and had lied about it.

However, Trump's desire to improve relations with Russia was not by itself evidence of collusion. After all, it had been Barack Obama, with Clinton as his secretary of state, who had announced his desire for a "reset" in 2009, who had ridiculed Mitt Romney for citing Russia as a major strategic threat in 2012, and who had done little in response to Russia's annexation of Crimea in 2014. Nevertheless, throughout 2017 there was a steady drumbeat of media reports, many of which had to be walked back, implying that investigators had found (or were on the verge of finding) the proof that Trump had colluded with Putin.

The best piece of news for Trump came at the end of the year. After giving up on the ACA repeal, Congress moved to another of House Speaker Paul Ryan's top priorities: a major tax cut and tax reform bill. Democrats almost unanimously announced their vehement and early opposition to the bill. This meant it would not have anything resembling bipartisan support, but Republicans also had freedom to ignore Democratic goals that might have otherwise been attained in negotiations. The end result was a bill that cut personal and corporate income tax rates. Prior to the tax bill, the United States had the highest global statutory corporate tax rate, the third highest average corporate tax rate, and the fourth highest effective corporate tax rate.[28] After the cut, the United States corporate tax rate fell significantly, coming in sixth out of the G7 leading economies and below both the G7 average and the OECD average.[29] Republicans recouped some of the revenue by capping the deduction for state and local taxes (the so-called SALT deduction) at $10,000. Hardest hit by that change were high-income individuals in high-tax (Democratic) states such as California, New York, New Jersey, and Connecticut. Scaling back the SALT deduction had been on the table during the development of the 1986 tax reform bill, but Democrats were heavily involved in the negotiations and could forestall that move with other compromises. In 2017, Democrats played themselves out at the beginning and were in no position to block the change. Polls showed most Americans skeptical of or opposed to the tax bill, which they did not believe would benefit them. Like Democrats who voted for the Affordable Care Act in 2010 despite bad polling, Republicans in 2017 plunged ahead anyway, convinced that views would change once people started seeing the benefits. As they pointed out, about 80 percent of income tax payers would be better off as a result of the bill. They forgot, however, that only slightly more than half of "tax units" in America pay income tax.[30] Polling on the bill did improve a bit over time, but not enough to make it popular.[31] Like the ACA for Democrats from 2010 to 2017, it became a burden that Republicans had to explain rather than a triumph they could boast.

In early 2018, a government shutdown resulted when Trump and Congress could not reach agreement on spending for Trump's desired border wall with Mexico. The issue was tied up in a broader question of immigration policy. The president had rescinded the Obama executive order legalizing children of illegal immigrants (creating the DACA program, or Deferred Action on Childhood Arrivals) and called on Congress to fashion a legislative solution. Congress, as usual on immigration issues, was stuck. Democrats did not want to fund the wall and resisted other restrictionist components that Trump made a condition of restoring legal DACA protections. From late 2017 until March 2018, a series of compromise proposals were floated. At the end, a solution looked possible but was (depending on whom you believed) blown up by Steven Miller, the immigration restrictionist who served as a key Trump advisor, or congressional Democrats, who tried to sneak in a provision allowing essentially unrestricted immigration for several months before the pact would take effect.[32] Finally, Trump signed the necessary appropriations without getting what he wanted. Instead, he declared an emergency on the border, allowing him to reprogram about $5 billion of Defense Department money to begin building the wall anyway, a maneuver that was challenged but ultimately upheld by the Supreme Court.

By this time, the immigration issue had become more polarized in other ways. Trump had ordered increased deportations and had sought to cut off federal law enforcement grants to cities and states that had declared themselves "sanctuary cities" for illegal aliens. He also declared a "zero tolerance" policy requiring prosecution of illegal border-crossers. Great controversy arose out of an administration decision on how to handle those with children. In theory, there were three basic ways to approach the issue: hold parents and children together; hold parents and children separately, placing children in shelters or foster homes; or do not hold them at all (what critics sometimes referred to as "catch and release") in the (usually vain) hope that they would voluntarily appear for their hearing rather than disappear into society. The final option was unacceptable to Trump. The first route, keeping families together in detention, was foreclosed by the Ninth Circuit Court's *Flores* settlement and subsequent rulings holding that children, whether accompanied or unaccompanied, could not be held in detention for more than twenty days.[33] The Trump administration went to court in 2018 to argue for termination of *Flores* but was unsuccessful. The remaining option—removing children from detention in keeping with the *Flores* settlement and placing them either in shelters or in foster homes—led critics to accuse Trump of ripping children away from their parents. Heart-rending stories of family separation moved elements of the Democratic Party to decry "concentration camps" on the border and to call for abolition of the Immigration and Customs Enforcement (ICE) bureau.[34] In an attempt to square the circle, the administration redoubled efforts to intercept asylum seekers as they were entering the United States, keeping them on the Mexican side of the border, where the *Flores* settlement did not operate.[35]

There was perhaps no other issue on which the chasm between the parties widened so much during the Trump years. Prior to 2017, both parties were relatively moderate on the issue, or at least internally conflicted. Republican presidents, including Reagan and both Bushes, had extolled immigrants in their rhetoric, and Reagan had signed an immigration act in 1986 that offered amnesty to those here illegally. Less than a decade later, Republicans had supported Proposition 187 in California seeking to end state benefits to illegal immigrants and had included in the national welfare reform legislation of 1996 a provision excluding legal immigrants, who must certify that they have a private means of support, from federal welfare payments. For their part, Democrats had objected to Prop 187 and the welfare exclusion, but President Obama had, at least for a time, supported vigorous deportation of illegal immigrants and, like Trump later, was slapped down by federal courts holding him to be in violation of the *Flores* settlement. Several news outlets were embarrassed in late 2019 when they cited a UN report claiming that 100,000 migrant children were detained by the United States in the current year only to retract the stories when it became clear that the figure was actually from 2015. The 2019 figure was closer to 69,000.[36] By 2020, whatever overlap between the parties might have been true was no longer evident or acknowledged. Trump was for tougher immigration policy across the board, legal or illegal, and Democrats were galloping toward a position of open borders.

In the summer of 2018, with the Russia investigation still swirling around him, Trump met Russian President Vladimir Putin in a summit meeting in Helsinki. He was harshly criticized across the spectrum when he seemed to compliment Putin and downplayed the U.S. intelligence community's assessment that Russia had interfered in the 2016 election to the degree that some saw him as more trusting of Putin than of the FBI and CIA. "I have great confidence in my intelligence people, but I will tell you that President Putin was extremely strong and powerful in his denial today," Trump asserted. "I hold both countries responsible. I think the United States has been foolish. We've all been foolish" (with regard to the U.S.-Russia relationship and the probe in particular). Trump went on to criticize the ongoing special counsel's investigation into Russian interference in the 2016 election as "a disaster for our country."[37]

On one side of the media aisle, CNN noted that "Trump's statements amounted to an unprecedented refusal by a US president to believe his own intelligence agencies over the word of a foreign adversary and drew swift condemnation from across the partisan divide."[38] On the other side, *National Review* opined that "the most alarming part of the presser was the palpable satisfaction the president took describing Putin's 'incredible' proposal. Trump is desperate to show that his entreaties to the Russian despot—amid the 'collusion' controversy and against the better judgment of his skeptical advisers and supporters—could bear real fruit. It made him ripe to get rolled."[39] It is never a good sign for a president when he manages to unite CNN and *National Review* against him.

At home, events cascaded toward the upcoming midterm elections, in which Republican control of Congress would be at stake. On June 27, U.S. Supreme Court Justice Anthony Kennedy, the court's "swing vote," announced his retirement, setting off a battle to fill the seat. Trump had already filled one vacancy early in 2017, the seat held by conservative jurist Antonin Scalia. When Scalia died in February 2016, Barack Obama had named Judge Merrick Garland to replace him. But Republicans had gained a Senate majority in the 2014 elections, and they chose not to act on Garland's nomination prior to the election. When Trump took office, he made his own nomination—Neil Gorsuch. Just before losing their Senate majority in 2014, Democrats had abolished the filibuster for lower court appointments, while retaining it for Supreme Court nominations. When some Democrats tried to launch a filibuster against Gorsuch, Republicans responded by finishing what Harry Reid had started, abolishing the filibuster for Supreme Court appointments as well. Gorsuch was approved, and the stage was set for the Supreme Court battle of 2018.

Although Democrats were angry that Obama's pick had been sandbagged, they were much more worried about this new vacancy. Gorsuch was a conservative who replaced a conservative (Scalia). If Trump succeeded in appointing a conservative to replace the moderate Kennedy, it could tilt the Court to the right. Trump named Brett Kavanaugh, a George W. Bush appointee to the

District of Columbia federal circuit court of appeals and a member of the Federalist Society. Kavanaugh had accumulated a strong record and had acquired a reputation as a careful jurist. Attempts by Democrats to divert him in the Senate Judiciary Committee hearings were generally unsuccessful, despite the best efforts of Kamala Harris, Cory Booker, and others. The week before the committee vote was scheduled, which almost all observers believed would result in success for Kavanaugh, the picture was turned upside down.

Democratic Senator Dianne Feinstein announced that one of her California constituents had contacted her months before with an allegation that thirty-six years before, when they were both in high school, Brett Kavanaugh had sexually assaulted her at a party. Within a few days, the woman's name became public—Christine Blasey Ford. Democrats and their supporters in the media, still in the midst of the "Me Too" moment, were outraged, and asserted that Blasey Ford's allegation had to be believed. Republicans found too suspicious both the timing of the announcement and the fact the Blasey Ford changed her story, could not confidently identify the year or the location of the assault, and had almost no evidence to support the accusation, which Kavanaugh flatly denied. The most corroboration she could muster was a set of notes from a session two and a half decades after the alleged event in which she discussed with her therapist an assault perpetrated in her youth by an unnamed assailant. Four people she identified as having been at the party in question—including her best friend, Leland Keyser—denied knowing anything about it. (Keyser would later say Ford's friends tried to pressure her into corroborating the story, but she refused.[40]) To those who believed Blasey Ford's account, Kavanaugh was a spoiled, entitled, and possibly alcoholic frat boy whose actions had disqualified him from the highest court in the land. To Kavanaugh's defenders, Blasey Ford was a liberal ideologue who was allowing herself to be used in a blatant smear of a good man and an accomplished jurist.[41]

Within days, other accusations against Kavanaugh sprang up. But these had even less support. The *New Yorker* published a piece featuring Deborah Ramirez, a woman who lived in Kavanaugh's dorm at Yale who claimed he had performed a lewd act on her while drunk at a dorm party.[42] The *New York Times*, it turned out, had passed on the story and reported that "the *Times* had interviewed several dozen people over the past week in an attempt to corroborate her story, and could find no one with firsthand knowledge. Ms. Ramirez herself contacted former Yale classmates asking if they recalled the incident and told some of them that she could not be certain Mr. Kavanaugh was the one who exposed himself."[43] Ramirez had only made the allegation after spending several days with Democratic lawyers and "memory specialists." Then there was celebrity attorney Michael Avenatti, who trotted out a woman, Julie Swetnick, who claimed that Kavanaugh had been part of a rape gang that made a habit of spiking the punch at parties and then taking advantage of drugged women.[44] The accuser soon walked back the allegations, "admitting that she cannot say for certain that Kavanaugh was part of, aware of or even witnessed the alleged sexual misconduct," though she had seen Kavanaugh standing close to a punch bowl at a party once.[45] And on it went.

Seeing in the media feeding frenzy their opportunity to stop Kavanaugh, Democrats demanded the reopening of hearings and an FBI investigation into Blasey Ford's allegations. When a couple of Republican senators agreed, the hearings were set, Blasey Ford in the morning, Kavanaugh in the afternoon. The day of hearings was a perfect encapsulation of the roller coaster of the Trump years. At lunch, the consensus of the pundits was that Blasey Ford was believable and had done irreparable damage to Kavanaugh's chances. By dinner, the broad agreement, if not quite consensus, was that Kavanaugh had come back, defended himself effectively, and would probably survive.

And survive he did. The renewed FBI investigation turned up nothing. In the end, Kavanaugh's nomination to the Supreme Court was on almost a party-line vote. Only one Democrat voted "yes"—Joe Manchin of West Virginia, who was up for reelection in a tough state. Only one Republican was opposed—Lisa Murkowski of Alaska—though she ultimate abstained to allow Republican Steve Daines of Montana to attend his daughter's wedding. Before the final vote was taken, though, disorder erupted around the country, as mobs on the left swarmed public officials, demanding that they oppose Kavanaugh. U.S. senators were even harangued in the Senate elevators by angry activists—a foretaste of things to come.[46] For a time, the Republican slogan "jobs, not mobs" seemed to have resonance.

MIDTERM DISRUPTION

The Kavanaugh fight cannot be separated from the approaching midterm elections, looming only a few weeks away. It became a major issue, especially in Senate races, where Republicans seemed to benefit. At just the moment leftist mobs began to be an effective issue for Republicans, however, another emotional issue took center stage instead. Starting in Central America and marching through Mexico toward the U.S. border was a caravan of refugees hoping—indeed vowing—to cross the border, with or without legal permission. In response, Trump sent 5,200 troops to the border and promised to repel the caravan.[47] By escalating the issue, the president promoted it to the front rank. While he clearly hoped to mobilize his supporters along with the troops, the actual effect seems to have been to dilute the message coming out of the Kavanaugh fight and to remind moderate suburbanites of the hard edges that had long alarmed them about Trump.

The theme of rampaging leftists was also thrown off by two episodes that demonstrated that anger and violence were not confined to the left. In one, Cesar Sayoc, a Florida convict whose van was plastered with Trump stickers, mailed explosive devices to several Democratic political figures and liberal media outlets, including Barack Obama, Hillary Clinton, George Soros, and the offices of CNN (none exploded). In the other, a violent anti-Semite killed eleven people at a Pittsburgh synagogue. He was no fan of Trump, but, like Sayoc, he did not fit the stereotype embedded in "jobs, not mobs." The temperature in the country was becoming uncomfortably high, and opponents of the Kavanaugh nomination were not the only ones with their fingerprints on the thermostat.

One of the most pronounced patterns in American politics is the tendency of the president's party to lose seats in the midterm congressional elections held halfway through his term. Republicans hoped to escape gravity, defying the midterm curse. Some hoped that economic improvements since January 2017 would buoy them, or that voters would finally come to appreciate the 2017 tax cut, or that gloomy polls were simply wrong. Trump's strongest supporters were firmly convinced he was playing "four-dimensional chess," and his tactical brilliance, though temporarily obscured, would shine through when the votes were tallied. Democrats, by contrast, were certain that Trump was so repugnant to most Americans, and had so thoroughly tarred the GOP, that the verdict on Election Day would be an unambiguous repudiation of the president and his party.

What actually emerged was a split verdict that illustrated the deep divisions in the country. In the House, Democrats gained a whopping forty seats, a win not as big as Republicans had enjoyed in 1994 (fifty-four seats) or 2010 (sixty-three seats), but impressive nonetheless. They did it by making significant gains in suburban districts and by cleaning up on the West Coast, where Republicans lost half of their fourteen House members in California. There, the SALT deduction cap was a deadly issue. While Democratic seat gains were found mostly in the suburbs, the Republican House vote eroded across the board, in suburbs, urban areas, and rural areas alike; among men and women, self-identified Republicans, Independents, and Democrats, whites and nonwhites, and across most income groups. In the House, Trump's "four-dimensional chess" was checkmated.

The House elections also brought to the foreground the leftward shift of the Democratic Party. Most notably, a group of four young progressive women, symbolically led by New York's Alexandria Ocasio-Cortez (AOC), won their primaries and entered the House. Ocasio-Cortez called herself a "democratic socialist" and immediately pushed radical positions on immigration and the environment.

The Senate, however, presented a different picture. There, Republicans made a net gain of two seats, defeating four Democratic incumbents while losing two seats of their own. In the House, all 435 districts hold elections at once, and there is nowhere to hide from national tides. In the Senate, only one-third of seats are up for election every two years, and the map of which states those are in matters a great deal. In 2018, though the GOP held a small majority in the Senate overall, twenty-six of the thirty-five seats up for election were held by Democrats, the most lopsided division in a Senate election in modern times. Moreover, several Democratic senators had to run for reelection in states that had voted for Trump in 2016, some of them by large margins. In the end, some of these, like Joe Manchin of West Virginia and Jon Tester of Montana, held on. Claire McCaskill of Missouri, Joe Donnelly of Indiana, Bill Nelson of Florida, and Heidi Heitkamp of North Dakota did not. Democrats had high hopes of winning Tennessee or perhaps even Texas, where the photogenic Robert Francis "Beto" O'Rourke spent $70 million trying to knock off Ted Cruz, but they fell short. In Utah, voters sent 2012 Republican presidential nominee Mitt Romney to the Senate—a win for Republicans, but not necessarily for Trump.

There have been other historical occasions on which the president's party lost seats in the House but gained seats in the Senate, but none where the outcomes diverged so greatly. To put it another way, the big population centers and the coasts had never been so disconnected from small-town, rural, middle America since the advent of popular election of senators. Another measure of the growing polarization of American politics was manifest in the steadily declining number of states that sent split delegations to the Senate. In 2018, another five states went from a split delegation to a unified party delegation; only one went in the other direction.

In the states, Republicans retained their edge in governorships and state legislatures, though by a reduced margin. Democrats gained seven governorships, but the GOP still held unified control of more state governments after their 2018 losses (twenty-three) than they had held after their big 2010 gains (twenty-one).

THE DISRUPTION CONTINUES:
RUSSIA, IMPEACHMENT, AND VIOLENCE

Optimists hoped that the altered lineup in Washington would settle the nation. Perhaps Trump would be chastened by his House losses; perhaps Democrats would be calmed by knowing that Trump's party did not hold all three elected branches. For a brief moment, the optimists seemed to be on to something. In the lame duck session of Congress held after the elections but before the new Congress took office, a spirit of compromise produced passage of the FIRST STEP Act, bipartisan legislation supported by Trump and endorsed by Black civil rights organizations, which retroactively applied reduced penalties for crack cocaine.[48]

This new Era of Good Feeling lasted about a month. For the next year, partisan warfare and social discombobulation were the themes: Russia, impeachment, and violence were the biggest stories.

Throughout 2018, the Russia investigation ground on, generating a large number of stories, many based on speculation and anonymous sources, and nearly as many presidential tweets. In 2019, the investigation finally reached its culmination. Trump's strongest critics entertained visions of him being frog-marched out of the White House, or at the very least removed from office constitutionally, on the basis of the Mueller probe, visions that the *New York Times* and MSNBC frequently intimated was the likely result. His defenders argued that such a result was unlikely. For one thing, the dubious—and even potentially illegal—origins of the Russia collusion story had become increasingly apparent. For another, Trump's foreign policy showed little sign of accommodation to Russia. Instead, he had supported increased defense spending, had approved military aid to Ukraine in its fight against Russian domination, had authorized military strikes against Russia's ally Syria when the Syrian regime had used chemical weapons against its people, had significantly increased the pressure against Russia's miscreant friends in Iran and Venezuela, and had pressured Germany to cancel its Nordstream 2 natural gas pipeline project with Russia, which together gave Trump a much stronger anti-Russian record than his predecessor. The whole investigation, this thinking went, was, at best, a "nothingburger," if not an attempted coup by the "deep state."[49]

When Mueller's report was finally issued, it fell somewhere in between the two extremes. It did not find evidence of collusion between the Trump campaign or Trump personally and Russia, the *raison d'être* of the whole exercise. The report summed up that "Although the investigation established that the Russian government perceived it would benefit from a Trump presidency and worked to secure that outcome, and that the Campaign expected it would benefit electorally from information stolen and released through Russian efforts, the investigation did not establish that members of the Trump Campaign conspired or coordinated with the Russian government in its election interference activities."[50] Mueller asserted that there were grounds to be concerned that the president had been engaged in obstruction of justice—that is, specifically, obstruction of the Mueller investigation itself, through firing of FBI Director James Comey and private threats (not carried out) to fire Mueller. Even here, Mueller declined to recommend action against Trump, citing the Justice Department's longstanding position that it could not indict a sitting president. Trump's defenders said that (1) Mueller's judgment was affected by his personal friendship with Comey, whose firing had been recommended by Deputy Attorney General Rosenstein; (2) the president, though sorely tempted, never actually carried out his threats against Mueller and had otherwise cooperated with the investigation; and (3) anyway, as chief executive, it was the president's constitutional right to fire subordinates in the executive branch. About two dozen people were indicted through the course of the investigation, but most were Russians who would never stand trial or figures such as General Michael Flynn or Paul Manafort accused of process crimes or (in Manafort's case) crimes committed before his affiliation with the Trump campaign.

Hoping to rescue something from the situation, Democrats scheduled hearings before the House Judiciary Committee and called Mueller as the only witness. Perhaps they could coax something more damning from him, maybe an admission that he thought the president was guilty of obstruction, though the report was more circumspect. This attempt failed. Even liberal commentators said that Muller appeared lackadaisical and even confused, and they acknowledged that he had failed to provide the ammunition Democrats needed to pursue the president further on these lines. From the left, *Vox* opined that "Former special counsel Robert Mueller's congressional testimony on Wednesday was a farce and a tragedy . . . Mueller either could not or would not perform the essential job of enlightening the American public about an issue of vital national importance"[51] The conservative website The Federalist contended that "Not only was Mueller often flustered and unprepared to talk about his own report—we now have to wonder to what extent he was even involved in the day-to-day work of the investigation—but he was needlessly evasive. In the end, he seriously undermined the central case for impeachment of President Donald Trump."[52]

Although Nancy Pelosi and other Democrats continued bringing up the alleged Russia connection from time to time, the Mueller hearing effectively marked the end of the Democratic quest to drive Trump out on that basis. From then on, Trump defenders said, Russia news told a different story: It became clear that the FBI investigation used a dossier of opposition research paid for by the Clinton campaign and was sustained on the basis of FISA court approvals that were later deemed by the Justice Department Inspector General to have been improperly obtained. The IG concluded that the FBI had wrongly obtained a FISA warrant to spy on Carter Page, reporting that the

FBI had "manipulated documents, concealed crucial exonerating evidence, and touted what it knew were unreliable if not outright false claims."[53] In the words of the IG report, "We identified multiple instances in which factual assertions relied upon in the first FISA application were inaccurate, incomplete, or unsupported by appropriate documentation, based upon information the FBI had in its possession at the time the application was filed."[54] The IG disclaimed political bias but identified a total of seventeen errors in the original FISA warrant application and renewals. Trump defenders also said that evidence lent credibility to General Michael Flynn's charge that he was railroaded by the FBI as a means to get at Trump[55] and that the Russian source that provided most of the information for the Steele Dossier may himself have been a Russian spy.[56] In the view of Trump and his supporters, it was the "biggest political scandal in American history,"[57] an attempt by a sitting president and the nominee of his party to use the FBI and CIA to destroy the opposition nominee (and then president).

Trump critics could point to other developments in the Russia story. In May 2019, Attorney General William Barr named Connecticut's U.S. attorney John Durham to investigate the origins of the FBI's Russia investigation. Trump reportedly hoped that the probe would produce a game-changing "October surprise," but by Election Day 2020, it had issued no report. A separate investigation looked into the question of whether officials in the Obama administration had improperly sought the identities of people whose names were blacked out in intelligence documents. It quietly ended without any findings of misconduct. Meanwhile, the bipartisan Senate Intelligence Committee turned up disturbing new information. It declared that Konstantin Kilimnik, with whom Trump campaign chair Paul Manafort had shared inside campaign information, was a Russian intelligence officer.[58] It added that Manafort harbored suspicions about Kilimnik's status but continued to work with him. The report also cast doubt on Trump's written denials that he remembered learning anything about WikiLeaks, the conduit for documents that Russian intelligence were believed to have stolen: "Despite Trump's recollection, the Committee assesses that Trump did, in fact, speak with [Roger] Stone about WikiLeaks and with members of his Campaign about Stone's access to WikiLeaks on multiple occasions."[59]

Almost as soon as the Russia investigation was exhausted, a new threat emerged to Trump's presidency. A whistleblower in the National Security Council staff alleged that Trump had made a phone call to the president of Ukraine, Volodymyr Zelensky, in which he attempted to use U.S. military aid to Ukraine as leverage to persuade the Ukrainian government to investigate the relationship between Hunter Biden and the Ukrainian energy firm Burisma. Biden, son of former vice president (and then Democratic front-runner) Joe Biden, had landed a position on Burisma's board of directors paying $83,000 a month, despite no experience in Eastern Europe and no knowledge of the oil and gas industry, at a time when his father was the administration's point man in Ukraine. The whistleblower allegation actually opened two questions: Was Trump improperly using his authority as president to pressure a foreign government into taking actions that would hurt the campaign of his most likely opponent for reelection? And had Hunter and Joe Biden been engaged in improper influence peddling?

The fact that Democrats immediately went on the attack and Republicans on the defensive was perhaps predictable, but it also demonstrated how thoroughly each side has become entrenched in its position and how little they seem capable of thinking institutionally or even thinking of things if the situation was reversed. When the IRS under President Obama applied extra scrutiny to conservative political groups seeking tax-exempt status, Republicans had recoiled in stern horror. One can only imagine their reaction if he had attempted to leverage a foreign government to investigate one of Mitt Romney's adult children. And, for Democrats, was there really nothing to see here? If, while he was vice president, Dick Cheney's daughter had acquired an $80,000-a-month position on the board of an Iraqi oil firm despite not knowing Arabic and knowing nothing about petroleum, there would have been no cause for concern?

In late September, the White House released a document that summarized the phone call but was not a verbatim transcript. The summary indicated that Trump had suggested Zelensky "look into" Hunter Biden and Burisma. There was no explicit mention of military aid being contingent on such an investigation, but Democrats argued a trade was implicit.[60]

Speaker Pelosi, who had resisted Democratic back-benchers' calls for impeachment on the basis of Russia, alleged violations of the emoluments clause of the Constitution, and other charges, finally gave in. Two sets of hearings were held, one by the House Judiciary Committee and the other by the Intelligence Committee. Democrats used their majority to the maximum effect, and Republicans complained that their witnesses were not permitted. The result was a foregone conclusion. On December 18, the House voted in favor of articles of impeachment on constitutional grounds of high crimes and misdemeanors, specifically "abuse of power" and "obstruction of Congress."[61] Many celebrities expressed their pleasure that Trump was now gone. Alyssa Milano, for example, tweeted that "I expected this moment but I expected to be more joyful. Maybe jump up & do a happy dance. Maybe. But I'm just sad and heartbroken. What he's left behind can't be erased with this vote."[62]

Of course, in reality outside of Hollywood, impeachment by the House is only the first step. To secure removal, the president must be found guilty of the charges by a two-thirds vote of the Senate. As Republicans had done in 1998–1999, Democrats now appealed to the memory of senators like Barry Goldwater, who had forsaken partisanship to tell Richard Nixon in 1974 that he had to go. However, while every Democrat voted in favor of removal, only one Republican senator—Mitt Romney—joined them in voting in favor of the abuse of power article.[63]

Trump and most Republicans had argued that the evidence—particularly the transcript of the phone call between Trump and President Zelensky—showed nothing amiss because there was no open discussion of a quid pro quo. Some conservatives, such as *National Review*'s legal expert Andrew McCarthy, argued that Trump was clearly pressuring Zelensky between the lines but that it didn't ultimately matter. There was no investigation of Hunter, and Trump resumed military aid to Ukraine shortly thereafter anyway.[64] Democrats and other Trump critics contended that the episode revealed a president who was dangerously comfortable abusing power for personal gain, even in the realm of foreign policy, where the interests of the United States must always be foremost.[65]

Throughout, the president's base of support held firm. Polls briefly showed a bare majority in favor of removal, but as time went on, the bare majority turned into a minority. In the meantime, Trump's job average RealClearPolitics approval rating slowly climbed from 41.8 percent on October 24 until it stood at 44.4 percent at the end of January. Perhaps a small subset of voters was giving Trump higher ratings in a negative reaction to impeachment itself. In 1997, Bill Clinton seemed similarly to gain favor partially because the public determined that removal was overkill, despite the president's guilt. Or perhaps Trump was finally reaping a little bit of the popularity that normally accrues to presidents when the economy strong.

And, at the end of December, the economy was strong. Unemployment had reached 3.5 percent, a fifty-year low. Black unemployment was the lowest ever recorded. Job creation was strong, GDP was strong, the stock market was strong. Polls showed that the economy was one of the few areas where a majority of Americans approved Trump's performance. Another parallel with Clinton: some Americans were willing to look the other way because the country was prospering.

Looked at in broader context, if Trump's acquittal was predictable—given fifty-three Republicans in the Senate—so was his impeachment. There had been three other successful House impeachment proceedings in American history. Two resulted in actual impeachments (Andrew Johnson and Bill Clinton), the other in a forced resignation (Richard Nixon). The three historical cases shared numerous political characteristics, which also applied to Trump.[66]

First, the presidents entered office with a question about electoral legitimacy. Johnson was entirely unelected; Nixon and Clinton were each first elected with only 43 percent of the nationally aggregated popular vote. Trump, of course, won in the electoral college despite finishing three million votes short of Hillary Clinton. Moreover, Nixon and Clinton, though reelected, were also dogged by election scandals that undermined their claims to mandate: Clinton in campaign finance in 1996, Nixon in Watergate itself. Similarly, despite the ambiguous end to the Mueller report, the odor of Russian interference continued to hang over Trump's 2016 victory for many Americans.

Second, their opponents saw the targets of impeachment as political flukes, usurpers in the White House. Prior to Nixon's win in 1968, Democrats had won seven of the previous nine presidential elections. Before Clinton crashed the White House gates, Republicans had won five of the previous six. And one cannot get more flukish than attaining the presidency as a result of assassination, as Johnson had done. For his part, Trump followed a string of four Democratic wins (and five leads in the popular vote) in the previous six elections. And of course almost no one believed Trump could win in 2016, so the fluke was not merely statistical. Each of these presidents, Trump included, were confronted by partisan opponents who thought the White House naturally belonged to them.

Third, each of the three impeached or nearly impeached presidents before Trump were seen by wide swaths of the American populace as fundamentally unfit for office from the beginning. Johnson was a hard-drinking pol who showed up to his own inauguration inebriated. Nixon's pejorative nickname, "Tricky Dicky," was earned long before he became president, as was Clinton's sobriquet, "Slick Willie." As we have seen, Trump had entered office after an election in which two-thirds of voters held that he could not be described as honest and trustworthy. In other words, in Trump's case, like the others, there was a widespread perception of moral failing before he had spent even a day in the White House.

Add to this the political environment. Johnson served in the immediate aftermath of a bloody Civil War, Nixon in the midst of the social tumult of the late 1960s and early 1970s, and Clinton toward the beginning of a long upsurge in partisan polarization. Two decades later, with Trump in the Oval Office, that polarization had grown significantly.

Seen through this historical lens, impeachments—including Trump's—may depend as much on political context as on the actual offenses allegedly committed by the president. It is not clear, for example, that Lyndon Johnson's dissembling about Vietnam or Ronald Reagan's defiance of the law in Iran-Contra were less serious than Trump's phone call or Clinton's grand jury perjury. But Johnson and Reagan had recently won big electoral victories, Congress was not eager to remove them, and, as most Americans saw it, they were not under the shadow of preexisting negative assumptions about their moral character. We are not making an argument here about the propriety of either Trump's impeachment or his acquittal—only a historical observation that the factors that led to his impeachment, like each of the others, went much deeper than the conduct in question.

Just before the Ukraine scandal broke, the nation endured another spasm of violence. On August 3, twenty-one-year-old Patrick Crusius walked into a Walmart in El Paso, Texas, and shot forty-six people, killing twenty-three—mostly Hispanic. Some political commentators immediately blamed Trump, pointing to a political manifesto believed to have been posted by the shooter in which he railed against the "invasion" of Mexican immigrants. He said, however, that his views predated Trump and that Trump was not responsible for them. The manifesto also showed him to be a more complicated figure. He sharply criticized both Democrats and Republicans, capitalism and industrial automation, and environmental degradation. He called for limits on immigration and supported a universal basic income and universal health care.[67] The next day, another shooting took place, this time in Dayton, Ohio, where twenty-four-year-old Connor Betts killed nine before being killed by police. Betts had a record of retweeting far left and pro-Antifa social media posts.[68] Together, the killers were emblematic of the general political deterioration and radicalization taking place in America, of which Trump was a part but far from the whole.

Many Americans began to feel extraordinarily vulnerable, though for a variety of reasons. Some saw themselves as potential victims of a mass shooting. Others feared their country was being overtaken by xenophobic violence stoked by a demagogic president. Yet others, hearing Beto O'Rourke (now running for president) promise to confiscate private firearms, feared that their constitutional right to self-defense was in jeopardy. It was another milestone on the road to the national nervous breakdown of 2020.

POLICY DISRUPTION AT HOME AND ABROAD

Throughout the first three years of the Trump presidency, foreign policy was also the scene of frequent disruption. Across that time, President Trump engaged in a trade war with China, a Twitter war with North Korea, and a brief shooting war with Iran, all of which had the potential to escalate out of control. When North Korea resumed missile tests, Trump derided the young dictator Kim Jong Un as "Rocket Man" and threatened to rain "fire and fury" down on him.[69] The high (or low) point of the extended crisis came when emergency officials in Hawaii accidentally triggered a statewide warning that missiles were incoming, along with the message "this is not a drill." But Trump then met with his North Korean rival in a surprise summit meeting, decided he liked him, and extracted an (unenforceable) agreement to stop tests. When the U.S. Embassy in Baghdad was besieged by pro-Iranian mobs in December 2019, the Iranians put General Qasem Soleimani, head of the Iranian Quds Force and director of the Iranian strategic operation from Lebanon to Yemen, on the ground in Iraq, presumably to organize additional trouble. Trump ordered that he be "taken out" with a drone strike. Critics of the move predicted it would lead to full-scale war with Iran, but the Mullahs backed off after launching one missile strike against a U.S. air base in Iraq that injured about a hundred U.S. servicemen but killed none. Around the world, Trump discombobulated traditional U.S. friends, pushing for greater defense spending by NATO allies, moving some U.S. troops out of South Korea and Germany, and scuttling a variety of multilateral agreements, including the Paris Climate Accords and the Iran nuclear deal. In Israel, Trump's decision to move the U.S. Embassy to Jerusalem carried out a promise made by presidents and congresses since the 1990s but never fulfilled because foreign policy experts had considered it too likely to inflame the region. Disruption did not stop at the water's edge.

Trump's economic policy mixed traditional Republican approaches with elements of disruption. The 2017 tax cut was the brainchild of Paul Ryan and represented a Republican commitment to tax cutting that went back at least as far as Ronald Reagan. Like Reagan, Trump also waged war on federal regulation. By the end of the Obama presidency, the *Federal Register*—the annual publication of proposed and promulgated regulations, executive orders, and the like—had reached nearly 100,000 pages. In the first year of the Trump presidency, pages in the *Federal Register* declined to about 62,000, though they edged up again to 72,000 by 2019.[70] Trump had announced that two regulations had to be repealed for each new one promulgated.

However, his spending policy—if there was one—could not have been further from the concerns of the Tea Party movement a few years before. Trump made no effort to match his tax cuts, even partially, with spending cuts, and he essentially abandoned the long (though intermittent) Republican drive to reform the entitlement programs before they bankrupt the country. The deficit soared with no apparent concern from Trump and no pushback from Republicans in Congress. He also discomfited traditional conservative economic analysts with a slew of tariffs designed, he said, to promote fairer free trade. In one case, he could plausibly claim that his strategy led to a new and (for the United States) better trade deal, when the old NAFTA was retired and replaced

by the U.S.-Mexico-Canada (or USMCA) agreement. In other instances, such
as the trade spat with China, the benefits were not so clear. By one estimate,
the trade war with China cost the United States 300,000 jobs and .3 percent of
GDP in exchange for cosmetic concessions on a few issues.[71]

ELEMENTS OF CONSTANCY

Despite this roller coaster of events, there were some elements of constancy
in the Trump presidency from January 2017 to January 2020.

The first was his standing with the public. He came into office after having won 46 percent of the nationally aggregated popular vote. His average
approval rating in public opinion polls as reported by RealClearPolitics did
not exceed that figure at any point in those thirty-six months. After a difficult
2017, when he languished in the high 30s from mid-May until the end of the
year, he also rarely fell below 40 percent approval. Trump's highest RCP
average came on February 3, 2017, at 46.0 percent; his lowest average was
37.1 percent approval on December 15, 2017.[72] Trump had the most stable
approval ratings of any president since polling began.[73] In contrast, Barack
Obama had ranged between 75 percent and 38 percent, George W. Bush between 91 percent and 27 percent.

Not only was Trump's national approval rating uncommonly stable, but
assessments of Trump by party were likewise quite stable. As Pew Research
noted in 2020, "Over the course of his presidency to date, an average of 87%
of Republicans have approved of Trump's handling of the job, compared
with an average of just 6% of Democrats."[74] This 81-percentage-point gap
was much larger than the partisan difference in average ratings for Barack
Obama (67 points) and George W. Bush (58 points). Of course, Bill Clinton,
George W. Bush, and Barack Obama had each in turn set new records in
partisan polarization before Trump, so it was not easy to untangle to what
degree Trump was cause and to what degree effect of polarization. Whatever the case, Republicans, who had only slowly warmed to Trump in 2016,
molded themselves to him throughout his presidency, while Democrats were
automatically repelled by nearly everything Trump proposed. Some analysts
contended that "cocooning"—the tendency of voters to seek news from media and social media sources aligned with their worldview—made voters not
only more partisan but also less likely to shift their opinions based on new
information. When one is cocooning, after all, the new information looks a
lot like the old information, regardless of the facts.

After a mixed appraisal of economic policy by poll respondents in 2017,
Trump established a clear pattern through early 2020. His approval rating on

the economy was higher—sometimes significantly higher—than his overall rating, reaching a peak of 56 percent in early February 2020.[75] Nevertheless, after almost a decade of dissatisfaction under Barack Obama, a solid majority of Americans remained generally dyspeptic under Donald Trump. Asked whether America was on the right track or the wrong track, the "right track" responses wobbled between 29.8 percent (the low, in October 2017) and 41.2 percent (the three-year high, achieved in September 2018).[76]

Another element of constancy, if it can be called that, was Trump's disregard for norms of presidential conduct. To be fair, those norms had been deteriorating for some time, starting with Bill Clinton's extracurricular uses for the Oval Office. Despite his carefully cultivated image of presidential grace and spotlessness, Barack Obama crashed through more than a few norms himself, whether it was publicly comparing House Republicans to domestic terrorists for exercising their constitutional power of the purse or using executive orders in ways that he had explicitly promised not to do.[77] Even in those cases, though, presidents respected the norms in the breach by trying to keep the destruction concealed. Trump openly reveled in the exercise. Whether it was continuing to decline to make public his income tax returns or producing an unceasing avalanche of insulting Tweets directed at political opponents, including wayward members of his own party, Trump simply did not care about traditional boundaries, whether informed by ethics, courtesy, or aesthetics.

Trump's conduct as president led to complaints throughout his presidency that he was tarnishing the office. Some saw him as a looming authoritarian, perhaps more on account of his rhetorical excesses, populist approach, and personal affinity for foreign strongmen than for any policy decision. Others simply saw him as an extreme manifestation of a downward trend observable for many years. Scholar Stephen Knott, for example, argued that Trump represented the nadir of a deterioration in the presidency that started when Thomas Jefferson claimed to speak for "the people" and fastened on to the role of party leader. In Knott's view, the distinctive element of the Founders' presidency was his role as head of state, the unifying, ceremonial head of the country—a role requiring humility, magnanimity, and nonpartisanship. The modern presidency, Knott noted, has largely eschewed this role, and the values undergirding it. Trump, in that sense, was a child of Jefferson, Woodrow Wilson, and Franklin Roosevelt, though an uncommonly crude and boisterous child.[78] The president's defenders were, on balance, less troubled by his explosion of norms. Charles Kesler argued that, "[B]reaking norms is neither good nor bad except as the norms themselves are good or bad. We elect presidents partly to separate the wheat from the chaff: to energize government by shedding or retiring norms that no longer serve the public good, and by adopting fresh ones that do." Moreover, "Most of Mr. Trump's alleged transgressions . . . offend against the etiquette of modern liberalism and modern liberal governance, not the Constitution."[79] Nevertheless, there was little disagreement among observers that the explosion was taking place—only over the degree of damage it was imposing and whether there were compensating benefits for the country.

A final constant was the unremitting hostility of most of the major media, the cultural establishment, and most of the permanent administrative apparatus of the federal government to Trump, and vice versa. From the beginning, Trump assailed the press as an "enemy of the people" and purveyor of "fake news," which seemed to include any news that reflected poorly on him. From the other side, numerous studies confirmed what could be plainly observed, which was that news coverage of Trump was in fact more negative than for any other president in the modern era. Unsourced stories were routinely published, as long as they portrayed Trump in a negative light; at one point after the El Paso shooting, the *New York Times* changed a headline because readers complained that it was too evenhanded toward the president.[80] In 2020, *Times* editor Bari Weiss resigned, saying the "woke" culture of the paper was more interested in promoting predetermined narratives than in reporting facts and giving readers the opportunity to reach their own conclusions.[81] Overall, the Media Research Center calculated that more than 90 percent of broadcast news coverage of Trump was negative.[82] For its part, the world of culture joined the fray when the cast of the musical *Hamilton* stopped a curtain call at a performance attended by Vice President Mike Pence so they could lecture Pence—before he and Trump had even taken office.[83]

Of greater import to the president was the opposition he stirred up in the permanent bureaucracy. In organizations as varied as the National Security Council and the Environmental Protection Agency, career bureaucrats went to atypical lengths to derail Trump's initiatives. Even some political appointees turned against the president after they left the administration—if not before. One anonymous writer who claimed to be currently in the administration wrote a notable piece in the op-ed page of the *New York Times* in the summer of 2019 claiming to be concerned about Trump's stability and reciting instances when he and other appointees conspired to block the president's wishes from being carried out. (In late 2020, it was revealed that "Anonymous" had been Miles Taylor, chief of staff for the secretary of Homeland Security.) Trump's defenders tended to see this phenomenon as evidence that the Washington Swamp was fetid indeed. The more the bureaucrats fought him, in this view, the more he must be doing right. His critics, however, saw the opposition of experienced civil servants or foreign service personnel as a sign that Trump was putting his gut instincts and selfish interests ahead of expert analysis and the public interest.

Above all, the long series of ups, downs, and somersaults meant that, for the first three years of the Trump presidency, disruption itself became a constant. And 2020 was about to become worse.

NOTES

1. Kenneth T. Walsh, "Trump Plays the Role of the Great Disrupter," *U.S. News & World Report*, June 2, 2017, https://www.usnews.com/news/ken-walshs -washington/articles/2017-06-02/president-donald-trump-plays-the-role-of-the-great -disrupter.

2. For an overview of the 2016 election, see James W. Ceaser, Andrew E. Busch, and John J. Pitney Jr., *Defying the Odds: The 2016 Elections and American Politics* (Lanham, MD: Rowman & Littlefield, 2017).

3. "Here's Donald Trump's Announcement Speech," *Time*, http://time.com/ 3923128/donald-trump-announcement-speech/.

4. Nicholas Confessore and Karen Youresh, "$2 Billion Worth of Free Media for Donald Trump," *New York Times*, March 15, 2016, http://www.nytimes.com/ 2016/03/16/upshot/measuring-donald trumps-mammoth-advantage-in-free-media .html?_r=0.

5. Aaron Blake, "Three dozen Republicans have now called on Trump to drop out," *Washington Post*, October 9, 2016, https://www.washingtonpost.com/news/the -fix/2016/10/07/the-gops-brutal-responses-to-the-new-trump-video-broken-down/.

6. https://www.realclearpolitics.com/epolls/other/direction_of_country-902.html.

7. https://www.cnn.com/election/2016/results/exit-polls.

8. Melanie Eversley, Aamer Madhani, and Rick Jervis, "Anti-Trump protests, some violent, erupt for 3rd night nationwide," *USA Today*, November 11, 2016, https://www.usatoday.com/story/news/nation/2016/11/11/anti-trump-protesters -pepper-sprayed-demonstrations-erupt-across-us/93633154/.

9. Diana Lambert, "Universities offer counseling and 'healing spaces' to students distraught over Trump win," *Sacramento Bee*, November 9, 2016, https://www .sacbee.com/news/local/education/article113811743.html.

10. Ed Pilkington, "'Faithless electors' explain their last-ditch attempt to stop Donald Trump," *The Guardian*, December 19, 2016, https://www.theguardian.com/ us-news/2016/dec/19/electoral-college-faithless-electors-donald-trump.

11. In 1872, Democratic nominee Horace Greeley died after the election but before the electors voted. A total of twenty-seven Democratic electors pledged to Greeley voted for someone else, and who could blame them?

12. Donald J. Trump, Inaugural Address Online by Gerhard Peters and John T. Woolley, American Presidency Project, https://www.presidency.ucsb.edu/node/ 320188.

13. For example, T. A. Frank, "TRUMP'S DARK, RAW INAUGURATION SPEECH SHOCKS WASHINGTON," *Vanity Fair*, January 20, 2017, https://www .vanityfair.com/news/2017/01/trump-inauguration-speech-shocks-washington.

14. Lydia Saad, "Trump Sets New Low Point for Inaugural Approval Rating," Gallup, January 23, 2017, https://news.gallup.com/poll/202811/trump-sets-new-low -point-inaugural-approval-rating.aspx.

15. https://www.whitehouse.gov/presidential-actions/executive-order-protecting -nation-foreign-terrorist-entry-united-states-2/.

16. https://www.theguardian.com/us-news/2017/jan/28/airports-us-immigration -ban-muslim-countries-trump.

17. See https://www.supremecourt.gov/opinions/17pdf/17-965_h315.pdf; http:// myattorneyusa.com/presidential-proclamation-9645-restrictions-on-entry-for-nationals -of-certain-countries-travel-ban.

18. Andrew E. Busch, "The Limits of Governmental Accomplishment," in Steven E. Schier, ed., *Debating the Obama Presidency* (Lanham, MD: Rowman & Little-field, 2016), 203–8.

19. Liz Hamel, Ashley Kirzinger, Cailey Muñana, Lunna Lopes, Audrey Kear-ney, and Mollyann Brodie, "5 Charts About Public Opinion on the Affordable Care Act and the Supreme Court," KFF, https://www.kff.org/health-reform/poll-finding/5 -charts-about-public-opinion-on-the-affordable-care-act-and-the-supreme-court/.

20. Molly Rubin, "Full text: Donald Trump says 'racism is evil' in his latest state-ment on Charlottesville," August 14, 2017, https://qz.com/1053270/full-text-donald -trumps-statement-on-charlottesville/.

21. "In Context: Donald Trump's 'very fine people on both sides' remarks (tran-script)," Politifact, https://www.politifact.com/article/2019/apr/26/context-trumps -very-fine-people-both-sides-remarks/.

22. See, for instance, Steve Cortes, "Trump Didn't Call Neo-Nazis 'Fine People.' Here's Proof," RealClearPolitics, March 21, 2019, https://www.realclearpolitics.com/ articles/2019/03/21/trump_didnt_call_neo-nazis_fine_people_heres_proof_139815 .html.

23. David Jackson, "Trump defends response to Charlottesville violence, says he put it 'perfectly' with 'both sides' remark," *USA Today*, April 26, 2019, https://www .usatoday.com/story/news/politics/2019/04/26/trump-says-both-sides-charlottesville -remark-said-perfectly/3586024002/.

24. Scott Clement and David Nakamura, "Poll Shows Clear Disapproval of How Trump Responded to Charlottesville Violence," *Washington Post*, August 21, 2017, https://www.washingtonpost.com/politics/poll-shows-strong-disapproval-of-how -trump-responded-to-charlottesville-violence/2017/08/21/4e5c585c-868b-11e7-a94f -3139abce39f5_story.html; Steven Shepard, "Poll: Majority Says Race Relations Have Gotten Worse under Trump," *Politico*, August 8, 2018, https://www.politico .com/story/2018/08/08/trump-race-relations-poll-766395; Quinnipiac University Poll, "Harsh Words for U.S. Family Separation Policy," July 3, 2018.

25. Peter Beinart, "The Rise of the Violent Left," *The Atlantic*, September 2017, https://www.theatlantic.com/magazine/archive/2017/09/the-rise-of-the-violent -left/534192/.

26. Luke Mullins, "The Terrifying Story of the Congressional Baseball Shoot-ing," *Washingtonian*, May 28, 2018, https://www.washingtonian.com/2018/05/28/ terrifying-story-of-the-congressional-baseball-shooting-steve-scalise/.

27. Michael Collins, "Indictment: Russians also tried to help Bernie Sanders, Jill Stein presidential campaigns," *USA Today*, February 17, 2018, https://www.usa today.com/story/news/politics/2018/02/17/indictment-russians-also-tried-help-bernie -sanders-jill-stein-presidential-campaigns/348051002/.

28. Congressional Budget Office, https://www.cbo.gov/system/files/115th -congress-2017-2018/reports/52419-internationaltaxratecomp.pdf.

29. Tax Policy Center, https://www.taxpolicycenter.org/briefing-book/how-do-us -corporate-income-tax-rates-and-revenues-compare-other-countries.

30. Howard Gleckman, "Remember the 47 Percent Who Pay No Income Taxes? They Are Not Who You Think," *Forbes*, August 6, 2019, https://www.forbes.com/ sites/howardgleckman/2019/08/06/remember-the-47-percent-who-pay-no-income -taxes-they-are-not-who-you-think/#1d6340be47d7.

31. Frank Newport, "U.S. Public Opinion and the 2017 Tax Law," Gallup, April 29, 2019, https://news.gallup.com/opinion/polling-matters/249161/public-opinion -2017-tax-law.aspx.

32. See https://www.theatlantic.com/politics/archive/2017/09/daca-deal-or -no-deal-trump-democrats-dreamers/539784/; https://www.buzzfeednews.com/ article/paulmcleod/senate-group-reaches-tentative-deal-to-protect-dreamers; https:// www.washingtonpost.com/politics/trump-blew-it-the-president-missed-his-best -chance-yet-to-get-funding-for-his-border-wall/2018/03/21/04993950-2d2b-11e8 -8688-e053ba58f1e4_story.html; https://www.washingtonpost.com/politics/trump -blew-it-the-president-missed-his-best-chance-yet-to-get-funding-for-his-border -wall/2018/03/21/04993950-2d2b-11e8-8688-e053ba58f1e4_story.html.

33. History of the Flores Settlement, Center for Immigration Studies, https://cis .org/Report/History-Flores-Settlement.

34. Caroline Kelly, "Ocasio-Cortez compares migrant detention facilities to concentration camps," CNN, June 19, 2019, https://www.cnn.com/2019/06/18/politics/ alexandria-ocasio-cortez-concentration-camps-migrants-detention/index.html.

35. https://academic.oup.com/publius/article-abstract/49/3/379/5530676?redirect edFrom=fulltext.

36. Bill Chappell, "U.N. Expert Clarifies Statistic on U.S. Detention of Migrant Children," November 20, 2019, https://www.npr.org/2019/11/20/781279252/u-n -expert-clarifies-statistic-on-u-s-detention-of-migrant-children; Zachary Evans, "Multiple Outlets Retract Stories on Trump-Admin Child Deportations That Relied on Obama-Era Data," November 20, 2019, https://www.nationalreview.com/news/ multiple-outlets-retract-stories-on-trump-admin-child-deportations-that-relied-on -obama-era-data/.

37. CNN, https://www.cnn.com/2018/07/16/politics/donald-trump-putin-helsinki -summit/index.html.

38. https://www.cnn.com/2018/07/16/politics/donald-trump-putin-helsinki -summit/index.html.

39. https://www.nationalreview.com/2018/07/helsinki-summit-trump-bites-on -putins-incredible-offer/.

40. Yaron Steinbuch, "Friend of Ford told FBI she was pressured into altering statement," *New York Post*, October 5, 2018, https://nypost.com/2018/10/05/

friend-of-ford-told-fbi-she-was-pressured-into-altering-statement/; Jerry Dunleavy, "'Just didn't make any sense': Friend of Kavanaugh accuser Christine Blasey Ford now challenges her story," *Washington Examiner*, September 16, 2019, https:// www.washingtonexaminer.com/news/just-didnt-make-any-sense-leland-keyser-now -challenges-story-of-kavanaugh-accuser-christine-blasey-ford.

41. Mollie Ziegler Hemingway and Carrie Severino, *Justice on Trial: The Kavanaugh Confirmation and the Future of the Supreme Court* (Washington, DC: Regnery, 2019).

42. Ronan Farrow and Jane Mayer, "Senate Democrats Investigate a New Allegation of Sexual Misconduct, from Brett Kavanaugh's College Years," *The New Yorker*, September 23, 2018, https://www.newyorker.com/news/news-desk/senate-democrats -investigate-a-new-allegation-of-sexual-misconduct-from-the-supreme-court-nominee -brett-kavanaughs-college-years-deborah-ramirez.

43. Becket Adams, "How to spot the New Yorker's irresponsible, slipshod reporting on Brett Kavanaugh," *Washington Examiner*, September 24, 2018, https:// www.washingtonexaminer.com/opinion/how-to-spot-the-new-yorkers-irresponsible -slipshod-reporting-on-brett-kavanaugh.

44. Davis Richardson, "New Accusations Against Kavanaugh Include 'Gang Rape,' According to Sworn Statement," *The Observer*, September 26, 2018, https:// observer.com/2018/09/brett-kavanaugh-gang-rape-accusation/.

45. Francesca Chambers, "Senate Judiciary Committee chairman asks DOJ to PROSECUTE Michael Avenatti and client who claimed Supreme Court Justice Brett Kavanaugh was present for high school 'gang rapes,'" *Daily Mail*, October 25, 2018, https://www.dailymail.co.uk/news/article-6317475/Republicans-seek-prosecution -Michael-Avenatti-Kavanaugh-gang-rape-accuser.html.

46. John Bacon and Caroline Simon, "59 arrested near Supreme Court as thousands nationwide rally against Kavanaugh nomination," *USA Today*, September 27, 2018, https://www.usatoday.com/story/news/politics/2018/09/27/brett-kavanaugh -protest-crucial-senate-hearing/1440738002/; Morgan Chalfant and Melanie Zanona, "Scores of Kavanaugh protesters arrested after descending on Senate building," *The Hill*, October 4, 2018, https://thehill.com/homenews/senate/409999-scores-of -kavanaugh-protesters-arrested-after-descending-on-senate-building.

47. Phil Stewart and Yeganeh Torbati, "Trump sends 5,200 troops to Mexico border as caravan advances," Reuters, October 29, 2018, https://www.reuters.com/ article/us-usa-immigration-trump/trump-sends-5200-troops-to-mexico-border-as -caravan-advances-idUSKCN1N31VG.

48. German Lopez, "Congress just passed the most significant criminal justice reform bill in decades," *Vox*, December 20, 2018, https://www.vox.com/policy -and-politics/2018/12/20/18148482/first-step-act-criminal-justice-reform-house -congress.

49. See Andrew C. McCarthy, *Ball of Collusion: The Plot to Rig an Election and Destroy a Presidency* (2019).

50. Special Counsel Robert S. Mueller III, *Report on the Investigation Into Russian Interference In The 2016 Presidential Election*, Vol. I, Department of Justice, March 2019, pp. 1–2.

51. https://www.vox.com/policy-and-politics/2019/7/24/20708503/robert-mueller-testimony-winners-losers.

52. https://thefederalist.com/2019/07/24/the-mueller-testimony-was-a-disaster-for-democrats/.

53. https://theintercept.com/2019/12/12/the-inspector-generals-report-on-2016-fb-i-spying-reveals-a-scandal-of-historic-magnitude-not-only-for-the-fbi-but-also-the-u-s-media/.

54. https://www.justice.gov/storage/120919-examination.pdf, p. viii.

55. Erik Larson and David Yaffe-Bellany, "Flynn Says New FBI Notes Show Misconduct Led to Criminal Charge," *Bloomberg*, July 10, 2020, https://www.bloomberg.com/news/articles/2020-07-10/flynn-judge-gets-reprieve-as-court-weighs-new-dismissal-hearing; Kyle Cheney and Josh Gersten, "Feds air FBI agent's gripes about Flynn probe," *Politico*, September 25, 2020, https://www.politico.com/news/2020/09/25/fbi-agents-michael-flynn-probe-421633.

56. Andrew Desiderio and Kyle Cheney, "Steele dossier sub-source was suspected of spying for Russia, DOJ reveals," *Politico*, September 24, 2020, https://www.politico.com/news/2020/09/24/steele-dossier-russia-doj-421536.

57. Mary Kay Linge, "Trump blasts FBI over Michael Flynn investigation: 'Treason!'" *New York Post*, May 2, 2020, https://nypost.com/2020/05/02/trump-blasts-former-fbi-officials-over-michael-flynn-investigation/.

58. U.S. Senate Select Committee on Intelligence, *Russian Active Measures Campaigns and Interference in the 2016 U.S. Election Volume 5: Counterintelligence Threats and Vulnerabilities*, August 18, 2020, https://www.intelligence.senate.gov/sites/default/files/documents/report_volume5.pdf, vi.

59. U.S. Senate Select Committee on Intelligence, *Russian Active Measures*, 245.

60. "Read Trump's phone call with Ukraine president: Full text," NBC News, September 25, 2019, https://www.nbcnews.com/politics/trump-impeachment-inquiry/read-full-transcript-trump-s-conversation-ukraine-s-president-n1058581.

61. https://www.cnn.com/interactive/2019/12/politics/impeachment-articles-annotated/.

62. Helen Murphy, "Celebrities Including Bette Midler, Cole Sprouse & More React After President Trump Is Impeached," *People*, December 19, 2019, https://people.com/politics/celebrities-react-after-trump-is-impeached/.

63. "How senators voted on Trump's impeachment," *Politico*, February 5, 2020, https://www.politico.com/interactives/2019/trump-impeachment-vote-count-senate-results/.

64. Andrew C. McCarthy, "Why Senate is entirely right to vote down House's impeachment charges," *New York Post*, February 4, 2020, https://nypost.com/2020/02/04/why-senate-is-entirely-right-to-vote-down-houses-impeachment-charges/.

65. Andrew Desiderio and Kyle Cheney, "'The Constitution's final answer': Why Dems say Trump must be removed," *Politico*, January 23, 2020, https://www.politico.com/news/2020/01/23/senate-impeachment-trial-arguments-102712.

66. Andrew E. Busch, "An Utterly Ordinary Impeachment," *Claremont Review of Books* (digital), January 20, 2020, https://claremontreviewofbooks.com/digital/an-utterly-ordinary-impeachment/.

67. https://randallpacker.com/wp-content/uploads/2019/08/The-Inconvenient
-Truth.pdf.

68. Paul P. Murphy, Konstantin Toropin, Drew Griffin, Scott Bronstein, and Eric
Levenson, "Dayton shooter had an obsession with violence and mass shootings, police say," CNN, August 7, 2019, https://www.cnn.com/2019/08/05/us/connor-betts
-dayton-shooting-profile/index.html.

69. Emily Tamkin, "Trump Threatens North Korea with 'Fire and Fury the
World Has Never Seen,'" *Foreign Policy*, August 8, 2017, https://foreignpolicy
.com/2017/08/08/trump-threatens-north-korea-with-fire-and-fury-the-world-has
-never-seen/.

70. Federal Register Pages Published Annually, https://www.llsdc.org/assets/
sourcebook/fed-reg-pages.pdf.

71. Rachel Layne, "Trump trade war with China has cost 300,000 U.S. jobs,
Moody's estimates," CBS News, September 12, 2019, https://www.cbsnews.com/
news/trumps-trade-war-squashed-an-estimated-300000-jobs-so-far-moodys-esti-
mates/.

72. https://www.realclearpolitics.com/epolls/other/president_trump_job_approval
-6179.html.

73. https://www.pewresearch.org/fact-tank/2020/08/24/trumps-approval-ratings
-so-far-are-unusually-stable-and-deeply-partisan/.

74. https://www.pewresearch.org/fact-tank/2020/08/24/trumps-approval-ratings
-so-far-are-unusually-stable-and-deeply-partisan/.

75. https://www.realclearpolitics.com/epolls/other/president_trump_job_approval_
economy-6182.html.

76. https://www.realclearpolitics.com/epolls/other/direction_of_country-902
.html.

77. For a thorough analysis of how Obama pushed the envelope on executive
power, see Louis Fisher, *President Obama: Constitutional Aspirations and Executive
Actions* (Lawrence: University Press of Kansas, 2018).

78. Stephen F. Knott, *The Lost Soul of the American Presidency: The Decline into
Demagoguery and the Prospects for Renewal* (Lawrence: University Press of Kansas,
2019).

79. Charles Kesler, "Breaking Norms Will Renew Democracy, Not Ruin It," *New
York Times*, August 23, 2018, https://www.nytimes.com/2018/08/23/opinion/trump
-democracy-norm-breaking.html.

80. Joan E. Greve, "New York Times changes front-page Trump headline after
backlash," *The Guardian*, August 6, 2019, https://www.theguardian.com/media/
2019/aug/06/new-york-times-front-page-headline-changed.

81. https://www.bariweiss.com/resignation-letter.

82. Jennifer Harper, "Broadcast coverage of Trump 95% negative, according to
new study," *Washington Times*, August 17, 2020, https://www.washingtontimes.com/
news/2020/aug/17/broadcast-coverage-of-trump-95-negative-according-/.

83. Jessica Taylor, "'Hamilton' to Pence: 'We Are the Diverse America Who Are
Alarmed,'" NPR, November 19, 2016, https://www.npr.org/2016/11/19/502687591/
hamilton-to-pence-we-are-the-diverse-america-who-are-alarmed.

Chapter Two

The Epic Journey of
Joseph Robinette Biden

The Democratic Nomination

In our book on the 2008 election, *Epic Journey*, we likened that race to Homer's *Odyssey*. One can describe the outcome of each story in mundane terms. Odysseus set out after the Trojan War to get home, and he got there. And in 2007, long before the parties had chosen their nominees, it seemed likely that John McCain would win the GOP nomination and that the Democrats would win the White House, which is what happened. Yet in each case, the journey to the expected outcome was full of twists and detours.

The quest for the 2020 Democratic nomination was another epic journey. Joe Biden started as the frontrunner and finished as the party's choice. In between, he went through a time where seemed to be an also-ran, fated to end his career with a humiliating loss. But as John McCain did in the 2008 GOP contest, the old man outlasted his rivals.

Biden's half-century in politics added another epic quality to the contest. He had won his first election, to a county office, in 1970. Two years later, Delaware elected him to the United States Senate. No one had ever gone so long between the start of an electoral career and a major-party presidential nomination.[1] When he took the oath for his Senate seat in 1973, he was the sixth-youngest senator in congressional history, having reached the constitutional minimum age of thirty shortly after Election Day.[2] During the 1988 election cycle, he sought the Democratic presidential nomination. If he had won, he would have been the third-youngest president in history, after Theodore Roosevelt and John F. Kennedy.

Instead, his 1988 campaign came to an early and awkward end. A rival campaign leaked a video showing that he had plagiarized a speech by a British political leader. The media piled on with other embarrassing stories, and he eventually withdrew from the race. Technology had helped spring the trap door. In the 1980s, C-SPAN had expanded its coverage to include campaign speeches, and growing availability of VCRs enabled reporters and political operatives to record them. Without these innovations, Biden's missteps might never have come to light.[3]

He ran again in 2008, only to lose the nomination to Barack Obama. Just when it looked as if his aspirations for national office were at an end, Obama picked him as his running mate. After eight years of loyal service to the much-younger man, Biden declined to run in 2016, citing grief over the untimely death of his son Beau. Until late on election night that year, the political community assumed that Hillary Clinton would be the next president and that Joe Biden would just be a beloved retiree. As we recount in *Defying the Odds*, that election turned out differently.

The shock presidency of Donald Trump brought Biden back into the fray. His historically long career was both an asset and a liability. On the one hand, he had deep experience over a wide range of issues and understood the mechanics of legislation better than any presidential contender since Bob Dole. On the other hand, America had changed since he began his Washington life. The Senate of the early 1970s still included unrepentant segregationists such as James Eastland of Mississippi. To pass bills, Biden had to get along with these people. His collegiality seemed unremarkable at the time, but it would expose him to criticism decades later. Similarly, his issue positions became a vulnerability. During his first twenty years in the Senate, violent crime was continuing the steep and deadly ascent that had begun in the early 1960s. Like many other liberal lawmakers, Biden responded to constituent worries by taking tough stances on criminal justice. By the second decade of the new century, crime was dropping and there was growing concern about mass incarceration and police violence. Biden's old positions clashed with the new demands of his party.

DAYS OF FUTURE PAST: DEMOCRATS 1988–2020

The entire Democratic Party was on an epic journey. The nation's demographic and political changes had transformed the party's makeup and the structure of political opportunity. Consider the party's 2020 candidates. More than two dozen Democrats entered the 2020 race, but by mid-November 2019, only Biden and nine others had enough support to get on the television debate stage. A tenth Biden rival, former New York City mayor Michael Bloomberg, would soon enter the contest. This field would have stunned a time traveler from 1988. As of that year, first-time major-party presidential nominees had fit a certain mold, exhibiting a narrow range of background characteristics. Specifically, all had been:

- White
- Male
- Not openly gay
- Christian or nondenominational
- Under seventy
- Experienced in the military or civilian public office

In 2020, *none* of the eleven Democrats checked all of these boxes. Even the most traditional member of the group broke the mold in one important way: our visitor from 1988 surely would have been bemused to learn that Joseph Biden was still running for president thirty-two years later. At age sixty-nine in 1980, Ronald Reagan had become the oldest person ever to win a first term in the White House. In 2016, Trump had pushed the envelope a bit by winning at age seventy. But if voters were to choose Biden in 2020, he would be seventy-eight on Inauguration Day—older when he took office than Reagan was when he left office. And by the time Reagan was preparing to retire, long before his diagnosis of Alzheimer's, there was already public concern about his mental fitness.[4] It seemed unlikely that anybody would think of starting a first term at that age.

Over time, though, Americans adapted to an aging workforce. In 1986, Congress had abolished mandatory retirement at age seventy for most workers, and thirty years later, the enormous baby boom generation started passing that milestone. Age discrimination still existed, but in certain white-collar occupations—especially academia—people became accustomed to gray hair.

A glance at Biden's rivals reinforces the point that the door was open to different kinds of candidates:

- Former Mayor Michael Bloomberg: age seventy-eight in 2020, Jewish
- Senator Cory Booker of New Jersey: African American
- Mayor Pete Buttigieg of South Bend, Indiana: gay
- Representative Tulsi Gabbard of Hawaii: female, Samoan American, Hindu
- Senator Kamala Harris of California: female, African American and Indian American
- Senator Amy Klobuchar of Minnesota: female
- Senator Bernie Sanders of Vermont: age seventy-nine in 2020, Jewish (nonobservant)
- Businessman Tom Steyer: no military or government experience
- Senator Elizabeth Warren of Massachusetts: female, age seventy-one in 2020
- Businessman Andrew Yang: Chinese American, no military or government experience

This field is emblematic of some important demographic and political changes. Start with the experience criterion. Through the 1980s, voters expected that experience as a governor, legislator, Cabinet member, or military officer would show that the candidate had the requisite knowledge and judgment.[5] The 1988 nominees could both boast of standard-issue resumes, but the experience norm was already weakening: Reverend Jesse Jackson showed great strength in the Democratic primaries. In the decades to come, other "inexperienced" candidates would play significant roles in nomination contests. Trump's election in 2016 showed that many voters were not only ready to waive the experience requirement but actively disdained it. Steyer and Yang would probably take offense at the notion that Trump had set a precedent for them—but he had.

Despite the symbolic runs of Margaret Chase Smith and Shirley Chisholm, no female candidate had ever been a serious contender for the presidency as of 1988. Geraldine Ferraro made history in 1984 as the first woman to receive a nomination for vice president, but the Mondale-Ferraro ticket lost forty-nine states and Ferraro never won another election. Representative Pat Schroeder considered running for the 1988 Democratic nomination, but after a tearful withdrawal speech, she endured sexist derision.

On the surface, public opinion seemed ready in 1988. Gallup found that 82 percent of respondents said that they would vote for a well-qualified woman candidate, and 12 percent said they would not.[6] The legacy of gender discrimination, however, had narrowed the pipeline of potential women candidates. In the 100th Congress, there were exactly two women in the United States Senate: Barbara Mikulski of Maryland and Nancy Kassebaum of Kansas. In 1988, there were only three women governors. The sole Democrat among the three, Madeleine Kunin of Vermont, was a naturalized citizen ineligible to be president.

By the second decade of the new century, the pipeline was wider. In 2019, there were nine women governors (six Democrats and three Republicans). Female representation in Congress went from just 5 percent in 1989 to 24 percent thirty years later. Elizabeth Warren and Amy Klobuchar were the first elected women elected to the Senate from their states.[7] And, of course, Hillary Clinton had cracked the glass ceiling by winning the popular vote for president in 2016.

No openly gay person had ever run for president as of the 1980s, and only a single member of Congress had voluntarily disclosed that he was gay. Some state laws made homosexual activity a crime, and in 1986, the Supreme Court had upheld such a law.[8] Public attitudes then changed. In 2007, 41 percent told Gallup that they would not vote for a well-qualified nominee of their own party if that person were a homosexual (the word that the survey used). By 2020, the share that would not vote for a well-qualified lesbian or gay person was down to 21 percent.[9] There was considerable opposition to same-sex marriage in the first decade of the century: in 2008, Californians passed a ballot measure to ban it. But in 2015, the Supreme Court's 5–4 decision in *Obergefell* seemed to settle the issue, and there was no serious effort to overturn it. During the 2020 nomination race, Buttigieg campaigned with his husband, something that would have been impossible in 1988 and extraordinary in 2012. In 2020, Democratic voters largely took it for granted.

In 1988, no Jew had ever been on a national ticket. (Barry Goldwater's father was Jewish, but he grew up in his mother's Episcopal faith.) Pennsylvania Governor Milton Shapp ran for the Democratic nomination in 1976, and Pennsylvania Senator Arlen Specter ran as a Republican twenty years later. Both campaigns sputtered down the memory hole. In 2000, Al Gore chose Senator Joseph Lieberman of Connecticut as his running mate. There was some speculation that the choice would come under attack from evangelical Christians, but most of them applauded the choice because of Lieberman's rectitude. From that point on, few considered Jewish identity as a major political impediment.

What really set Bernie Sanders apart was not his religious background but his embrace of democratic socialism. For more than a century, scholars had puzzled as to why there was no major, durable socialist movement in the United States.[10] Socialists had run as third-party candidates, winning lower-level offices here and there, but no serious candidate for a major party presidential nomination had ever embraced the socialist label. The Cold War deepened Americans' aversion to socialism, as many equated it with communism. It was a grave insult to call a politician a socialist, as the House of Representatives acknowledged. In a House floor speech on April 15, 2011, Representative Mo Brooks (R-AL) referred to "socialist members of this body." Representative Keith Ellison (D-MN) objected, demanding that the words be taken down, a procedural move that could have kept Brooks from speaking on the floor again for the rest of the day. Brooks instead agreed to have the word *socialist* stricken from the record.[11]

Sanders was always forthright about his beliefs, which is why his 1981 election as mayor of Burlington, Vermont, made national news. In 1988, he traveled to the Soviet Union to establish a sister city relationship between Burlington and the Russian city of Yaroslavl.[12] (Though he was a newlywed and his wife accompanied him, the trip was an official visit and not his honeymoon, as critics later charged.[13]) He praised aspects of Soviet society, which would have been politically risky even in the waning years of the Cold War.

By the second decade of the twenty-first century, Cold War memories had gone cold. Especially among the young, what voters did remember vividly was the Great Recession, which darkened public views of capitalism. In 2010, Gallup started asking respondents whether they had positive views of socialism and capitalism. Among Democrats, it was a tie: 53 percent had a positive view of both. Eight years later, Democrats were significantly more positive toward socialism, 57 percent to 47 percent.[14] There is an important caveat: what respondents *meant* by the term differed from the textbook definition—that is, public ownership of the means of production. Americans were more likely to define socialism as ensuring equality for everyone or providing benefits and social services.[15] And high on the list of those benefits was health care. In his 2016 campaign, Sanders had run on single-payer health insurance, which he branded as "Medicare for All." The broad concept—if not the difficult details—found a following in the Democratic Party. In 2016, nearly three-quarters of Democratic identifiers told Gallup that they favored replacing the Affordable Care Act with a federally funded program providing health insurance for all Americans.[16]

In 2018, Representative Joseph Crowley (D-NY), chair of the House Democratic Caucus and the Queens County Democratic Party, suffered a stunning primary defeat at the hands of Alexandria Ocasio-Cortez, who had worked Sanders's 2016 campaign. The election got national attention because the winner was young (age twenty-eight at the time), charismatic, and media savvy. And she was a self-described democratic socialist. In an interview, she explained her understanding of democratic socialism: "We're talking about single-payer health care that has already been successful in many different models, from Finland to Canada to the UK." It also encompassed such measures as a living wage, "so that no person in America is too poor to live," she said. "That's what democratic socialism means in 2018, and not this kind of McCarthyism Red Scare of a past era."[17] But her "Green New Deal" program would greatly increase federal power over the economy. By her own estimate, it would cost at least $10 trillion, and critics put the figure several times higher.[18]

Her victory was also a sign of the growing power of Hispanic voters. That power had not yet reached its full potential, in part because Hispanic voter registration lagged behind population numbers and also because of the diverse interests of Hispanic Americans. Cuban Americans in Florida, for instance, do not necessarily identify with Mexican Americans in Texas. Such political obstacles helped explain why the one Hispanic candidate in the 2020 contest, former San Antonio mayor and HUD secretary Julian Castro, did not get enough support to make the debate stage in late 2019.

By contrast, African Americans had long established their clout in Democratic nomination politics. Once again, the 1988 election provides a point of departure. In the Democratic primaries, Jesse Jackson had much more success in consolidating African American support than he had four years before. He also reached beyond his demographic base to bring in white progressives. Bernie Sanders, who had never before taken part in Democratic politics, gave a nominating speech for Jackson at a party caucus in Burlington.[19] At one point, Jackson pulled even with Michael Dukakis in the delegate count, and he finished the nomination contest with enough delegates to demand platform concessions from the winner. Although Barack Obama would later eclipse him in the party's collective memory, the 1988 Jackson campaign marked the emergence of African American influence rooted not just in symbolism and moral suasion but also in hard vote totals.

Between 1992 and 2016, no candidate won the Democratic presidential nomination without winning a majority of the Black vote.[20] As New South Democrats, Bill Clinton and Al Gore had long supported civil rights legislation and had deep connections to African American leaders. Some even called Clinton the nation's "first Black president." In 2004, John Kerry courted Black voters. In the 2008 nomination contest, as we explain in *Epic Journey*, Hillary Clinton initially had more support among African Americans than Barack Obama. Though they liked Obama, many wondered whether he could actually win the nomination. His strong showings in Iowa and New Hampshire erased those doubts, and African American voters swung massively in his favor.[21] Eight years later, Black voters helped Clinton overcome a challenge from Sanders. Despite his early involvement in the civil rights movement and his 1988 support for Jackson, Sanders represented an overwhelmingly white state and did not have a strong African American base. This problem would prove consequential in 2020.

At the same time that Black voters gained strength within the party, conservative white Southerners switched to the GOP. Their departure removed a counterbalance to the party's growing liberal wing. In a 1994 Gallup survey, nearly half of Democratic respondents called themselves moderates, with the rest split evenly between liberal and conservatives. By 2018, the liberal share reached 51 percent, marking the first time a majority of Democrats adopted this term. It ticked down to 49 percent in 2019, but liberalism remained the dominant persuasion in the party.[22] In both the 1988 and the 2020 campaigns, Biden had a reputation as a party centrist, but the Democratic center had moved leftward, and he had moved along with it. On issues such as civil rights and criminal justice, his new positions were more progressive than his old ones. His competitors would try to use the earlier Joe Biden against the latest version.

MANY ARE CULLED

According to a count by the *New York Times*, twenty-eight people ran for the Democratic nomination.[23] Why so many? One answer is Donald Trump. From the first day of his presidency, rank and file Democrats loathed Trump and were unusually eager to take him down. Democratic politicians drew encouragement from their party's takeover of the House in 2018. Granted, midterm elections have limited predictive power: Reagan, Clinton, and Obama all won reelection after severe midterm setbacks. In this case, though, polls provided additional reason for Democratic optimism. In most national surveys, Trump's approval rating never topped 50 percent. Unpopular presidents seldom win.

The Democratic nomination was a prize worth fighting for, and nobody had a prohibitive claim to it. Despite winning a plurality of the popular vote in 2016, Hillary Clinton enjoyed little support for another run in 2020. Many Democrats believed that her campaign errors and ethical issues had cost them an election that they should have won, thus saddling the nation with Donald Trump. Early in 2019, she nodded to reality and announced that she would forgo a race in 2020.[24] Joe Biden, the next in line to be the party's frontrunner, did scare not off rival candidates. During his half-century in politics, Biden had never won a general election on his own outside of his small home state of Delaware. His two presidential campaigns had ended in failure. His vice-presidential service had earned him the gratitude of President Obama and the affection of Democratic politicians. It also included a number of verbal blunders, such as his hot-mic comment to Obama that passage of the Affordable Care Act was "a big [expletive deleted] deal." An ambitious would-be candidate could reasonably guess that the elderly, gaffe-prone Biden would eventually stumble. There seemed to be room at the top.

With the erosion of political and demographic barriers, even unlikely candidates could imagine a path forward. The last two presidents had been an African American freshman senator with an unusual name and a reality-TV star with a shady past, so a large group of Democrats thought to themselves, "Why not me?" Some came out of the House of Representatives, which had not sent a sitting member to the White House since James A. Garfield in 1880. On July 28, 2017, Representative John Delaney (D-MD) made the earliest official presidential candidacy declaration in history. His only moment in the sun was a burn. At a debate, he cautioned progressive candidates against making unrealistic promises. Elizabeth Warren got applause with a smackdown: "I don't understand why anybody goes to all the trouble of running for president of the United States just to talk about what we really can't do and shouldn't fight for."[25] When he withdrew in January 2020, practically no one noticed. Three other House members came and went with barely a ripple: Tim Ryan of Ohio, Seth Moulton of Massachusetts, and Eric Swalwell of California. So did former representative Joe Sestak of Pennsylvania, a retired admiral.

Robert Francis "Beto" O'Rourke of Texas, caused a brief stir. In 2018, he had passed up reelection to the House for a race against Senator Ted Cruz, who was among the Republican lawmakers that Democrats most despised. During a campaign town hall, a questioner asked O'Rourke whether he thought that it was disrespectful for professional football players to kneel during the national anthem. He gave a stirring answer that defended their patriotism and their right to protest racial injustice. The resulting YouTube clip went viral, thrilling Democrats who resented GOP emphasis on the issue.[26] He narrowly lost to Cruz but hoped that his strong showing in a GOP state could propel a presidential campaign. After several months on the trail, he learned the limits of being almost-a-giant-killer. "It's not good enough to not be Ted Cruz anymore," Republican media strategist Matt Gorman told journalist Peter Hamby. "In a state, you have a baseline of party support that's with you no matter what if you're running against a Republican. Not in a primary. He needs to make an identity for himself."[27] He never did.

Representative Tulsi Gabbard of Hawaii did make an identity that registered in national polls. At the same time, that identity capped her support in low single digits. At the 2016 Democratic convention, she had given the nominating speech for Bernie Sanders. With Sanders running again in 2020, she needed support from outside the progressive wing. Her positions guaranteed that she would not get it. She had attacked President Obama's policies on terrorism, and, in 2017, she traveled to Syria for a meeting with the country's murderous dictator, Bashar al-Assad. These moves did help her popularity—in Russia. A content analysis found that Kremlin-controlled outlets RT and Sputnik gave her more favorable coverage than any other candidate.[28] When the House took up the impeachment of President Trump, she voted "present," explaining that she was taking a stand against partisanship.[29] Democratic partisans did not like it. In a *Saturday Night Live* parody of the next debate, Cecily Strong appeared as Gabbard, announcing her arrival by saying "present." She added, "Democrats, I'll get you, my party, and your little mayor too," She then gave an evil laugh as lights flashed before she left the stage.[30] Hillary Clinton called Gabbard a "Russian asset" in a televised interview, and Gabbard fought back by calling Clinton a "warmonger."[31]

Current and former governors, who had dominated presidential nomination politics in years past, were barely visible in the 2020 cycle. Jay Inslee of Washington stressed climate change and environmental issues, which did not distinguish him from other candidates. John Hickenlooper of Colorado got scant attention by running as a moderate and switched to running for the Senate. Former governor Deval Patrick of Massachusetts entered late and left no footprints even in neighboring New Hampshire.

If Democrats wanted to make up lost ground in red states and rural areas, there was no better candidate than Governor Steve Bullock of Montana. He had won three statewide races, most recently by a four-point margin as Trump was carrying the state by twenty. Notwithstanding his demonstrated appeal to Republican voters, he took mainstream Democratic positions on major issues. In contrast to Trump's lackadaisical attitude toward governance, Bullock was dedicated to effective management. In the end, he was too dedicated for his own good. He put off his campaign launch campaign until mid-May 2019 in order to get an extension of Medicaid expansion through Montana's Republican-controlled legislature. By then, it was too late to raise enough money and establish an effective national organization. Like Hickenlooper, he eventually decided to run for the Senate instead.

A pair of senators failed to gain altitude. Michael Bennet of Colorado had gained respect among colleagues and C-SPAN viewers for his thoughtful speeches and deep grasp of policy, but he generated little attention from the general public. Kirsten Gillibrand of New York initially appeared to be a top-level contender, in part because of her fundraising base in her home state. Two problems, however, weighed her down. Governor David Paterson had originally named her to fill the vacancy stemming from Hillary Clinton's appointment as secretary of state in 2009. Before then, she had been a House member from Upstate New York, and she had a relatively conservative voting record on gun control and other issues. As a senator, she had abruptly shifted to the liberal side of the spectrum, raising questions about opportunism.[32] More recently, she had been the first Democratic senator to call for the resignation of Senator Al Franken in the wake of sexual misconduct allegations. Many feminists supported her move, but some Democratic contributors thought that she had betrayed a leading progressive colleague.[33]

No big-city mayor had ever become president, and none would do so in 2020.[34] As mentioned earlier, former San Antonio mayor and HUD secretary Julian Castro struggled to rally Latino voters nationwide.[35] Bill de Blasio of New York had a strong progressive record, but his arrogant personal manner had become too much for voters in his home city, which is saying something.[36] His campaign folded before the first day of autumn 2019. Eric Garcetti of Los Angeles had a much more genial personality, as well as an intriguing demographic background as a Jewish Hispanic with an Italian surname. He tested the waters in states with early contests, even making the dubious claim that "Iowa and Los Angeles have a ton in common."[37] Voters did not buy it, and he opted out of the race. It was just as well. The city's problems, ranging from rampant homelessness to rat-borne typhus, would have been a bonanza to opposition researchers.[38]

Some candidates never stood a chance. Former West Virginia state senator Richard Ojeda, a retired Army paratrooper, ended his campaign just ten days after starting it. Besides his obscurity, his major problem was his 2016 vote for Trump, a dealbreaker for most Democrats.[39] Mayor Wayne Messam of Miramar, Florida (population 122,000), lacked a distinctive appeal. His policy positions were standard Democratic fare and his status as an African American was of little help in a field that included much better-known Black candidates. Finally, New Age guru Marianne Williamson did get enough support to make the first two debates. She unintentionally provided comic relief by disdaining detailed policy positions in favor of eccentric sermonettes. In the second debate, she proclaimed what she would tell Donald Trump: "I'm going to harness love for political purposes. I will meet you on that field. And, sir, love will win."[40]

Marianne Williamson was not going to win. But several of her competitors did seem to have a real chance, and they had been working at it for a long time.

EARLY MOVES

Representative Tom Cole (R-OK), the respected former chair of the National Republican Congressional Committee, made a remarkably candid admission late in 2017: "There's no illusion about the storm that's coming. If you had any doubts, they were wiped away after New Jersey, Virginia and Alabama."[41] In the first two states, Democrats had scored big victories in the scheduled off-year gubernatorial elections. In a special election for the Alabama Senate seat previously held by Attorney General Jeff Sessions, Democrat Doug Jones upset Roy Moore, a former judge who faced accusations of inappropriate behavior involving minors. The results provided a lift to Democrats who were still reeling from Trump's victory a year before.

There was also a more tangible consequence. Jones's victory added to Democratic strength in the Senate, and the resulting shift in committee ratios opened up a seat on the Judiciary Committee. So had the resignation of Senator Al Franken (D-MN). With two seats to fill, Senate Democrats acknowledged Black political power by appointing the only African American Democrats currently serving in the Senate: Cory Booker and Kamala Harris. They were the first African American members of the committee since Carol Moseley Braun (D-IL) nearly twenty years earlier. Both coveted the appointment. The Judiciary Committee deals with not only nominations to federal courts but also high-profile social issues such as civil rights and criminal justice. For a Democrat contemplating a presidential run in 2020, the Judiciary Committee offered an opportunity to get publicity and talk about concerns that motivate Democratic primary voters. And Booker and Harris each needed to shore up support on the party's left wing.

When he was mayor of Newark years earlier, Booker had worked closely with Republican Governor Chris Christie, who by 2017 was a Trump supporter and the object of Democratic contempt. Despite his progressive positions on most issues, Booker was attentive to business interests and had strong support on Wall Street. (When he ran for reelection to the Senate in 2014, he was the chamber's top recipient of contributions from the hedge fund industry, far ahead of number-two recipient, Mitch McConnell.[42]) Early in 2017, liberals praised him for breaking tradition and testifying against the nomination as attorney general of his colleague Jeff Sessions. Then Booker alienated them by voting to kill a measure that aimed at reducing prescription drug prices. One critic said, "This is classic Booker—stand out front on feel-good social issues, regardless of his past positions, and align with big money everywhere else."[43]

Like Booker, Harris faced skepticism from progressive Democrats. As San Francisco district attorney and attorney general of California, she had developed a reputation for caution. Even though she now supported elimination of cash bail as part of a broader agenda for criminal justice reform, she had said little on the issue as a prosecutor.[44] During her tenure in Sacramento, the attorney general's office defended the death penalty in court, which helped her win the political support of law enforcement groups. She explained, with justification, that she was carrying out her sworn duty to uphold the laws of California regardless of whether she agreed with them. "I have a client, and I don't get to choose my client," she said.[45]

With the Supreme Court nomination of Brett Kavanaugh, the Judiciary Committee took center stage. Harris's prosecutorial experience came into play as she asked tough, sharp questions that unsettled the nominee and went viral among liberals. Insisting that Kavanaugh clarify his views of *Roe v. Wade*, she asked, "Can you think of any laws that give the government power to make decisions about the male body?" Kavanaugh was uncharacteristically at a loss for words: "I'm not aware—I'm not—thinking of any right now, senator."[46] (Harris also stirred controversy when she played a tape of Kavanaugh that had been edited, altering the substance of his remarks.[47]) Booker had less success. When a senior Republican threatened him with sanctions for releasing documents relating to Kavanaugh's thoughts on racial profiling, other Democrats came to his defense: "This is about the closest I'll ever have in my life to an 'I am Spartacus' moment,' said Booker."[48] He was referring to a scene in the Stanley Kubrick classic in which slaves conceal the identity of their rebel leader by all shouting "I am Spartacus!" Booker's well-known affection for popular culture served him poorly in this case. The line instantly became a joke in the political community, and the documents at issue contained no explosive revelations.

A third member of the committee would run in 2020. Amy Klobuchar of Minnesota was casting herself more as a practical problem-solver than a champion of liberal causes. Her most telling moment in the Kavanaugh hearings involved the allegations of sexual assault against him. She mentioned that her father was a recovering alcoholic and then asked Kavanaugh whether he had ever drunk so much that he could not remember what happened the night before.

> KAVANAUGH: It's—you're asking about, you know, blackout. I don't know. Have you?
>
> KLOBUCHAR: Could you answer the question, Judge? I just—so you—that's not happened. Is that your answer?
>
> KAVANAUGH: Yeah, and I'm curious if you have.
>
> KLOBUCHAR: I have no drinking problem, Judge.[49]

The exchange made Kavanaugh look nasty, and he quickly apologized. Democrats gave Klobuchar high marks for keeping her cool.[50] A few months later, though, her demeanor became a problem when news stories detailed her abusive treatment of congressional aides.[51] It is unlikely that a significant share of the electorate read these accounts. Still, the contrast with her "Minnesota Nice" public image gave pause to the activists and professionals who play an important part in the early days of a primary contest. Her alleged behavior reportedly prompted at least three people to withdraw from consideration to manage her campaign.[52] "I doubt it will [affect voters] much," one national Democratic consultant told *Politico*. "But does it mar her rollout and her getting support from important people, like donors and elected officials? Yes. And in the long run, that's a problem with getting voters."[53]

Several weeks after the Kavanaugh hearing, Democrats had a spectacular showing in House elections, taking control of the chamber with a net gain of 40 seats. Republicans exceeded expectations in Senate races, expanding their majority by two seats. As we explain in the midterm update to *Defying the Odds*, the Kavanaugh hearings may have hurt red-state Democratic senators by galvanizing Republican voters.[54] The split 2018 results would shape the 2020 presidential race. Democratic control of the House raised the possibility of a presidential impeachment and Republican control of the

Senate effectively foreclosed the possibility of a conviction. In the summer of 2018, a year before the Ukraine controversy, one poll found that 75 percent of Democrats wanted the House to start impeachment proceedings against Trump.[55] Billionaire Tom Steyer had already been trying to capitalize on this sentiment by mounting a public relations campaign called "Need to Impeach." Such action was not imminent. Incoming House Speaker Nancy Pelosi was reluctant even to discuss impeachment, in part because she understood the near-impossibility of getting a two-thirds majority to convict Trump in a Republican Senate.

For the time being, Democratic politicians were focusing more on the looming presidential race than a hypothetical impeachment. The first announcement from a top-tier candidate came on December 31, 2018, when Senator Elizabeth Warren of Massachusetts formed an exploratory committee. Her immediate task consisted of dealing with an unforced error. Years before, she had drawn on family legend to claim Cherokee heritage, which led to unverified accusations that she had gamed affirmative action to advance her academic career. Trump referred to her derisively as "Pocahontas." Although her ancestry was not a major issue by 2019, she took a DNA test and proudly announced that it confirmed her claim. The test showed that she was, at most, 1/64th Native American, prompting a new round of criticism and ridicule.[56] She eventually apologized to the Cherokee Nation, and the controversy receded. For Warren, it was an unfortunate distraction. She had an inspiring biography, having risen from humble origins in Oklahoma to become an important legal scholar and then a member of the Senate. Instead of highlighting her genuine accomplishments, she had to spend much of the early weeks of 2019 discussing DNA.

Warren ran on a detailed set of policy proposals, and her tagline was "I've got a plan for that." On economic inequality, one of her plans was a wealth tax: 2 percent a year on household net worth between $50 million and $1 billion and a 4 percent annual surtax (6 percent overall) on household net worth above $1 billion.[57] The plan would have been a fundamental departure from the current federal tax system, which focuses on income instead of wealth. Because the plan promised vast revenues (more than $3 trillion over 10 years) by targeting a tiny portion of the population, it was a hit with much of the progressive Democratic base.

She had competition for that base. Bernie Sanders had fared well against Hillary Clinton in the 2016 primaries and had never really stopped running. After that campaign, he founded Our Revolution, a 501(c)(4) political advocacy group, as well as the Sanders Institute, a 501(c)(3) think tank. Both helped him keep his name in the news. Most important, he retained a list of millions of small-dollar donors, who could keep replenishing his campaign treasury. Sanders, the oldest candidate in the race, had shown a strong appeal to younger voters in 2016 and was counting on them to carry him over the line in 2020.

Warren and Sanders had similar positions on many issues, but there was an important difference between them. Warren was in the capital-P Progressive tradition of Theodore Roosevelt, whom she identified as her favorite president.[58] The Progressives wanted to regulate business in the public interest and curb special-interest power through political reform. Socialists have always favored more fundamental change. Later in the year, Sanders said in a television interview, "Elizabeth I think, as you know, has said that she is a capitalist through her bones. I'm not. . . . And I think business as usual, and doing it the old fashioned way is not good enough. It's not regulation. Now what we need is, in fact, I don't want to get people too nervous, we need a political revolution."[59]

The most obvious capitalist among potential Democratic candidates was Michael Bloomberg. Before his 2001 election as mayor of New York City, Bloomberg had become a billionaire by pioneering the use of technology to provide financial information. In 2018, he had spent lavishly to support Democratic congressional candidates.[60] The question for 2020 was whether that money could buy him party love. After all, he had won his first and second mayoral terms as a Republican before becoming an Independent in 2007. His tough crime policies followed in the path set by his predecessor, Rudolph Giuliani—a distinctly unappealing record for the Democratic electorate of 2020. In March 2019, he announced that he would not run. He would later change his mind.

The unlikeliest major contender was the mayor of South Bend, Indiana, a city of slightly more than 100,000 souls. What accounted for the phenomenal rise of Pete Buttigieg? In several ways, he could claim to be the antithesis of Donald Trump. Whereas Trump was in his seventies (like Biden, Warren, Sanders, and Bloomberg), Buttigieg was vying to be the youngest-ever president, having just turned thirty-seven. Trump was a flaming heterosexual, with three wives and countless sleazy affairs. Buttigieg was a gay man who was happily married to one spouse. Trump was infamous for his atrocious spelling and grammar, as well as his refusal to read anything much longer than a tweet. Buttigieg was a Rhodes Scholar who spoke several languages, including Norwegian, which he taught himself in order to read more novels by a favorite author. Trump had used dubious means to avoid the Vietnam-era military draft. Buttigieg was a veteran who had enlisted in the Navy Reserve and went on active duty as an intelligence officer in Afghanistan.

Buttigieg's poise and eloquence enthralled Democrats who wanted a clean break with recent past of American politics. He got highly favorable coverage from the start, in part because he had a generational and cultural connection with the young, well-educated reporters who cover presidential campaigns. He was also at home online. In March 2019, a social media analytics company found that he was generating more Facebook and Twitter interactions per article than any other candidate.[61]

Buttigieg was part of the Millennial generation, who came of age after the year 2000. Biden, born in 1942, was a product of the previous century. On the good side, his age and decades of public service had given him firsthand exposure to a large portion of American history. To paraphrase a popular insurance ad, he knew a thing or two because he'd seen a thing or two. On the bad side, his language and mannerisms sometimes seemed out of place in twenty-first century America. He frequently used old-fashioned terms such as "malarkey" and "record players." More seriously, he was too casual about touching people, which caused multiple women to complain that he had crossed a line.[62] In the era of #MeToo, such behavior could severely damage a candidate, and he sought to fix the problem. "I want to talk about gestures of support that I've made to women and some men that have made them uncomfortable," Biden said in a video. "The boundaries of protecting personal space have been reset. I get it. I get it. I hear what they're saying, and I understand it. I'll be much more mindful. That's my responsibility and I'll meet it."[63]

Biden stood in the twentieth-century Democratic tradition of Harry Truman and Hubert Humphrey, pitching his appeal to white working-class voters. In 2016, his bloc had tipped key Rustbelt states to Trump, and Biden thought that he was just the candidate to get them back in the fold. His hardscrabble upbringing in Scranton, Pennsylvania, had given him a special empathy for blue-collar workers. To drive the point home, he held his first campaign rally in Pittsburgh, where he spoke of the people who "transport our goods, build our bridges and repair our roofs, keep our water system safe, people who race into burning buildings, people who race into danger to protect us, people who pick up our garbage off our streets, ironworkers, steel workers, boilermakers, plumbers, electrical workers, salespeople."[64]

This base would once have been enough to clinch the party nomination. As late as 1996, 58 percent of Democrats and Democratic-leaning Independents were whites without a college degree. By 2019, that figure was down to 30 percent.[65] The dominant elements of the Democratic coalition were now racial minorities and educated white professionals. Many progressive activists considered Biden a relic, a pathetic old man seeking to lead a party that no longer existed. They overlooked a couple of important Biden advantages. The first was Barack Obama. Although the forty-fourth president did not endorse a candidate in the primaries, Biden's eight years of loyal service to him had strongly reinforced his credibility with African American voters. The second was Donald Trump. The Monmouth University Poll asked voters, "Would you prefer a strong nominee who could defeat Mr. Trump, even if you disagree with that candidate on most issues—or a candidate with whom you see eye to eye, but who would have difficulty overcoming the president?" By nearly a two-to-one margin, Democrats consistently chose the first option.[66] And in polls taken throughout 2019, they considered Biden the strongest candidate against Trump.[67] The question was whether those advantages would hold long enough to carry Biden through the nomination contest

DEBATE SEASON

Once the field took shape, two well-known old men led the polls. Biden stood in first place, though his support among Democrats fell far short of a majority. Because he already enjoyed near-universal name identification in the party, he had the luxury of putting off his formal announcement until April. Bernie Sanders came in second. He was also a familiar face in the party, and campaign finance figures from the first quarter of 2019 showed that he could keep up the fight. (Biden would not have to file until the second quarter.) Sanders placed first among the announced candidates, gathering $18.2 million from 525,000 donors and transferring another $2.5 million from his Senate campaign account. Most of his money came from people giving less than $200 each, which was significant because he could keep soliciting these same donors until they reached the legal limit of $2,800.[68]

Harris had an impressive launch, coming in second in fundraising and holding third place in the national polls. She got a great deal of buzz because of her effective performance on the Judiciary Committee as well as her diverse background as the daughter of immigrants from Jamaica and India. As winter turned to spring, however, the buzz fizzled. "You don't get elected because you're a list of qualities," said Gil Duran, a former Harris advisor. "What's the big idea she's carrying? That's what she's trying to figure out. She's having trouble figuring out what she represents."[69]

Warren did have big ideas, and once the DNA kerfuffle died down, she inched up in the polls. So did Buttigieg, who also raised millions in small donations. Like all the other candidates, they eagerly awaited the first debate in hopes that it would vault them to the top. To get onto the stage, they had to meet the criteria that the Democratic National Committee had set: registering 1 percent or more support in three public polls (either nationwide or in early-voting states) or raising donations from at least 65,000 donors, with a minimum of two hundred donors per state in at least twenty U.S. states.[70] In all, twenty candidates ended up in the debate, with the DNC randomly allocating them to two nights: June 26 and 27.

Harris luckily drew a spot on the same night as Biden, and she made the most of the opportunity. She alluded to his Senate career in the 1970s, when he worked with segregationist senators James Eastland (D-MS) and Herman Talmadge (D-GA) and opposed mandatory busing for racial balance in public schools.

> I'm going to now direct this at Vice President Biden, I do not believe you are a racist, and I agree with you when you commit yourself to the importance of finding common ground. But I also believe, and it's personal—and I was actually very—it was hurtful to hear you talk about the reputations of two United States senators who built their reputations and career on the segregation of race in this country. And it was not only that, but you also worked with them to oppose busing. And, you know, there was a little girl in California who was part of the second class to integrate her public schools, and she was bussed to school every day. And that little girl was me.[71]

Biden's less-than-dynamic response was that she had distorted his position. (His problem was that he had in fact opposed racial-balance busing in the 1970s.[72]) The dramatic exchange became the top story of the first debate, and Harris's poll numbers went up. The confrontation illustrated an emerging dynamic of contemporary politics: the interaction between social media and television. Links to video of the exchange proliferated on Twitter and Facebook, which in turn encouraged more media coverage. "You don't have to be in Des Moines or Manchester to have a viral moment and if that happens you're in front of millions of people and can raise potentially millions of dollars," Democratic strategist Tad Devine told Jonathan Martin of the *New York Times*.[73]

The episode also illustrated the limits of viral moments. Despite the renewed attention, Harris still had difficulty with identifying a message that set her apart from the other candidates. Alluding to her role as a fearsome questioner on the Judiciary Committee, she said that she would "prosecute the case" against Trump. But she was running for president, not prosecutor. Americans elect a chief executive not to ask tough questions but to make tough decisions. And in this case, the issues at hand did little lasting damage to Biden. Few Democrats really believed that Barack Obama's vice president sympathized with racists. As for busing, a 2007 Supreme Court decision had forbidden the use of racial classifications in student assignment plans for the purpose of racial balance.[74] The matter was moot, and the Harris surge was short-lived.

A couple of weeks after the debate, the second quarter fundraising numbers came out. Buttigieg surprised the political community by topping the list with $25 million.[75] Biden came in second with $22 million, with Warren and Sanders a few million dollars behind. Harris was fifth at $11.8 million. Booker's relatively meager $4.5 million haul suggested that his previous fundraising success was not carrying over into the presidential campaign and that he had failed to make the top tier of candidates.

Buttigieg was now firmly in that top tier, and he learned that prominence brings scrutiny. On June 16, a white South Bend police officer shot and killed a Black man during an investigation of vehicle thefts. The incident led to local protests and cast a national spotlight on longstanding racial tensions in the city. Buttigieg, whose following was overwhelmingly white, now had a political liability. During the June debate, he frankly acknowledged that he had not done enough to recruit African American officers, and in July, he tried to shore up his credibility on civil rights with a plan to combat racism in the federal government.[76] Several months later, it turned out that his campaign website had illustrated the plan with a stock photo of a Kenyan woman.[77] Removing the photo did not solve his underlying problems with race, which would trail him into 2020.

The second debate was another two-parter on July 30 and 31. While not changing the contours of the contest, it suggested that the progressive candidates might have a hard time with the issue of health care. Jake Tapper posed a tough question to Warren, who had joined Sanders in backing Medicare for All: "Now, Senator Sanders has said that people in the middle class will pay more in taxes to help pay for Medicare for All, though that will be offset by the elimination of insurance premiums and other costs. Are you also, quote, 'with Bernie' on Medicare for All when it comes to raising taxes on middle-class Americans to pay for it?"[78] She sidestepped, claiming that billionaires and corporations would pay more, while the middle class would come out ahead in the end. Her evasiveness was understandable, since major change in health care policy always entail direct and indirect costs, which are unpopular. This basic fact of life plagued President Obama when he got Congress to pass the Affordable Care Act, and then hit congressional Republicans just as hard when they tried to repeal it. The other key moment of those debates occurred when Tulsi Gabbard mounted an intense attack on Harris's record as a prosecutor in California.

For the third debate on September 12, the Democratic National Committee set tighter polling and fundraising criteria that deliberately winnowed the field This time, just ten candidates made it, and they were all on one stage for one night. Biden got the greatest amount of speaking time, largely because he got to respond to attacks from other candidates.[79] Journalists noted that Biden did well, while Warren got the best grades from the debate audience.[80] She went up in the national polls, passing Sanders for third place, and briefly reaching a statistical tie with Biden for first place.[81]

On October 1, Sanders entered a Las Vegas hospital after feeling chest pain at a campaign event. Doctors then inserted two stents in a blocked artery. On October 4, his campaign confirmed that he had suffered a heart attack. If supporters worried that the incident would capsize his campaign, they got a dose of reassurance eleven days later, when he appeared at the fourth Democratic debate. He was as vigorous as ever, and applause indicated that had the sympathy of the audience. In the short run, the heart attack gave him a political boost.

In the meantime, Warren's rise in the polls had made her a target. At the debate, she came under crossfire about her support for Medicare for All. After she declined to address the tax consequences, Buttigieg said, "Well, we heard it tonight, a yes or no question that didn't get a yes or no answer. Look, this is why people here in the Midwest are so frustrated with Washington in general and Capitol Hill in particular. Your signature, Senator, is to have a plan for everything. Except this."[82] Klobuchar said, "At least Bernie's being honest here and saying how he's going to pay for this and that taxes are going to go up. And I'm sorry, Elizabeth, but you have not said that, and I think we owe it to the American people to tell them where we're going to send the invoice." Both Buttigieg and Klobuchar forcefully reminded viewers that Warren's plan would take millions of Americans off the insurance plans that they already had. That argument drew blood. As long as people thought Medicare for All was just an enlargement of an existing popular program, they liked it. When pollsters mentioned that it could raise taxes or eliminate existing plans, support dropped.[83]

Warren's standing in the polls fell as quickly as it had risen, and within a few weeks, she was back in third place. In November, she changed her health care plan. Now she proposed to delay the implementation of a single-payer system and, in the interim, give people the ability to opt into Medicare. She evidently hoped that her shift to the center would increase her appeal. It did the opposite. Moderate Democrats were still wary of Medicare for All, even in slow motion. Her shifting stance disappointed progressives who had admired her clarity and firmness.[84] Her campaign never recovered.

As Warren lost ground, Biden held steady. For a frontrunner, he had a modest level of support, with surveys showing less than a third of Democrats in his corner. Campaign finance numbers also suggested weakness, with his third-quarter fundraising total far behind Sanders's and Warren's.[85] And Buttigieg, who was born during Biden's *second* term in the Senate, edged him out for third place in fundraising. (One consolation prize for Biden was that he raised more than Harris, who dropped out on December 3.) Neither Biden nor anyone else had a commanding lead, and some commentators were writing about the possibility of a contested convention. Additional debates in the last two months of 2019 failed to shake things up.

A couple of potential "game changers" did catch the candidates' attention. One was impeachment. For all the passion on both sides of the issue, the December 18 House vote to impeach Trump had practically no effect on his approval rating, which stayed within the same narrow band that had been in place since early 2017. Few voters changed their minds about Trump, and it was evident that the 2020 general election would turn on other issues. The real impact of impeachment would be much more immediate. The Senate would hold a trial early in 2020, meaning that the senators remaining in the field (Sanders, Warren, Klobuchar, and Booker) would have to spend a good deal of time in the U.S. Capitol instead of Iowa or New Hampshire. To make matters worse, Senate rules would forbid them to speak on the floor until the end of the proceedings. With the senators mute and absent much of the time, Biden and other candidates might gain a comparative advantage.

Meanwhile, Biden faced a daunting threat in the person of Michael Bloomberg. After his earlier announcement that he would not run, Bloomberg changed his mind and officially entered the contest on November 24. "There is a greater risk of having Donald Trump reelected than there was before," Bloomberg explained. "I looked in the mirror and said, 'I just cannot let this happen.'"[86] Because of his late entry, he chose to skip the first four contests (Iowa, New Hampshire, Nevada, and South Carolina) and instead focus on the states voting on Super Tuesday, March 3. Bloomberg, the wealthiest person ever to run for president, had the money to pull off such a risky and unorthodox strategy. He was hoping to convince Democrats that he would have a much better chance of beating Trump than Sanders or Warren—which was the argument that Biden had been hoping to make.

As the new year began, a titanic game changer had not yet caught the attention of the American political community. Only a small number of experts noticed reports of a disease outbreak in the Chinese city of Wuhan.

"JOE BIDEN IS COLLAPSING"

Short on funds and low in the polls, Cory Booker pulled out of the race on January 13. On the following day, six Democrats met in the last debate before the Iowa caucuses. By this point, regular viewers knew the candidates' soundbites by heart, and the only news that emerged was the sniping between

Warren and Sanders, who had previously been on cordial terms. The next three weeks would be frustrating for them, as well as for Klobuchar. Stuck in the Senate chamber for hours on end, they had to make do with remote television interviews and town halls where they would literally phone it in. Biden and Buttigieg, meanwhile, were free to campaign the old-fashioned way. "I sit there knowing that I'm off the campaign trail while some of my opponents are running around everywhere," Klobuchar said. "I think to myself, 'you know—this is my job.'"[87]

In a primary, people vote either by mailing in their ballots or by casting them at a polling place. The Iowa caucuses were different. As in previous campaigns, Iowans spent hours in gyms, rec rooms, and other public spaces in each of state's 1,678 precincts. People expressed preferences by physically gathering with other supporters of the same candidate. If a candidate got less than 15 percent in a precinct, her or his supporters would then move over to another candidate's group. The 2020 caucuses had a couple of new features. For elderly people, students, and others who could not get to the regular caucuses, the state party set up eighty-seven "satellite caucuses" at places such as nursing homes and colleges.[88] Another change involved procedures for reporting results. In the past, the party's precinct leaders simply called in the results to state headquarters. This time, they had a smartphone app, which would presumably make it easy for the state party to calculate three numbers: the initial vote totals, the totals after switches, and the "state delegate equivalents" (the number of delegates for each candidate at the state convention). In the past, Democrats had only reported the last number, and they were counting on technology to provide greater accuracy and transparency in revealing voter choice.

It seemed like a good idea at the time.

On caucus night, many precinct leaders found that the app did not work. When they tried to use the telephone as a backup, they had a hard time getting through. A dirty trick was at least partially to blame for the telephone chaos: a fringe internet message board posted the phone number to report Iowa caucus results and encouraged its followers to "clog the lines."[89] Candidates and their supporters went to bed that night with the results in limbo, and the uncertainty persisted. Within a couple of days, it seemed that Buttigieg and Sanders were in a statistical dead heat, which normally would have been a psychological victory for Buttigieg. But the murkiness of the numbers dampened his post-Iowa momentum. It would take until the end of the month—and after the New Hampshire primary—to sort out the final numbers. One thing was already clear: Biden was in fourth place. "I'm not going to sugarcoat it," he said two days after the caucuses. "We took a gut punch in Iowa. The whole process took a gut punch. But this isn't the first time in my life I've been knocked down."[90] Nor would it be the last.

National polls soon showed Biden falling back and Sanders pulling ahead. With the end of the impeachment trial on February 5, the senators in the race could again campaign freely. A debate in New Hampshire confirmed Sanders's new frontrunner status, as other candidates aimed attacks at him albeit with few "defining moments." In the primary on February 11, he led with 25.6 percent. It was a wobbly victory for the Vermont senator, who had trounced Hillary Clinton in the state with 60 percent of the vote four years earlier. Buttigieg was less than two points behind, and Klobuchar hoped that her third-place finish (19.7 percent) would reenergize her campaign. Elizabeth Warren only got 9.2 percent, a humiliating score for a former frontrunner and a candidate from a nearby state. Biden was fifth at 8.4 percent—another unspinnable loss. He had not always campaigned well—at one point rather oddly berating a young woman who asked him a question as a "lying dog-faced pony soldier."[91] He had sought to lower expectations before the vote, telling the debate audience, "I took a hit in Iowa and I'll probably take a hit here. Traditionally Bernie won by 20 points last time. And usually it's the neighboring senators that do well."[92] But he also finished behind two Mid-westerners, and in single digits. "This is horrendous. We're all scared," a Biden adviser told *Politico*.[93]

The New Republic had already run a piece predicting that a fifth-place win would spell doom: "In politics, universally known and liked former vice presidents don't win by losing badly in both Iowa and New Hampshire." The title of the article was "Joe Biden Is Collapsing."[94] As his national numbers sank further, many Democratic activists assumed that Biden would soon withdraw from the race.

Then he had some luck in Las Vegas. Democrats were debating there in advance of the Nevada caucuses, and for the first time, Michael Bloomberg was on stage. The former mayor had spent hundreds of millions on radio and television ads all over the country, and it looked as if he would soon overtake Biden for second place in the national polls. A strong debate performance might have enabled Bloomberg to become the mainstream alternative to Sanders and hasten Biden's exit. Instead, he did badly—very, very badly.

Journalist Hallie Jackson asked Bloomberg about sexual harassment suits that had ended in nondisclosure agreements. Like Trump, he tried to wave away the issue by talking about opportunities that he had provided for women. Warren answered, "I hope you heard what his defense was. 'I've been nice to some women.'" Bloomberg rolled his eyes—a reaction that conveyed disrespect for Warren and a dismissive attitude toward the whole issue. He refused to answer her repeated questions about how many women had signed the agreements. Nevertheless, she persisted: "We are not going to beat Donald Trump with a man who has who knows how many nondisclosure agreements and the drip, drip, drip of stories of women saying they have been harassed and discriminated against. [Applause.] That's not what we do as Democrats." Biden jumped in, saying that Bloomberg could simply release the women from the agreements. Bloomberg responded impatiently, "I've said we're not going to get—to end these agreements because they were made consensually, and they have every right to expect that they will stay private." People in the audience booed loudly. They also booed a little later when Bloomberg responded to a Sanders proposal for worker co-ownership of large corporations: "Other countries tried that. It was called communism, and it just didn't work."[95]

The event drew 19.7 million viewers, making it the most-viewed Democratic debate in history.[96] For many of those viewers, it was their first chance to see Bloomberg in live action—and unfortunately for the former mayor, the cliché held true: you don't get a second chance to make a first impression. Shortly after the debate, a poll showed that his support had slipped slightly. More serious was the change in his net favorability among Democratic voters, the share with favorable views of him minus those with unfavorable views. That figure fell twenty points from a pre-debate poll. Among self-described moderates—the constituency that Bloomberg had to win over from Biden— he fell thirty points.[97] By botching his debut, the former mayor had left the door open for the former vice president.

That door was open just a crack. As expected, Sanders won the Nevada caucuses, his third big win—and Biden's third big loss—in three weeks. An entrance survey showed that he had beaten Biden among nearly every demographic category except senior citizens and African Americans. In South Carolina, the latter group was about to have a say.

SUDDENLY

All along, Biden supporters could cling to a few threads of hope. He maintained strong favorability ratings among Democrats, and he posted decent fundraising numbers after the third quarter of 2019, especially once he could inherit contributors from Harris and Booker.[98] And in spite of his reputation for verbosity, he tightened his speeches in the wake of New Hampshire. One reason for his shift in rhetoric was frank advice from his old friend, Representative James Clyburn of South Carolina. Clyburn later explained to a reporter, "I said, 'There's a reason preachers deliver their sermons in threes. You know, Father, Son and Holy Ghost?'" Clyburn said, "Zero in on how to make this personalized, talk about their families, and talk in terms of people's communities."[99] During a CNN town hall, Biden took a question about faith from a African American pastor whose wife had died at the hands of a white supremacist in the 2015 Charleston massacre. Biden talked about religion and forgiveness. He blinked back tears as he got very personal:

> I've learned the only way—I don't know how you've dealt with it, Reverend, but the way I've been able to deal with when my wife was killed and my daughter were killed and then my son died, I've only been able to deal with it by realizing they're part of my being.
>
> My son, Beau, was my soul. And what I found was, I had to find purpose, purpose. And what was the purpose? . . . I think you know this about my boy, that I ask myself, I hope he's proud of me today, because he asked me when he was dying, promise me, dad, promise me, dad, promise me.
>
> He said, I know no one loves me more than you do, Dad, but promise me you'll stay engaged. He knew I would take care of the family, but he worried what I would do is I would pull back and go into a shell and not do all the things I've done before. It took me a long time to get to the point to realize that that purpose is the thing that would save me. And it has.[100]

The moment went viral. It had an effect because it was moving and genuine, and also because it set an implicit but powerful contrast with Trump, who would never express such feelings.

Besides his rhetorical advice, Clyburn gave Biden something more concrete: his endorsement. In presidential campaign politics, endorsements seldom matter much. Clyburn was an exception. As a House majority whip, Clyburn was the highest-ranking African American in Congress. The depth of his roots in the civil rights movement were evident in one simple anecdote: he met his wife in jail, when she brought him food after his arrest at a civil rights march.[101] Most South Carolina Democrats were African American, and Clyburn's words carried weight with them. In an exit poll, 61 percent of voters said that the endorsement was an important factor in their decision, and 27 percent who called it "the most important factor."[102]

The primary took place on Saturday, February 29, and it was not close. Biden beat Sanders 48 percent to 20 percent. The impact of the victory was all the greater because so many people had counted him out just a couple of weeks earlier. And something else added significance to the result: in his three races for the presidency, dating back to the 1988 campaign, he had never before won a presidential primary. Although Democrats had always liked Biden, they wondered whether he could count on him to win. Now they had a peg on which to hang their affection.

South Carolina helped clear his path. Tom Steyer, who had not been a major player anywhere else, got 11 percent and promptly quit the race. Buttigieg, despite campaigning hard in the state, got only 8 percent. It was a clear sign that he would do poorly in the Super Tuesday contests on March 3, in which African Americans would account for a large share of the vote. He had come further than anyone could have imagined a year earlier, but his single semi-victory in Iowa was hardly enough to keep a campaign going. Klobuchar fared worse in South Carolina and had done no better than third anywhere else. Within a couple of days, both dropped out. On the eve of Super Tuesday, they both joined former candidate Beto O'Rourke at a Texas rally, where they all endorsed the former vice president. News reports indicated that all three were responding to tacit signals from Barack Obama. Biden hinted as much: "He's not going to get involved in endorsing anyone for this nomination. But I think he will make sure that, you know, the party is united at the end of the day, and as I will, whether I win or not."[103]

Biden's epic journey to the nomination abruptly turned into a rocket ride. On Super Tuesday, he won Alabama, Arkansas, Massachusetts, Maine, Minnesota, North Carolina, Oklahoma, Tennessee, Texas, and Virginia. The Minnesota victory was particularly striking because he had not campaigned there: the Klobuchar endorsement apparently made a difference. Sanders won California, Colorado, Utah, and his home state of Vermont. Biden now led the delegate count in what had effectively become a two-person contest. As we explained in earlier books in this series, Democratic rules on proportional allocation make it hard for a lagging candidate to catch up in such circumstances.

Bloomberg, whose hundreds of millions in campaign spending bought him a single victory—in American Samoa—withdrew the next day and endorsed Biden. Warren quit the day after that. Despite her early promise, she had not won anywhere, including her home state. Given a clear choice between the two remaining candidates, the party electorate quickly coalesced around Biden. By the end of the week, he was consistently topping 50 percent in national polls of Democrats. Over the rest of March, Biden built an insurmountable lead by winning several other primaries, including the big states of Florida, Illinois, and Michigan, which Sanders had won in a surprise in 2016. Sanders did get a morale boost from a late endorsement by Jesse Jackson, whose 1988 candidacy had brought him into Democratic Party politics for the first time. Few noticed. Jackson's power had long ago evaporated. More newsworthy was a Biden endorsement from Kamala Harris.

By this time, the pandemic started reshaping the campaign as states rescheduled primaries. The last debate of the nomination contest took place at a CNN studio, minus an in-person audience. The absence of cheers and catcalls helped elevate the dignity of the event, where Sanders and Biden had a substantive discussion of their differences. Perhaps the most important short-term impact was to bring traditional campaign rallies to an end. Sanders had enjoyed large and enthusiastic crowds of young supporters, and webcams were no substitute for the love of a live audience. The primary in Wisconsin in early April put the exclamation point on Biden's nomination victory.

With Biden as the inevitable nominee and his favorite means of campaigning suddenly closed to him, Sanders endorsed Biden on April 13. The race was effectively over.

WHAT HAPPENED

So why did Biden win?

In 2020, African American voters reconfirmed their status as the nominating wing of the Democratic Party. Biden struggled in Iowa and New Hampshire in part because those states had relatively few African Americans. Things changed when the race moved to South Carolina and other states with large Black electorates.

Notwithstanding his collegiality with segregationists in the 1970s, Biden had a decades-long connection with African American voters, which grew deeper during his service to President Obama. Said Representative Clyburn in his endorsement, "We know Joe. But more importantly, he knows us."[104] His competitors could not match him on this point. Harris and Booker found that Black voters do not automatically vote for Black candidates: unlike Barack Obama in 2008, the two senators were unable to show that they were viable in the broader Democratic electorate. Buttigieg and Bloomberg faced serious questions about policing in the cities that they had led. Sanders did have a history of supporting civil rights, but his connections had grown cold during his

Table 2.1. Biden Percentage in States with Large (>20%) Black Democratic Primary Electorates

	Black Share of Democratic Electorate	Biden Share of Black Voters
South Carolina	56%	61%
Alabama	49%	72%
Florida	29%	74%
Illinois	26%	67%
Mississippi	69%	87%
North Carolina	27%	62%
Tennessee	26%	57%
Texas	20%	58%
Virginia	28%	59%

Source: CNN, "Entrance and Exit Polls," https://www.cnn.com/election/2020/entrance -and-exit-polls/

long tenure representing a monochrome state. During the campaign, he erred badly by failing at outreach. "I knew that our campaign had not done the work it needed to do," one aide put it, adding that the Sanders effort was "geared toward white progressives," leaving African American voters behind.[105] And African American Democrats tended to be more practical and less dogmatic than Sanders's white progressive base.[106]

Fear of Trump came also into play. For a long time, many Democrats had fantasized that the impeachment process would end in Trump's removal. By early 2020, they knew that the election would be their only chance to oust him, and victory was not certain. Before the pandemic killed so many Americans and crashed the economy, it looked as if Trump had at least an even-money chance to win reelection. In appraising candidates, Democrats placed a high value on the ability to beat him. After New Hampshire, Biden briefly lost his electability edge.[107] He got it back after South Carolina.

Some evidence suggests that the pandemic may have given Biden a final boost. James Bisbee and Dan Honig compared counties with and without reported cases in their local media market, before and after the outbreak of the virus. COVID-19 anxiety apparently resulted in diminished support for Sanders as compared with his support in the 2016 primaries.[108] Though this study is far from definitive, it makes intuitive sense. During an existential crisis, voters might be leery of a seventy-eight-year-old socialist who freely spoke of revolution and had recently suffered a heart attack. For all his gaffes and faults, Biden probably seemed a safer pick.

To people watching at home, the 2020 nomination contest may have looked like a canceled TV series whose showrunners had to wrap up elaborate plotlines in a hastily written final episode. This analogy assumes that the ending was inevitable and that the twists and turns were just devices to maintain audience interest. Could things have turned out differently? Perhaps. If Kamala Harris had shown message discipline and focused her campaign on an issue such as income inequality, she might have been able to sustain her early surge, which in turn might have given her entrée to the African American vote. If Elizabeth Warren had thought through the political implications of Medicare for All and offered a more moderate plan right from the start, she might have been able to build a coalition of mainstream and progressive Democrats. If Michael Bloomberg had humbly acknowledged fault and released women from their nondisclosure agreements, he might have supplanted Biden as the candidate of moderate Democrats. And most of all, if Bernie Sanders had resolved after the 2016 campaign to focus on African American voters, he might have survived South Carolina and gone on to win the nomination.

Of course, all of these scenarios are in the realm of pure speculation. Back in the real world, Joe Biden became the Democratic nominee. Amid an historic set of crises, he was now hoping that his epic journey would take him to the White House.

NOTES

1. Ronald Brownstein, "Biden's Been in Politics Longer Than Any US Presidential Nominee Ever. Here's Why That Matters," CNN, May 14, 2019, https://www.cnn.com/2019/05/14/politics/joe-biden-career-longevity/index.html.

2. Senate Historical Office, "Youngest Senator: November 16, 1818," https://www.senate.gov/artandhistory/history/minute/Youngest_Senator.htm.

3. John J. Pitney Jr., *After Reagan: Bush, Dukakis, and the 1988 Election* (Lawrence, Kansas: University Press of Kansas, 2019), 120.

4. William J. Eaton, "Reagan's 77 Years Are Beginning to Show: A Tired President Jokes about His Age," *Los Angeles Times*, June 4, 1988, https://www.latimes.com/archives/la-xpm-1988-06-04-mn-3863-story.html.

5. One exception to the pattern was 1940 Republican nominee Wendell Willkie, who had never held office. But even Willkie had served in the military, as a junior officer at the end of World War I.

6. Carole Kennedy, "Is the United States Ready for a Woman President? Is the Pope Protestant?" in *Anticipating Madam President*, ed. Roberta Ann Johnson (Boulder, CO: Lynne Rienner, 2003), 135.

7. Muriel Humphrey had briefly served as an appointed senator from Minnesota, succeeding her deceased husband Hubert Humphrey.

8. *Bowers v. Hardwick*, 478 U.S. 186 (1986). The Supreme Court overturned this decision in *Lawrence et al. v. Texas*, 539 U.S. 558 (2003).

9. "Gay and Lesbian Rights," Gallup, https://news.gallup.com/poll/1651/gay-lesbian-rights.aspx.

10. Werner Sombart, *Why Is There No Socialism in the United States*, trans. Patricia M. Hocking and C. T. Husbands (London: Macmillan, 1976 [1906]), https://link.springer.com/book/10.1007/978-1-349-02524-4.

11. House session, April 15, 2011, https://www.c-span.org/video/?298969-1/house-session.

12. Michael Kranish, "Inside Bernie Sanders's 1988 10-Day 'Honeymoon' in the Soviet Union," *Washington Post*, May 3, 2019, https://www.washingtonpost.com/politics/inside-bernie-sanderss-1988-10-day-honeymoon-in-the-soviet-union/2019/05/02/db543e18-6a9c-11e9-a66d-a82d3f3d96d5_story.html.

13. Dan Evon, "Did Bernie Sanders 'Honeymoon' in Soviet Russia?" Snopes, February 29, 2020, https://www.snopes.com/fact-check/bernie-sanders-honeymoon-russia.

14. Frank Newport, "Democrats More Positive About Socialism Than Capitalism," Gallup, August 13, 2018, https://news.gallup.com/poll/240725/democrats-positive-socialism-capitalism.aspx.

15. Frank Newport, "The Meaning of 'Socialism' to Americans Today," Gallup, October 4, 2018, https://news.gallup.com/opinion/polling-matters/243362/meaning-socialism-americans-today.aspx.

16. Frank Newport, "Majority in U.S. Support Idea of Fed-Funded Healthcare System," Gallup, May 16, 2016, https://news.gallup.com/poll/191504/majority-support-idea-fed-funded-healthcare-system.aspx.

17. Nisha Stickles and Barbara Corbellini Duarte, "Exclusive: Alexandria Ocasio-Cortez Explains What Democratic Socialism Means to Her," *Business Insider*, March 4, 2019, https://www.businessinsider.com/alexandria-ocasio-cortez-explains-what-democratic-socialism-means-2019-3.

18. Eliza Relman, "Alexandria Ocasio-Cortez Says Her Green New Deal Climate Plan Would Cost at Least $10 Trillion," *Business Insider*, June 5, 2019, https://www.businessinsider.com/alexandria-ocasio-cortez-says-green-new-deal-cost-10-trillion-2019-6; Doug Holtz-Eakin, "How Much Will the Green New Deal Cost?" Aspen Institute, June 11, 2019, https://www.aspeninstitute.org/blog-posts/how-much-will-the-green-new-deal-cost.

19. Pitney, *After Reagan*, 126–27.

20. Steve Kornacki, "Journey to Power: The History of Black Voters, 1976 to 2020," NBC News, July 29, 2019, https://www.nbcnews.com/politics/2020-election/journey-power-history-black-voters-1976-2020-n1029581.

21. James W. Ceaser, Andrew E. Busch, and John J. Pitney Jr., *Epic Journey: The 2008 Elections and American Politics* (Lanham, MD: Rowman & Littlefield, 2009), 116.

22. Lydia Saad, "The U.S. Remained Center-Right, Ideologically, in 2019," Gallup, January 9, 2020, https://news.gallup.com/poll/275792/remained-center-right-ideologically-2019.aspx.

23. Alexander Burns et al., "Who's Running for President in 2020?" *New York Times*, April 8, 2020, https://www.nytimes.com/interactive/2019/us/politics/2020-presidential-candidates.html.

24. Shane Goldmacher, "Hillary Clinton Says She Is Not Running for President in 2020," *New York Times*, March 4, 2020, https://www.nytimes.com/2019/03/04/us/politics/hillary-clinton-not-running.html.

25. Thomas Kaplan, "Elizabeth Warren's Slam on John Delaney Was Called the Line of the Night. Here's What She Said," *New York Times*, July 30, 2019, https://www.nytimes.com/2019/07/30/us/politics/elizabeth-warren-debate.html.

26. Dartunorro Clark, "Democrat Beto O'Rourke, In Viral Video, Defends NFL Protests," NBC News, August 23, 2018, https://www.nbcnews.com/politics/politics-news/democrat-beto-o-rourke-goes-viral-response-nfl-players-kneeling-n903176.

27. Peter Hamby, "'You Have to Have a Plan to Deal with Them': How the Media Fell Out of Love with Beto O'Rourke," *Vanity Fair*, May 15, 2019, https://www.vanityfair.com/news/2019/05/how-the-media-fell-out-of-love-with-beto-orourke.

28. Clint Watts, "Russia Mentions of Democratic Candidates," Foreign Policy Research Institute, November 19, 2019, https://www.fpri.org/fie/russia-media-mentions.

29. Beatrice Peterson, "Hawaii Rep. Tulsi Gabbard Defends Voting 'Present' on Impeachment as 'An Active Protest,'" ABC News, December 20, 2019, https://abc news.go.com/Politics/hawaii-rep-tulsi-gabbard-defends-voting-present-impeachment/ story?id=67820214.

30. Aris Folley, "'SNL' mocks Tulsi Gabbard after 'present' vote on impeachment: 'Democrats, I'll Get You, My Party, and Your Little Mayor Too,'" *The Hill*, December 22, 2019, https://thehill.com/blogs/in-the-know/in-the-know/475640-snl -mocks-tulsi-gabbard-after-present-vote-democrats-ill-get.

31. Marc Caputo and Daniel Strauss, "The 'Russian Asset' and the 'Warmonger': The Roots of the Clinton-Gabbard Dispute," *Politico*, October 23, 2019, https://www .politico.com/news/2019/10/23/tulsi-gabbard-hillary-clinton-dispute-054398.

32. Elena Schneider, "Why Gillibrand Crashed and Burned," *Politico*, August 29, 2019, https://www.politico.com/story/2019/08/29/kirsten-gillibrand-drops-out-2020 -race-1477845.

33. Natasha Korecki and Laura Nahmias, "Franken Scandal Haunts Gillibrand's 2020 Chances," *Politico*, November 26, 2018, https://www.politico.com/ story/2018/11/26/al-franken-kirsten-gillibrand-2020-1014697.

34. Grover Cleveland did serve as mayor of Buffalo, but during his tenure, the city had a population of 155,000.

35. A National Latino Voter Poll put Castro third among Latino voters, at 12 percent, behind Biden at 22 percent and Sanders at 20 percent. Todd J. Gillman, "Why Is Julián Castro, the Only Latino Candidate for President, Struggling to Catch On, Even with Latinos?" *Dallas Morning News*, November 9, 2019, https://www.dallasnews .com/news/politics/2019/11/09/julian-castros-balancing-act-yet-to-pay-off-court -latinos-without-getting-pegged-as-the-brown-guy/.

36. Emily Stewart, "Why Bill de Blasio Is So Hated, Explained," *Vox*, July 31, 2019, https://www.vox.com/policy-and-politics/2019/7/16/20694916/bill-de-blasio -2020-polls-eric-garner.

37. Maeve Reston, "LA and Iowa Have 'a Ton in Common,' LA's Mayor Garcetti Tells Iowa Voters," CNN, April 16, 2018, https://www.cnn.com/2018/04/15/politics/ garcetti-iowa-visit/index.html.

38. Soumya Karlamangla, "Long Before City Hall Rats, L.A. Has Struggled with the Rise of Typhus," *Los Angeles Times*, February 17, 2019, https://www.latimes .com/local/california/la-me-ln-typhus-20190217-story.html.

39. Dan Merica, "Richard Ojeda Ends Short-Lived 2020 Campaign," CNN, January 25, 2019, https://www.cnn.com/2019/01/25/politics/ojeda-ends-2020-campaign/ index.html.

40. "Transcript: Night 2 of the First Democratic Debate," June 27, 2019, https:// www.washingtonpost.com/politics/2019/06/28/transcript-night-first-democratic -debate.

41. Jonathan Martin and Alexander Burns, "Rebelling Republican Suburbs Offer Democrats Path to House Control," *New York Times*, December 18, 2017, https://

www.nytimes.com/2017/12/18/us/politics/house-control-2018-suburbs-trump-republicans-democrats.html.

42. Contributors with Ties to Hedge Funds Gave $450,750 to Booker, $272,150 to McConnell. Center for Responsive Politics, "Hedge Funds: Top Recipients," https://www.opensecrets.org/industries/recips.php?ind=F2700&cycle=2014&recipdetail=S&Mem=Y&sortorder=U.

43. Walter Bragman, "Cory Booker and 12 Other Dems Just Stopped Bernie Sanders' Amendment to Lower Prescription Drug Costs," *Paste*, January 12, 2017, https://www.pastemagazine.com/politics/cory-booker/thirteen-democrats-just-stopped-bernie-sanders-ame/.

44. Juliet Linderman and Tami Abdollah, "Harris Eyes Reform as Candidate, Was Cautious as Prosecutor," Associated Press, April 1, 2019, https://apnews.com/0e7dd2e5b2564a25b6266f0632da651e.

45. Emily Bazelon, "Kamala Harris, a 'Top Cop' in the Era of Black Lives Matter," *New York Times Magazine*, May 25, 2016, https://www.nytimes.com/2016/05/29/magazine/kamala-harris-a-top-cop-in-the-era-of-black-lives-matter.html.

46. Filipa Ioannou, "Kamala Harris Goes Viral Grilling Kavanaugh on Laws Restricting the Male Body," *San Francisco Chronicle*, September 6, 2018, https://www.sfgate.com/politics/article/kamala-harris-kavanaugh-male-body-roe-abortion-13209859.php.

47. Ken Kurson, "Kamala Harris Slammed for 'False' Video About Kavanaugh," September 12, 2018, https://californiaglobe.com/congress/kamala-harris-slammed-for-false-video-about-kavanaugh/.

48. Tim Marcin, "Cory Booker Says He's Having 'I Am Spartacus' Moment at Kavanaugh Hearing," *Newsweek*, September 6, 2018, https://www.newsweek.com/cory-booker-i-am-spartacus-moment-kavanaugh-hearing-claims-watch-1109658.

49. "Kavanaugh Hearing: Transcript," *Washington Post*, September 27, 2018, https://www.washingtonpost.com/news/national/wp/2018/09/27/kavanaugh-hearing-transcript.

50. Annmarie Timmins, "Voters in N.H. Thank Klobuchar For Her Composure During Kavanaugh Hearings," *Boston Globe*, February 18, 2019, https://www.bostonglobe.com/metro/2019/02/18/voters-thank-klobuchar-for-her-composure-during-kavanaugh-hearings/6S1Ydc7WfTJP8XdKWuIpZL/story.html.

51. Matt Flegenheimer and Sydney Ember, "How Amy Klobuchar Treats Her Staff," *New York Times*, February 22, 2019, https://www.nytimes.com/2019/02/22/us/politics/amy-klobuchar-staff.html.

52. Molly Redden and Amanda Terkel, "Sen. Amy Klobuchar's Mistreatment of Staff Scared Off Candidates to Manage Her Presidential Bid," *Huffington Post*, February 7, 2019, https://www.huffpost.com/entry/amy-klobuchar-abuse-staff-2020_n_5c5a1cb1e4b0871047588649.

53. Elena Schneider, "Klobuchar's Opening Pitch Sidetracked by Staff Horror Stories," *Politico*, February 10, 2019, https://www.politico.com/story/2019/02/10/amy-klobuchar-2020-staff-horror-stories-1160780.

54. James W. Ceaser, Andrew E. Busch, and John J. Pitney Jr., *Defying the Odds: The 2016 Elections and American Politics, Post-2018 Election Update* (Lanham, MD: Rowman & Littlefield, 2019), 204–5.

55. Philip Rucker and Scott Clement, "Poll: 60 Percent Disapprove of Trump, While Clear Majorities Back Mueller and Sessions," *Washington Post*, August 31, 2018, https://www.washingtonpost.com/politics/poll-60-percent-disapprove-of-trump-while-clear-majorities-back-mueller-and-sessions/2018/08/30/4cd32174-ac7c-11e8-a8d7-0f63ab8b1370_story.html.

56. Chris Cillizza, "Elizabeth Warren Might Have Actually Made Things Worse with Her DNA Gambit," CNN, October 17, 2018, https://www.cnn.com/2018/10/16/politics/elizabeth-warren-donald-trump-pocahontas/index.html.

57. "Ultra-Millionaire Tax," Warren Democrats, https://elizabethwarren.com/plans/ultra-millionaire-tax.

58. Emily Bazelon, "Elizabeth Warren Is Completely Serious," *New York Times Magazine*, June 17, 2019, https://www.nytimes.com/2019/06/17/magazine/elizabeth-warren-president.html.

59. ABC News, "'This Week' Transcript," October 13, 2019, https://abcnews.go.com/Politics/week-transcript-10-13-19-treasury-secretary-steven/story?id=66243200.

60. Stephanie Saul and Rachel Shorey, "How Michael Bloomberg Used His Money to Aid Democratic Victories in the House," *New York Times*, November 30, 2018, https://www.nytimes.com/2018/11/30/us/politics/michael-bloomberg-democrats-donate.html.

61. Neal Rothschild and Sara Fischer, "Interest in Pete Buttigieg Is Exploding," Axios, April 2, 2019, https://www.axios.com/2020-presidential-election-pete-buttigieg-mayor-pete-3427076d-f8e5-4000-99d6-7adceb2f3bcc.html.

62. Jonathan Martin and Alexander Burns, "Biden Didn't Rush into 2020. The Race Came to Him Anyway," *New York Times*, April 6, 2019, https://www.nytimes.com/2019/04/06/us/politics/biden-2020.html.

63. Tara Law, "Biden Promises to Be 'More Mindful' of Women's Personal Space," *Time*, April 3, 2019, https://time.com/5563770/joe-biden-women.

64. "Joe Biden Holds Presidential Rally," CNN, April 29, 2019, https://time.com/5563770/joe-biden-women/http://transcripts.cnn.com/TRANSCRIPTS/1904/29/cg.02.html.

65. Pew Research Center, "In Changing U.S. Electorate, Race and Education Remain Stark Dividing Lines," June 2020, https://www.pewresearch.org/politics/2020/06/02/the-changing-composition-of-the-electorate-and-partisan-coalitions.

66. "National: Washington, Obama, and Trump, Oh My!" Monmouth University Poll, December 10, 2019, https://www.monmouth.edu/polling-institute/documents/monmouthpoll_us_121019.pdf.

67. Ronald Brownstein, "How Pundits May Be Getting Electability All Wrong," *The Atlantic*, September 12, 2019, https://www.theatlantic.com/politics/archive/2019/09/electability-democrats-2020-joe-biden/597904.

68. Raymond Arke, "One Quarter Down: How the Packed 2020 Democratic Presidential Field Fared in Fundraising," Center for Responsive Politics, April 16, 2019, https://www.opensecrets.org/news/2019/04/how-2020-democratic-presidential-fundraising.

69. Melanie Mason and Mark Z. Barabak, "After Dazzling Debut, Kamala Harris Falls from Top of Presidential Pack," *Los Angeles Times*, May 31, 2019, https://www

.latimes.com/politics/la-na-pol-kamala-harris-campaign-california-20190531-story
.html.

70. Democratic National Committee, "DNC Announces Details for the First Two Presidential Primary Debates," February 14, 2019, https://democrats.org/news/dnc-announces-details-for-the-first-two-presidential-primary-debates.

71. "Full transcript: 2019 Democratic Debate Night Two," NBC News, June 27, 2019, https://www.nbcnews.com/politics/2020-election/full-transcript-2019-democratic-debate-night-two-sortable-topic-n1023601.

72. Astead W. Herndon and Sheryl Gay Stolberg, "How Joe Biden Became the Democrats' Anti-Busing Crusader," *New York Times*, July 15, 2019, https://www.nytimes.com/2019/07/15/us/politics/biden-busing.html.

73. Jonathan Martin, "'You Don't Have to Be in Des Moines': Democrats Expand Primary Map, Spurred by Social Media," *New York Times*, June 1, 2019, https://www.nytimes.com/2019/06/01/us/politics/2020-democratic-primaries.html.

74. *Parents Involved in Community Schools v. Seattle School District No. 1*, 551 U.S. 701 (2007), https://supreme.justia.com/cases/federal/us/551/701.

75. Reid Champlin and Jessica Piper, "Top Tier of 2020 Democrats Forms after Q2 Fundraising," Center for Responsive Politics, July 16, 2019, https://www.opensecrets.org/news/2019/07/top-tier-of-2020-democrats-forms-after-q2-fundraising.

76. Reid J. Epstein and Richard A. Oppel Jr., "Buttigieg, Struggling with Black Voters, Releases Plan to Address Racial Inequities," *New York Times*, July 11, 2019, https://www.nytimes.com/2019/07/11/us/politics/pete-buttigieg-racism.html.

77. Stephanie Saul, "Buttigieg Campaign Used Stock Photo of Kenyan Woman to Illustrate Plan for Black America," *New York Times*, November 18, 2019, https://www.nytimes.com/2019/11/18/us/politics/buttigieg-stock-photo-kenya.html.

78. "Transcript: The First Night of the Second Democratic Debate," July 30, 2019, https://www.washingtonpost.com/politics/2019/07/31/transcript-first-night-second-democratic-debate.

79. "Who Talked the Most during the Third Democratic Debate," *Washington Post*, September 13, 2019, https://www.washingtonpost.com/graphics/2019/politics/who-spoke-most-at-democratic-debate-september.

80. Aaron Bycoffe, Sarah Frostenson and Julia Wolfe, "A Final Look at Who Won the Third Democratic Debate," FiveThirtyEight, September 16, 2019, https://projects.fivethirtyeight.com/democratic-debate-september-poll.

81. "Warren Continues to Climb while Biden Slips Quinnipiac University National Poll Finds; Democratic Primary Is Neck And Neck," Quinnipiac University, September 25, 2019, https://poll.qu.edu/images/polling/us/us09252019_umpj13.pdf/.

82. "The October Democratic Debate Transcript," *Washington Post*, October 15, 2019, https://www.washingtonpost.com/politics/2019/10/15/october-democratic-debate-transcript.

83. Amber Phillips, "Why 2020 Democrats Are Backing Off Medicare-For-All, In Four Charts," *Washington Post*, August 21, 2019, https://www.washingtonpost.com/politics/2019/08/21/why-democrats-are-backing-off-medicare-for-all-charts.

84. Annie Linskey, Jeff Stein, and Dan Balz, "How a Fight Over Health Care Entangled Elizabeth Warren—and Reshaped the Democratic Presidential Race,"

Washington Post, November 30, 2019, https://www.washingtonpost.com/politics/how-a-fight-over-health-care-entangled-elizabeth-warren—and-reshaped-the-democratic-presidential-race/2019/11/29/40f4d30e-0bb0-11ea-97ac-a7ccc8dd1ebc_story.html.

85. Karl Evers-Hillstrom, "Biden Far from Frontrunner in Q3 Fundraising," Center for Responsive Politics, October 4, 2019, https://www.opensecrets.org/news/2019/10/joe-biden-far-from-frontrunner-fundraising.

86. Evan Halper, "Michael Bloomberg Brings His Billions—and His Baggage—to Presidential Race," *Los Angeles Times*, November 25, 2019, https://www.latimes.com/politics/story/2019-11-25/bloomberg-election-kickoff-news-conference.

87. Cheyenne Haslett, "How the Impeachment Trial Has Changed the Iowa Plan for Warren, Sanders and Klobuchar," ABC News, January 30, 2020, https://abcnews.go.com/Politics/impeachment-trial-benches-senators-seeking-time-2020-trail/story?id=68595824.

88. Sixty of the satellite caucuses were in-state, twenty-four were in out-of-state sites in the United States, and three were in foreign countries. Iowa Democratic Party, "2020 Iowa Democratic Party Caucus: Satellite Caucuses," https://www.thecaucuses.org/satellite-caucuses.

89. Ben Collins, Maura Barrett and Vaughn Hillyard, "'Clog the Lines': Internet Trolls Deliberately Disrupted the Iowa Caucuses Hotline for Reporting Results," NBC News, February 6, 2020, https://www.nbcnews.com/tech/security/clog-lines-iowa-caucus-hotline-posted-online-encouragement-disrupt-results-n1131521.

90. Stephen Gruber-Miller and William Cummings, "Joe Biden, in New Hampshire, Calls Preliminary 4th Place Finish in Iowa Caucuses 'A Gut Punch,'" *Des Moines Register*, February 5, 2020, https://www.desmoinesregister.com/story/news/elections/presidential/caucus/2020/02/05/joe-biden-calls-4th-place-iowa-caucus-finish-gut-punch/4669943002.

91. Anna North, "Biden's 'Lying Dog-Faced Pony Soldier' Moment, Explained," *Vox*, February 10, 2020, https://www.vox.com/2020/2/10/21131327/biden-dog-faced-pony-soldier-new-hampshire.

92. "New Hampshire Democratic Debate Transcript," February 7, 2020, https://www.rev.com/blog/transcripts/new-hampshire-democratic-debate-transcript.

93. Natasha Korecki, Marc Caputo, and Maya King, "'Blood in the Water': Biden Campaign Reels after New Hampshire Trouncing," *Politico*, February 12, 2020, https://www.politico.com/news/2020/02/12/biden-new-hampshire-primary-114291.

94. Walter Shapiro, "Joe Biden Is Collapsing," *The New Republic*, February 8, 2020, https://newrepublic.com/article/156510/joe-biden-collapsing.

95. "Full transcript: Ninth Democratic Debate in Las Vegas," February 19, 2020, https://www.nbcnews.com/politics/2020-election/full-transcript-ninth-democratic-debate-las-vegas-n1139546.

96. Dino-Ray Ramos and Ted Johnson, "Democratic Debate Draws Record Audience of 19.7 Million Viewers for NBC and MSNBC," *Deadline*, February 20, 2020, https://deadline.com/2020/02/democratic-debate-criminal-minds-tv-ratings-wednesday-1202864463.

97. Eli Yokley, "Bloomberg Loses Ground Following Debate Debut in Las Vegas," *Morning Consult*, February 21, 2020, https://morningconsult.com/2020/02/21/michael-bloomberg-polling-post-debate-las-vegas.

98. "Sanders Takes Top Spot in Dem Primary as Biden Falls, Quinnipiac University National Poll Finds," Quinnipiac University, February 10, 2020; https://poll.qu.edu/national/release-detail?ReleaseID=3655; Ben Wieder, "Joe Biden Receives Surge of Support From Donors of Former 2020 Rivals," McClatchy News Service, February 3, 2020, https://www.mcclatchydc.com/article239878223.html.

99. Matt Viser and Cleve R. Wootson Jr., "Eighteen Days That Resuscitated Joe Biden's Nearly Five-Decade Career," *Washington Post*, February 29, 2020, https://www.washingtonpost.com/politics/eighteen-days-that-resuscitated-joe-bidens-nearly-five-decade-career/2020/02/29/c18a5130-5a7d-11ea-ab68-101ecfec2532_story.html.

100. "Town Hall with Democratic Presidential Candidate, Former Vice President Joe Biden," February 26, 2020, http://transcripts.cnn.com/TRANSCRIPTS/2002/26/se.02.html.

101. Gillian Brockell, "A Civil Rights Love Story: The Congressman Who Met His Wife in Jail In 1960," *Washington Post*, January 10, 2020, https://www.washingtonpost.com/history/2020/01/10/clyburn-recounts-1960-meet-cute-with-his-future-wife-jail/.

102. Chris Kahn, "Key Black Lawmaker's Backing Factors Big in Biden's South Carolina Win: Poll," Reuters, February 29, 2020, https://www.reuters.com/article/us-usa-election-south-carolina-poll/clyburns-endorsement-of-biden-a-factor-for-a-majority-of-south-carolina-voters-poll-idUSKBN20N13S.

103. Carol E. Lee, Kristen Welker, Josh Lederman and Amanda Golden, "Looking for Obama's Hidden Hand in Candidates Coalescing Around Biden," NBC News, March 2, 2020, https://www.nbcnews.com/politics/2020-election/looking-obama-s-hidden-hand-candidate-coalescing-around-biden-n1147471.

104. Jim Clyburn, Twitter post, February 26, 2020, https://twitter.com/ClyburnSC06/status/1232674035076681728?s=20.

105. Sean Sullivan, "Insiders Recount How Sanders Lost the Black Vote—and the Nomination Slipped Away," *Washington Post*, March 25, 2020, https://www.washingtonpost.com/politics/insiders-recount-how-sanders-lost-the-black-vote—and-the-nomination-slipped-away/2020/03/24/2b7b8b8e-685e-11ea-b313-df458622c2cc_story.html.

106. Amina Dunn, "5 Facts about Black Democrats," Pew Research Center, February 27, 2020, https://www.pewresearch.org/fact-tank/2020/02/27/5-facts-about-black-democrats.

107. Ursula Perano, "Poll: Joe Biden Loses Status as Most Electable Democrat," Axios, February 13, 2020, https://www.axios.com/biden-electability-sanders-2020-democrats-dcf4a53b-1a5d-4cde-9a79-41389975229d.html.

108. James Bisbee and Dan Honig, "Flight to Safety: 2020 Democratic Primary Election Results and COVID-19," *COVID Economics*, April 10, 2020, https://cepr.org/file/9011/download?token=OYF-efkM.

Chapter Three

Disease, Disorder, Downturn

The Interregnum

Until the 1990s, nomination contests typically lasted deep into springtime, and voters did not think of the final presidential race as starting until Labor Day.[1] Since then, there has been a span of three to six months between the clinching of the nomination and the nominee's official coronation at the national convention. We call this period "the interregnum."[2]

When an incumbent president is running without serious competition for the party nomination, the interregnum ought to be a season of plenty. Fundraising is not a huge challenge, because nearly everyone with an interest in federal policy wants access to the chief executive. Campaign operatives like to say that when the president enters a room, it fills up with money. Even more important, the president can use the powers of the office to dominate the news cycle. In the words of the lead character in the 1995 movie *The American President*, "The White House is the single greatest home court advantage in the modern world." Conversely, the interregnum can be tough on the outparty. Once the press has judged that the nomination is a done deal, the challenger must struggle for public attention. The choice of a running mate offers the best chance at breaking through, and even that opportunity can blow up if the vice presidential candidate turns out to be badly flawed.

As 2020 began, the Trump team was hoping that the interregnum would be both short and profitable. A rough, prolonged Democratic nomination contest seemed to be in the offing. By the time the Democratic nominee emerged, she or he would be dealing with an empty war chest and a fractured party. In the meantime, once Trump won his certain acquittal in the Senate impeachment trial, he could focus the nation's attention on steady economic growth and low unemployment. He faced only token opposition in the Republican primaries, several of which had actually been cancelled and replaced with delegate selection by party insiders.

It was not going to be that kind of interregnum. Instead of building up his political advantages, Trump had to deal with a deadly pandemic, a sudden recession, and outbreaks of civil disorder. The triple crises undercut him in several ways.

First, they convinced many Americans that the country was on the wrong track—always a bad situation for an incumbent president. For three years, good economic times had given Trump a bit of political insulation from the many controversies of his tenure. He never enjoyed majority approval in polling averages, but as long as the economy was humming and the United States was avoiding a new war, some voters were willing to overlook his scandals and missteps. This setting changed during the interregnum. Everyone felt the effects of the pandemic and the subsequent shutdowns. Nearly 200,000 died during this period, and millions underwent bouts of unemployment. Some lost jobs and businesses for good. Incidents such as the killing of George Floyd brought renewed attention to police misconduct and the nation's troubled race relations. Protests were widespread, and in certain places, they turned violent. When the country is in such pain, a president needs to show care and concern. The New York real estate business produces few empaths, so Trump had little experience on this score. He had spent his adult life trying to project ruthlessness, and he had once tried to trademark his tagline, "You're fired!"[3]

Trump had a salesman's instincts, constantly downplaying bad news, hyping good news, and stretching the truth beyond the breaking point. Those habits, which had brought him prominence in business and entertainment, served him poorly in 2020. National crisis, as Franklin Roosevelt said, "is preeminently the time to speak the truth, the whole truth, frankly and boldly."[4] Instead, Trump deliberately distorted the dangers of the pandemic. When Americans needed to trust what their president was telling them, many could not.

For several months after the March shutdowns, social distancing restrictions forced both candidates to curtail the kind of campaigning that they loved most. For four years, Trump's enormous rallies had won few converts to his cause, but they did keep his spirits up and gave a morale boost to his core supporters. Without with energy of the rallies, mid-2020 was a time of great frustration for him. Meanwhile, Biden kept to his home in Wilmington, Delaware, and communicated with people from a makeshift studio in his basement. Normally, such limitations would hobble a challenger. Not in 2020. Biden led Trump before the shutdown, and his lead held steady throughout the interregnum. And Biden's basement campaign worked to his advantage in another way. Biden had always been prone to verbal blunders, which had forced him out of the 1988 presidential race. Now at an advanced age, he occasionally had "senior moments" when he seemed to lose his train of thought. Accordingly, the reduced campaign schedule limited the risk of public embarrassments.

For all his political troubles, Trump still retained formidable assets. First, he enjoyed the fervent loyalty of core supporters, who had stuck with him through the *Access Hollywood* tape of 2016, the impeachment of 2019, and countless other episodes. Second, the flip side of a firm base was a flawed opposition. Although Biden got fairly good ratings as a person, some prominent voices in his party espoused positions that were much less popular. Biden's low profile during the spring and summer created a vacuum that these voices filled. Phrases such as "Green New Deal" and "Defund the Police" would provide the GOP with a good deal of ammunition for the fall campaign.

The final asset was the awesome power of the presidency. All chief executives had used their authority for political advantage, but none had so openly mobilized the machinery of government to serve a reelection campaign. Trump boldly took actions that other presidents would not have even considered, such as staging his acceptance speech on the White House lawn. He had spent a lifetime disregarding norms and defying the odds, and he had no intention of stopping now.

PRELUDE TO A SHUTDOWN

On January 27, Biden published an op-ed in *USA Today*: "The possibility of a pandemic is a challenge Donald Trump is unqualified to handle as president . . . Trump's demonstrated failures of judgment and his repeated rejection of science make him the worst possible person to lead our country through a global health challenge."[5] At the time, the piece got little attention. The political community was focusing on the impeachment trial and the upcoming Iowa caucuses, and Biden's prospects for the nomination seemed shaky at best. But Biden was speaking to the issue that would dominate politics in 2020.

Trump seemed unconcerned. On the evening of February 4, he proclaimed in his State of the Union address that good times were rolling: "Jobs are booming, incomes are soaring, poverty is plummeting, crime is falling, confidence is surging, and our country is thriving and highly respected again. America's enemies are on the run, America's fortunes are on the rise, and America's future is blazing bright."[6] Notwithstanding the Trumpian hyperbole, the proclamation had some truth to it: in a number of ways, America really had been doing well. The day after the speech, the Senate ended his impeachment trial by voting acquittal, with only Mitt Romney of Utah breaking party ranks. Despite his low approval ratings, he appeared to be in good shape to start a reelection campaign. According to a Monmouth University poll one week after his Senate trial, two-thirds of voters thought that he would win in November.[7]

Coronavirus did not yet dominate public attention, and he made only passing reference to it in his State of the Union. "We are coordinating with the Chinese government and working closely together on the coronavirus outbreak in China," he said. "My administration will take all necessary steps to safeguard our citizens from this threat."[8] One of the steps, a ban on travel from China, had just gone into effect. Biden was already faulting Trump's response to the pandemic, tweeting, "We need to lead the way with science—not Donald Trump's record of hysteria, xenophobia, and fear-mongering."[9] Trump would later cite this attack to say that Biden opposed the travel ban, though Biden would claim that he was speaking broadly about Trump's attitude toward other countries. It did, however, immediately follow the announcement of the ban. Biden did not explicitly support that ban until April 3.[10]

From an early date, there was an inconsistency between Trump's public confidence and private concern. "Well, we pretty much shut it down coming in from China," Trump told Sean Hannity on Fox.[11] He tweeted that the Chinese attack on the virus "will be successful, especially as the weather starts to warm & the virus hopefully becomes weaker, and then gone. Great discipline is taking place in China, as President Xi strongly leads what will be a very successful operation. We are working closely with China to help!"[12] Behind closed doors, Trump took a different tone. "You just breathe the air and that's how it's passed," Trump told journalist Bob Woodward on February 7. "And so that's a very tricky one. That's a very delicate one. It's also more deadly than even your strenuous flus."[13] White House aides also made private comments that belied what they said on television. On February 24, on CNBC, economic adviser Larry Kudlow said, "We have contained this, I won't say airtight but pretty close to airtight."[14] At a meeting of the Hoover Institution board, however, he reportedly said that the virus was "contained in the U.S., to date, but now we just don't know."[15] The attendees got the hint. Word spread in the financial community, and a stock market selloff ensued.

The crisis was getting worse. Loopholes in the travel restrictions allowed thousands to arrive on direct flights from China.[16] Many more were coming in from Europe, where the virus was spreading rapidly. Though it would not be public knowledge until months later, COVID was already claiming American lives.[17] Dr. Nancy Messonnier, an official with the Centers for Disease Control and Prevention, said at the end of the month, "Ultimately, we expect we will see community spread in this country. It's not so much a question of if this will happen anymore but rather more a question of exactly when this will happen and how many people in this country will have severe illness."[18] She bluntly warned Americans to prepare for school closures and cancellation of mass gatherings. Trump reportedly threatened to fire her for sounding that alarm, and Health and Human Services Secretary Alex Azar repeated the line that the virus had been "contained."[19] In a press conference, Trump said, "I think every aspect of our society should be prepared. I don't think it's going to come to that, especially with the fact that we're going down, not up. We're going very substantially down, not up."[20]

Cases were going up. During what critics would call the "lost month" of February, the United States had failed to take several steps that could have curbed the spread of the virus.[21] The first was a ban on travel from Europe, which did not occur until March 11, too late to do much good. The second was a surge in medical supplies and protective equipment. Severe shortages plagued hospitals during the early months of the pandemic, and while production of ventilators and masks eventually ramped up, other critical supplies remained scarce.[22] The third was mass testing. On March 6, Trump visited the Atlanta headquarters of the Centers for Disease Control and Prevention (CDC) and said that "anybody that needs a test gets a test. We—they're there. They have the tests. And the tests are beautiful. Anybody that needs a test gets a test."[23] That claim was inaccurate: there was a severe shortage of tests.[24] The fourth failure lay in public education. Despite the efforts of officials such as Dr. Messonnier, the federal government did not send clear and consistent messages about the severity of the disease or the need for preventive measures such as social distancing.

It was not just a federal failure or a Republican one. The New York metropolitan area was the epicenter of the problem at the start, and both the state and the city governments were slow to react. Dr. Thomas R. Frieden, the former head of the CDC and former commissioner of the city's Health Department, told the *New York Times* that if state and local authorities had adopted social-distancing measures a week or two earlier than they did, the estimated death toll from the outbreak might have been only half as large.[25] Governor Andrew Cuomo also came under criticism for his administration's March advisory requiring nursing homes to accept the readmission of patients from hospitals, even if they were positive for COVID. Many blamed the advisory for deaths at nursing homes, a charge that Cuomo disputed. American and global health officials sometimes gave inconsistent advice. The U.S. surgeon general, Jerome Weeks, declared in February that mask wearing by the general public was "NOT helpful," a conclusion that he reversed by summer.[26] For a time, health experts held that COVID could be easily spread on surfaces, before concluding it could not.[27]

Across the country, state governments responded with increasingly drastic steps, including the closure of schools and non-essential businesses, which were justified as a short-term measure intended to "flatten the curve." On

March 11, Trump gave an address to the nation in which he sketched federal actions against the rapidly spreading disease. The speech erred on important details, overstating the extent of the European travel ban and falsely claiming that insurers had agreed to waive copayments for COVID treatment. (The agreement involved testing, not treatments.[28]) The stock market, which had been slipping, fell further after the speech. This development probably dismayed Trump, who had previously taken a rising Dow Jones industrial average as a key indicator of his economic success.

In one respect, though, Trump's speech did strike a customary note for a president in crisis: "We are all in this together. We must put politics aside, stop the partisanship, and unify together as one nation and one family."[29] In a press briefing a week later, he likened the national emergency to the Second World War and explicitly labeled himself a "wartime president." He continued: "And now it's our time. We must sacrifice together because we are all in this together and we'll come through together. It's the invisible enemy. That's always the toughest enemy: the invisible enemy. But we're going to defeat the invisible enemy. I think we're going to do it even faster than we thought. And it will be a complete victory. It'll be a total victory."[30]

He got the customary public response, as his approval ratings rose modestly for the next few weeks.[31] However, his unity theme would not last long, and neither would the rally effect.

DARKNESS AT SPRINGTIME

Trump was surely hoping that the 2020 race would become something like a khaki election. After all, Abraham Lincoln and Franklin Roosevelt had won reelection during times of existential conflict. Patriotic appeals and warnings against changing horses in midstream enabled both of them to defeat strong opponents. Trump, however, overlooked a crucial part of the wartime political equation: bipartisanship. In 1864, the GOP chose a Democratic senator from the South as Lincoln's running mate. During the Second World War, FDR's secretary of state was a Republican and his navy secretary had been the GOP candidate for vice president in 1936. The rough equivalent for Trump would have consisted of giving a cabinet post to Senator Tim Kaine (D-VA), the 2016 Democratic vice presidential nominee.

Such a move would have been almost unimaginable for Trump. As it turned out, he had little interest even in symbolic efforts to rise above partisanship and reach across the aisle. On the same day that he proclaimed himself a wartime president, he tweeted, "95% Approval Rating in the Republican Party, 53% overall. Not bad considering I get nothing but Fake & Corrupt News, day and night. 'Russia, Russia, Russia', then 'the Ukraine Scam (where's the Whistleblower?)', the 'Impeachment Hoax', and more, more, more. . . . Also, according to the Daily Caller, leading Sleepy Joe Biden in Florida, 48% to 42%."[32] Throughout the entire interregnum, Trump did not have a single meeting with House Speaker Nancy Pelosi. The last time that they had spoken face to face was October 16, 2019. After a contentious meeting that day, Trump tweeted a photo of Pelosi literally standing up to a conference room full of Trump officials. He thought it would embarrass her, but it instantly became a hit among her supporters. Pelosi made her contribution to frosty relations when she ostentatiously tore up a copy of Trump's State of the Union Address as he finished delivering it.

With the physical campaign trail off limits for the time being, Trump increased his presence on television. More visibility did not translate into greater popularity, as he reverted to the habits that had held his approval rating below 50 percent since his inauguration. When a reporter asked him whether he took responsibility for the lag in testing, he said, "Yeah, no, I don't take responsibility at all, because we were given a—a set of circumstances and we were given rules, regulations, and specifications from a different time."[33] The phrase "I don't take responsibility" grated on Americans who expected the chief executive to do just that, and it would provide grist for attack ads for the rest of the year. At the press conference at which he invoked national unity, he shrugged off reports that athletes could get COVID tests that were not yet widely available to ordinary Americans: "perhaps that's been the story of life." He pivoted away from his earlier deference to the Chinese government, and now blamed it for the virus. The Beijing regime was blameworthy indeed, but some heard a racial undertone when he spoke of "the Chinese virus." Reporter Yamiche Alcindor asked him about a White House official who had used the term "Kung flu." He asked her to repeat the term.

Q—term "Kung flu." My question is—

THE PRESIDENT: "Kung flu"?

Q—do you think that's wrong? "Kung flu." And do you think using the term "Chinese virus"—that puts Asian Americans at risk, that people might target them?

THE PRESIDENT: No, not at all. No, not at all. I think they probably would agree with it 100 percent. It comes from China. There's nothing not to agree on.[34]

Trump apparently wanted people to remember "Kung flu," and they did, much to his delight. During a June event with youthful supporters, he noted that the disease had different names. An audience member shouted, "Kung

flu!" and Trump responded, "'Kung flu,' yeah. [Applause.] Kung flu. . . .
Some people call it the 'Chinese flu,' the 'China flu.' Right?"[35]

By the end of March, he was in political attack mode. In a phone conversation with campaign surrogates, communications director Tim Murtaugh
reportedly said, "This is the bottom line: President Trump is leading the nation in this war against the coronavirus, and Joe Biden, the Democrats and
the media have decided to be the opposition in that war."[36] His reelection
campaign produced a minute-long digital ad attempting to link Joe Biden
to China. "During America's crisis, Biden protected China's feelings," the
ad said, amid a series of clips showing Biden praising the Chinese.[37] The ad
backfired. Democrats pointed to Trump's recent praise for Xi Jinping and
noted that one of the "Chinese" leaders pictured in the ad was Gary Locke, a
Chinese American who had served as governor of Washington.

Trump erred when he told a Fox News town hall that he hoped "to have
the country opened up and just raring to go by Easter."[38] Public health experts noted that the target date was unrealistic and that hard times lay ahead.
Of course, the pandemic itself mattered more than anything that Trump
said. By April 29, COVID-19 infections had topped one million and deaths
had reached 58,355—more than the entire Vietnam War.[39] Knowing that
the shutdown would cause severe economic damage, Congress had already
passed the Coronavirus Aid, Relief, and Economic Security (CARES) Act.
Providing $2.2 trillion in tax relief and outlays, the measure was the biggest
spending bill in American history. But it would take time before Americans
could feel its effects. During the month of April, the unemployment rate increased by 10.3 percentage points to 14.7 percent. Those figures represented
the highest jobless rate and the largest over-the-month increase in the history of the data, going back to 1948.[40] Division and mistrust spread further
as some Republicans expressed suspicions that Democratic governors had
strictly locked down their economies to damage Trump's reelection effort or
that they were using the COVID crisis to permanently "reset" the economy
on a more statist course.

The pandemic was infecting every corner of American life. Businesses
closed, sometimes permanently. Schools went online, with uneven results.
Students faced the heartbreak of cancelled sports seasons and commencement
events. Couples had to postpone weddings, at best settling for tiny, socially
distanced ceremonies. Worst of all, suicides and drug overdoses soared and
many COVID victims died alone, because their loved ones could not visit
hospitals and hospices to say goodbye. In May, a nationwide survey found
that 90 percent of respondents reported emotional distress stemming from the
pandemic.[41] Around the same time, more than half of respondents told the
Kaiser Health Tracking Poll that "the worst is yet to come."[42]

Trump had once suggested that COVID, like seasonal flu, would disappear with warm weather. He told governors back in February, "you know, a lot of people think that goes away in April with the heat—as the heat comes in. Typically, that will go away in April."[43] Although the daily count of new cases had declined somewhat by the middle of May, the pandemic was not going away. Trump blamed Democrats. He told the *New York Post* that he opposed a bailout for states facing budget problems stemming from the pandemic: "It's not fair to the Republicans because all the states that need help—they're run by Democrats in every case."[44] At first, Democratic areas did indeed suffer the most. Much of the death toll occurred in large urban communities, especially the New York metropolitan area.[45] Then the geography of COVID started to change, as more and more "red" counties reported high prevalence.[46]

The "red shift" did not necessarily change the behavior of individual Republicans when it came to masking and social distancing. Trump's messaging on the topic was inconsistent. He sometimes spoke about need for masking, but at other times, he mocked the practice. At a press conference, he asked a reporter to remove a mask so he could hear the question more clearly. When the reporter declined, Trump said, "Oh, okay, because you want to be politically correct. Go ahead."[47] He retweeted a video of a maskless young man saying at a crowded Florida bar, "Uh oh, wouldn't want the Commies in blue states to see us Floridians all out at bars having a good time with no face masks."[48] (A few weeks after the video, COVID outbreaks forced Florida to close its bars.) A *Wall Street Journal* poll found that, of voters who always wore a mask outside the house, two-thirds supported Biden. Among those who never or seldom wore a mask, 83 percent were for Trump. Although these data do not prove that Trump caused his supporters to forgo masking, they do show that his disparagement of masks found a receptive audience.[49]

Trump made other comments that disturbed the public health community. At a briefing with members of his coronavirus task force, an official talked about the use of bleach and other disinfectants to clean indoor surfaces. Trump misunderstood the remarks. He said, "And then I see the disinfectant, where it knocks it out in a minute. One minute. And is there a way we can do something like that, by injection inside or almost a cleaning. Because you see it gets in the lungs and it does a tremendous number on the lungs. So it would be interesting to check that."[50] Contrary to Democratic attacks, Trump was not explicitly advising Americans to chug bleach, but manufacturers worried that people could read his comments that way. A Clorox spokesperson issued a statement: "Bleach and other disinfectants are not suitable for consumption or injection under any circumstances. People should always read the label for proper usage instructions."[51] On other occasions, Trump pitched hydroxychloroquine as a potentially game-changing medication for COVID. FDA initially granted an emergency use authorization, which it revoked after concluding that it was ineffective against the virus and could be dangerous if people took it for off-label purposes.[52]

An internet survey by the Centers for Disease Control and Prevention found that one-third of adults had unsafely used disinfectants and other topical chemicals to ward off COVID.[53] It was not clear how many suffered serious injury as a result. As for the other purported cure, one man died after ingesting a cleaning compound under the mistaken impression that it contained hydroxychloroquine. Trump's advocacy of the medication did cause a shortage, which created problems for those who needed it to treat lupus.[54] His gaffes put him on the wrong side of public opinion. A *Morning Consult* poll in May found that only 23 percent of registered voters supported using hydroxychloroquine for COVID, down from 29 percent in April.[55] Trump still continued to support it, dismissing an FDA warning as a "Trump enemy statement."[56] A couple of months later, after he retweeted video promoting the drug, a HarrisX poll found that 59 percent disapproved of his action.[57]

As the weather got warmer, it was clear that the pandemic was hurting Trump's political standing. Events that started in late May gave him an opportunity to change the subject.

LAW AND ORDER, THEN AND NOW

On May 25, 2020, Minneapolis police arrested an African American man named George Floyd for allegedly using a counterfeit bill. Although Floyd was in handcuffs and lying facedown on the pavement, one of the officers knelt on Floyd's neck for several minutes, killing him. A bystander recorded the incident on video, which soon went viral and triggered massive demonstrations across the country. Some of the protests turned violent. For a time, this turmoil partially eclipsed the pandemic in the mass media, and Trump tried to frame it as an issue of "law and order," a phrase that he often repeated. Many Americans saw it differently, focusing on police misconduct and racial inequality. To understand these divergent perspectives, we need step back for a moment and examine Trump's background. We should also consider the ways in which American society had changed during his public life.

A political leader's worldview is, at least in part, the product of the setting in which that person came of age. Born in 1946, Trump was eligible to cast his first presidential vote in 1968. (In those days, the voting age in New York and most other states was twenty-one.) During the previous eight years, the rate of violent crime had nearly doubled. Waves of urban riots had swept across the country, most recently after the assassination of Dr. Martin Luther King Jr. Protests against the Vietnam War were growing, and they sometimes resulted in clashes with police. Whereas crime and civil unrest were non-issues as recently as 1960, they were now at the center of national debate. Public opinion surveys from the period are revealing. In early 1968, for the first time since the start of scientific polling in the 1930s, the public saw crime and lawlessness as the nation's top domestic problem.[58] In a CBS poll, 70 percent of whites thought that police should be "tougher than they have been" in handling riots, compared with just 17 percent of African Americans.[59] A survey of major Northern cities found that African Americans tended to blame riots on urban economic problems while whites blamed outside agitators and news coverage.[60] After Chicago police attacked anti-war protesters at the 1968 Democratic convention, survey respondents overwhelmingly sided with the police.[61]

Accordingly, "law and order" became a major theme for many political speeches. The rawest version of this rhetoric came from third-party presidential candidate George Wallace. At a Madison Square Garden rally, he claimed that violence originated with "a few anarchists, a few activists, a few militants, a few revolutionaries, and a few Communists." He suggested that Supreme Court decisions on the rights of criminal defendants had "handcuffed" the police and promised that his election would "put some backbone in the backs of some mayors and governors I know."[62] Republican nominee Richard Nixon offered a more sophisticated version of the "law and order" message: "Let us always respect, as I do, our courts and those who serve on them. But let us also recognize that some of our courts in their decisions have gone too far in weakening the peace forces as against the criminal forces in this country and we must act to restore that balance."[63] Nixon and Wallace together won 57 percent of the popular vote.

Two years later, members of the Ohio National Guard killed four antiwar protesters at Kent State University. One Gallup poll about the massacre found that 58 percent blamed the demonstrators, not the National Guard.[64] Another Gallup survey found that campus unrest scored higher on the public's list of national problems than the Vietnam War.[65] The Kent State killings sparked more demonstrations, one of which took place in Manhattan. This time, hundreds of construction workers struck back, beating up student protesters, as the police stood by and let them do it. Wearing hardhats, waving American flags and carrying signs that said, "America: Love It or Leave It," the hardhat rioters became symbols of white working-class America. Nixon understood which side his supporters were on, so he staged a White House meeting with their union leaders, who gave him a hardhat labeled "Commander in Chief."

Young Trump was in the vicinity of the hardhats, working in his father's New York real-estate development business. At the time, much of the city was becoming an urban hellscape, and Trump's "American Carnage" inaugural address reflected the impressions that he still carried decades later. By and large, his business customers in the 1970s associated Black people with crime and did not want to live near them. In 1973, the Justice Department charged the Trump Organization with racial discrimination in apartment rentals, steering African Americans away from predominately white buildings. In his first appearance on the front page of *The New York Times*, Trump called the charge "absolutely ridiculous" but eventually settled out of court.[66]

New York remained a dangerous place for years, and its rate of violent crime in the late 1980s was even higher than in the early 1970s. In 1989, five youths—four Black and one Hispanic—faced charges for the brutal "wilding" assault on a woman in Central Park. In an already-fearful city, the story caused a media frenzy—and Trump was part of the story. "Mayor Koch has stated that hate and rancor should be removed from our hearts," Trump said in a full-page newspaper ad. "I do not think so. I want to hate these muggers and murderers."[67] In an interview with Larry King, he pressed the theme: "Of course I hate these people and let's all hate these people because maybe hate is what we need if we're gonna get something done." He denied that he was "prejudging" the suspects but merely saying that they should get the death penalty if the victim died and they were found guilty.[68] Soon afterward, former prosecutor Rudy Giuliani ran a "law and order" campaign for New York mayor and nearly defeated Democrat David Dinkins—an extraordinary feat for a Republican in an overwhelmingly Democratic city. In 1993, with crime still at catastrophic levels, Giuliani again ran the same issue and narrowly won a rematch with Dinkins. For someone in Trump's position, the lessons of the previous decades were clear: Americans feared crime and resented street protests. They would vote for politicians who promised tough action to restore law and order.

But then things got more complicated.

In 1992, 83 percent of respondents told Gallup that the criminal justice system was "not tough enough." By 2016, that figure was down to 45 percent.[69] During the same time span, there was growing public concern about police violence, though it was more intense among African Americans than whites.[70] Why the shift in attitudes? On the one hand, Americans simply had less reason to fear for their safety. The rate of violent crime had started to fall in the mid-1990s, and by the time of Trump's run for the presidency, it had dropped to about half of its peak level.[71] On the other hand, people had more reason to believe charges of police misconduct. In the 1960s, such accusations typically pitted the word of police officers against the word of civilians, and the public gave the benefit of the doubt to the people with badges. By the twenty-first century, though, the ubiquity of smartphones and bodycams meant that there was often a video record of encounters with law enforcement. Americans increasingly acknowledged the possibility of police violence because they had seen it on television. And finally, the core constituency for "get-tough" policies was shrinking. White voters without college degrees made up just 39 percent of the electorate in 2018, compared with 71 percent in 1976.[72]

As with so many other things, Trump's beliefs about crime and disorder tended not to evolve with the times. He continued to suggest that cities were as dangerous as they were in the 1970s, telling African Americans in 2016, "We will make your streets safe so when you walk down the street, you don't get shot, which is happening now."[73] He even kept insisting that the Central Park Five were guilty, despite their exoneration on the basis of DNA evidence and the real perpetrator's confession.[74] So it is not surprising that Trump's worldview proved problematic to many voters in the late spring and summer of 2020.

The day after George Floyd's death, the demonstrations started. In Minneapolis, there was peaceful protest, but there was also arson and vandalism. Rioters damaged 1,500 buildings and set fire to 150 buildings in the city, including the Third Precinct police headquarters.[75] Trump attacked the city government for not putting down the disorder more forcefully. He tweeted, "These THUGS are dishonoring the memory of George Floyd, and I won't let that happen. Just spoke to Governor Tim Walz and told him that the Military is with him all the way. Any difficulty and we will assume control but, when the looting starts, the shooting starts. Thank you!"[76] Twitter took the unusual step of flagging the tweet for "glorifying violence." (As Trump critics quickly pointed out, the phrase about looting and shooting dated back to 1967, when the police chief of Miami used it to threaten rioters with deadly force.[77]) Biden tweeted back, "I will not lift the President's tweet. I will not give him that amplification. But he is calling for violence against American citizens during a moment of pain for so many. I'm furious, and you should be too."[78]

Protest spread to other cities, including Washington, DC. When a demonstration near the White House got out of hand, the Secret Service briefly moved Trump to an underground bunker for his own safety. (He later claimed that he was merely inspecting the facility.) In a tweetstorm, he praised the Secret Service for its professionalism. If he had stopped there, no one could have faulted his response. But he tweeted on about the "professionally organized" crowd that had failed to breach the White House fence: "If they had they would have been greeted with the most vicious dogs, and most ominous weapons, I have ever seen. That's when people would have been really badly hurt, at least. Many Secret Service agents just waiting for action. 'We put the young ones on the front line, sir, they love it, and good practice.'"[79] Washington, DC, mayor Muriel Bowser claimed to hear an echo of the 1960s: "I thought the president's remarks were gross. To make a reference to vicious dogs is no subtle reminder to African Americans of segregationists who let dogs out on innocent [people]."[80] And like Trump's other "sir stories," his quotation from a nameless official was almost certainly a fabrication: the Secret Service never welcomes violence.

Protests continued, and Trump reportedly wanted to use the military to put them down. Advisers cautioned against the idea, but he wanted to make a dramatic gesture.[81] He focused on Lafayette Square, a small park across from the White House, which was still full of demonstrators. Acting on a suggestion from his daughter Ivanka, Trump planned to walk across the park to a church building that had suffered arson damage. In a Rose Garden statement, he called himself "the president of law and order" and urged governors "to deploy the National Guard in sufficient numbers that we dominate the streets."[82] He also repeated his claim that the Antifa movement had instigated disorder.[83] Meanwhile, with National Guard troops nearby, riot officers and mounted police were forcing demonstrators out of the park by using chemical spray as well as smoke and flash grenades. Accompanied by senior administration officials, Trump made his symbolic walk, then posed in front of the church building while holding a Bible.

Criticism ran hot, and not just from the usual suspects. James Mattis, Trump's former secretary of defense and retired Marine Corps general, wrote, "Donald Trump is the first president in my lifetime who does not try to unite the American people—does not even pretend to try. Instead he tries to divide us."[84] More subtle but equally significant was a statement by General Mark Milley, chairman of the Joint Chiefs of Staff. In a memo to the chiefs, he said that the Constitution "gives Americans the right to freedom of speech and peaceful assembly. We in uniform—all branches, all components, and all ranks—remain committed to our national values and principles embedded in the Constitution."[85] He later apologized for his presence at Trump's walk across the park.

Decades earlier, as we have seen, the public tended to support forceful action against protesters. But if Trump was hoping for a replay, he was in for disappointment. In a *USA Today*/Ipsos survey, 63 percent of respondents opposed the show of force in Lafayette Square, with 44 percent saying that they "strongly" opposed it.[86] A *Washington Post*/Schar School poll asked more generally about the demonstrations that followed the killing of George Floyd. Sixty-one percent disapproved of Trump's response.[87] Consistent with previous surveys, ABC found that two-thirds of Americans disapproved of his handling of race relations.[88] As protests continued nationwide in the weeks after Lafayette Square, Trump's overall approval ratings also dipped.

Most Americans expressed broad support for the protests and the Black Lives Matter movement, and a number went further.[89] Surveys taken in June suggested that between 15 million and 26 million people in the United States had joined in the marches and rallies, an historic level of participation.[90] Driving this activism was an increasing perception of racial injustice. Three-quarters of Americans now said that racial and ethnic discrimination was a big problem in the United States, compared with just half in 2015.[91]

Despite indications that his "law and order" strategy was not changing the trajectory of the presidential campaign, Trump persisted. The GOP had hemorrhaged support in the suburbs during his tenure, so now he argued that Democrats were planning to spread urban disorder to those areas. "The crime and chaos in Democrat-run cities have gotten so bad that liberals are even getting out of Manhattan's Upper West Side," said a *Wall Street Journal* op-ed bearing the bylines of Trump and HUD Secretary Ben Carson. "The plan is to remake the suburbs in their image so they resemble the dysfunctional cities they now govern. . . . That's why we stopped the last administration's radical social-engineering project that would have transformed the suburbs from the top down."[92] Trump and Carson were referring to his scrapping of a 2015 regulation requiring any community that wanted HUD funding to document and report patterns of racial bias. Trump tweeted, "The 'suburban housewife' will be voting for me. They want safety & are thrilled that I ended the long running program where low income housing would invade their neighborhood. Biden would reinstall it, in a bigger form, with Corey [*sic*] Booker in charge!"[93] Booker, the former mayor of Newark and the first African American senator from New Jersey, responded with a tweet that mocked the misspelling of his first name and suggested that Trump was blowing a dog whistle: "Donaled, your racism is showing. —Cory."[94] Few voters probably noticed the Twitter exchange, but, in any event, Trump's suburban tactic fell short. Most suburban women told pollsters that they would not worry if new apartments, subsidized housing developments, or people with housing vouchers came to their neighborhoods.[95] Overall, suburbanites continued to disapprove of Trump's performance in office. Like other Americans, they worried about COVID and the economy.

If Trump overreached on race and crime, some progressives and Democrats overreached as well. Trump failed to grasp the growing support for civil rights and concern about police misconduct. This shift, however, did not amount to an embrace of the full progressive agenda. In California, for instance, Democrats took the opportunity to put up a ballot measure reversing the state ban on racial preferences. They miscalculated. Polls showed that Americans approved of the general idea of "affirmative action," and yet 72 percent opposed giving preference to Black Americans in hiring and promotion, including 43 percent who said they opposed strongly.[96] And even if crime was no longer as pressing a concern as it was three decades earlier, Americans still cared about it, and they recoiled from scenes of street violence. Most of the protests in the summer of 2020 were just as peaceful as Democrats claimed, but there was also rioting that resulted in at least a billion dollars in paid insurance claims—the most expensive civil disorder in insurance history.[97] Aside from run-of-the-mill riots, radicals in Seattle seized a piece of territory for several weeks, driving out the police and calling themselves the Capitol Hill Autonomous Zone (CHAZ); in Portland, radicals besieged the Mark O. Hatfield federal courthouse, assaulting it on a nightly basis throughout the summer. Protestors also tore down or damaged monuments around the country. Trump posted many tweets mocking Democratic and media descriptions of "peaceful protests," and some voters surely thought that he had a point.

A prominent protest slogan was "Defund the police." In Minneapolis, a majority of city council members embraced the concept, quickly pledging to replace the city's police department with a vaguely defined department of community safety and violence prevention. Endorsements of the idea came from prominent figures on the left, including Representative Ilhan Omar (D-MN), whose district included Minneapolis. Defunding sounded extreme because the term means "withdraw money from," which often translates into "disband." When Congress defunded the Office of Technology Assessment, for instance, the organization effectively ceased to exist. Some advocates of "defunding" argued that they were not proposing the abolition of police forces; instead, they proposed to redirect some portion of police budgets to social services. Not all activists got the memo. Mariame Kaba, a community organizer, wrote an article in the *New York Times* titled "Yes, We Mean Literally Abolish the Police."[98]

Whatever its intended meaning or its policy merits, the slogan "defund the police" was a political loser. In June, four surveys found that Americans opposed "defunding police departments" or the "defund the police" movement by an average of 58 percent to 31 percent.[99] A Gallup survey indicated that 81 percent of Black Americans wanted either the same or greater level of police presence in their neighborhoods.[100] Republicans immediately realized that the activists had handed them a political gift. Trump tweeted, "LAW & ORDER, NOT DEFUND AND ABOLISH THE POLICE. The Radical Left Democrats have gone Crazy!"[101] At a House Judiciary Committee hearing, Representative Jim Jordan (R-OH) said, "Americans know that it is pure insanity to defund the police. . . . This Congress started off with Democrats on the left saying we should Abolish ICE, then abolish the Department of Homeland Security, now they're talking about abolishing the police. This is wrong!"[102] Recognizing the political danger, practical-minded Democrats tried to tamp down the "defunding" talk. "When you allow people to use incendiary terms, we create a climate within which we can't get much done," said Representative James Clyburn (D-SC), whose support had enabled Biden to win the Democratic nomination. "For me, the word *defund* means what Merriam-Webster says that it means. So if you're talking about reallocating resources, say that. If you mean reimagining policing, say that. If you're going to reform policing, say that. Don't tell me you're going to use a term that you know is charged—and tell me that it doesn't mean what it says."[103] Biden made clear that he did not support defunding, though he advocated reforms to curb police misconduct. Unfortunately for the Democrats, the "defund" voices were louder and more insistent than that of their party's presumptive nominee, who was maintaining his low public profile.

Eventually, defunding lost steam. After a summer surge in violence, members of the Minneapolis City Council tiptoed away from the idea, with some explaining that they did not mean it literally.[104] Nevertheless, Republican opposition researchers already had all the material they needed for the fall campaign.

SUMMER OF DIVISION

As the protests were under way, the economic news provided Americans with a pleasant surprise. Many economists had feared that the unemployment rate could rise to 20 percent. But on June 5, the Bureau of Labor Statistics reported that total nonfarm payroll employment had risen by 2.5 million in May, and the unemployment rate had actually dropped by 1.4 percentage points, down to 13.3 percent.[105] What happened? Some states had taken tentative steps to reopen, and many workers were able to resume their jobs. On the national level, the effects of the CARES Act were kicking in. The $2.2 trillion measure had provided $300 billion in one-time cash payments to individual taxpayers (with the paper checks bearing Trump's name), $260 billion in increased unemployment benefits, and billions more for corporations and state and local governments. The bill also set up a Paycheck Protection Program providing small businesses with forgivable loans as an incentive to keep their workers on payroll.

This jobs report was the first of several that would keep ratcheting the unemployment number down from its April peak. The good news did not stop there. The Dow Jones Industrial average was recovering from the crashes of

March, and consumer spending would rise during every month of the summer. In mid-July, Trump tweeted, "The Economy is coming back fast!"[106]

It was a bouquet with a thorn. The statistics had improved from the early weeks of the pandemic, but they were still much weaker than they had been when Trump made his triumphant State of the Union Address in February. In what some called a "K-shaped recovery," affluent professionals fared much better than blue-collar workers. The percentage of American with stock had declined since the Great Recession a dozen years earlier, and stock ownership was concentrated among people with college degrees and high incomes.[107] They reaped most of the benefit of the Dow's bounceback. Similarly, white-collar professionals were able to shift their work from physical offices to home computers. Blue-collar employees did not have that luxury: their jobs required them to show up in factories, kitchens, and other unglamorous workplaces. According to the Federal Reserve, 63 percent of workers with college degrees worked entirely from home, compared with only 20 percent of those with a high school diploma or less.[108]

It was not clear that the economic upheaval would lead to a political one. If voters compared the economy with its March trough, they would see growth and recovery. If their benchmark was early February, they would see gloom. What would happen in the latter case? The Great Depression and the Great Recession had prompted voters to oust the party in power and lurch to the left, at least temporarily. Progressives were hoping for a similar outcome this time, and they took heart from the public acceptance of the enormous COVID relief package.[109] They overlooked some key differences, however. The crashes of 1929 and 2008 were arguably failures of capitalism, and people on the left could contend that these disasters pointed out the need for government intervention. The shutdowns of 2020, by contrast, were the proximate *result* of government intervention. Moreover, when it came to business closures, the key decisionmakers were state and local officials, not the president. As for the COVID relief package, its purpose was not to restructure economic power in the United States, merely to restore some semblance of the pre-pandemic status quo.

Instead of rearranging the partisan and ideological lines, the pandemic's economic fallout reinforced them. Eighty-nine percent of Democrats and Democratic leaners and 71 percent of Independents told an NBC/Survey Monkey poll that they were more concerned that businesses were reopening too quickly than too slowly, compared with just 34 percent of Republicans and GOP leaners.[110] One reason for the divide was that partisans were responding to messages from the top. Whereas leading national Democrats urged caution and put the emphasis on safety, Trump relentlessly spoke of the need to reopen the economy. Another reason was the changing makeup of the party coalitions. Between 1996 and 2019, the Pew Research Center found, the share of Democratic voters with at least a four-year degree grew from 22 percent to 41 percent. During the same time frame, the share of Republican voters with a four-year college degree changed little, from 27 percent then to 30 percent.[111] In other words, Democrats were much more likely to be in the educational category that suffered least from the shutdowns.

During the summer, massive wildfires broke out on the West Coast, and some scientists blamed climate change.[112] Environmental activists in the Democratic Party used the occasion to talk up "the Green New Deal," an extensive progressive agenda of economic and environmental reform, which included a rapid shift away from fossil fuels. While not endorsing all elements of the plan, Biden and Democratic congressional leaders did support a move toward zero carbon emissions. At first glance, it seemed as if they were appealing to a broad public consensus, as polls showed growing acceptance of the reality of climate change and the need to do something about it. Beneath the surface, there were political costs. The pandemic had taken a painful toll on transportation and other industries that relied on fossil fuels. People in those industries—oil and gas workers, bus drivers, airport employees—had either suffered job losses or feared them. For many of these workers, "the Green New Deal" seemed like a bad deal: real, immediate loss in exchange for a vague promise of a "green job" sometime in the future. As with many other issues, there were deep partisan differences, with Democrats placing a much greater priority on climate change than Republicans. Regional divides mingled with partisan ones. People in coastal areas were more likely than inlanders to think that climate change affected their local community and to favor a ban on offshore drilling. And 37 percent of Democrats lived within 25 miles of a coastline, compared with just 25 percent of Republicans.[113]

For a brief time late in the spring, there were hopes that businesses and schools might soon start edging toward normality. Daily counts of new COVID cases were declining. Some states either eased or contemplated easing their restrictions, and colleges made tentative plans for partial in-person instruction during the fall semester. Then came the summer surge. By July, COVID was rising again, causing many states to pause or reverse their plans for reopening.[114] The surge sped up the "red shift" in new cases: in July and August, states that had voted for Trump in 2016 reported a much higher rate than those that had voted for Clinton.[115] Frustration mounted, divisions deepened, and protests against COVID restrictions, which had begun months earlier, continued apace. The anti-shutdown protesters were especially resentful that Democratic politicians had criticized their events as COVID-risky even though these same figures had praised the densely crowded Black Lives Matter protests. A video from Stand Up Michigan juxtaposed audio clips of

Governor Gretchen Whitmer faulting the shutdown protesters with images of her taking part in a BLM demonstration.[116]

Events in Michigan foreshadowed the January 2021 Washington riot. In April 2019, Trump approvingly reacted to a demonstration in Michigan's capital city of Lansing: "LIBERATE MICHIGAN!"[117] A couple of weeks later came another, more ominous protest. Hundreds of shutdown opponents, some visibly carrying firearms, gathered on the grounds of the State Capitol. Michigan is an open-carry state, and it was lawful for them to bring weapons into the building. But when some tried to get onto the State Senate floor, sergeants-at-arms and state police blocked them. The show of weapons and the extreme tone of the protesters' rhetoric got national attention. So did Trump's reaction: "The Governor of Michigan should give a little, and put out the fire. These are very good people, but they are angry. They want their lives back again, safely! See them, talk to them, make a deal."[118] Demonstrations continued and, at one point, forced cancellation of a legislative session. In October, the FBI arrested thirteen suspects for an alleged plot to kidnap Governor Whitmer and overthrow the state government. Several of them had taken part in the armed protest.[119]

By late August, the COVID surge was tapering off, but a second surge of civil rights protests was starting. On August 23, a twenty-nine-year-old Black man named Jacob Blake had a confrontation with police in Kenosha, Wisconsin. As he was getting into his car, a white officer shot fired seven shots at him. The resulting injuries left him paralyzed from the waist down. There had been other controversial incidents of police violence since May, but this one—like the George Floyd killing—was on video. A recording by a neighbor appeared to show that Blake was not brandishing a weapon and that the police officer shot him in the back, though he later acknowledged having held, dropped, and then reached for a knife.[120] Demonstrations again swept the country. As with the George Floyd aftermath, there was violence, with Kenosha suffering millions of dollars in property damage. There was also dangerous pushback. An Illinois teenager brought a rifle to Kenosha, killing two protesters and injuring a third. (The shooter claimed self-defense.) In St. Louis, a couple drew firearms on demonstrators who had broken through a gate and were nearing their house: they later faced a felony charge of unlawful use of a weapon, though the governor of Missouri said he would pardon them if convicted.

The two candidates reacted in predictably different ways. Trump visited a riot-damaged area of Kenosha and said, "Violent mobs demolished or damaged at least 25 businesses, burned down public buildings, and threw bricks at police officers—which your police officers won't stand for, and they didn't stand for it. These are not acts of peaceful protest, but really domestic terror."[121] Biden spoke by phone with Jacob Blake and met with his family. "What I came away with was the overwhelming sense of resilience and optimism that they have about the kind of response they're getting," Biden said at a forum in Kenosha. "His mom talked about—my wife asked to say a prayer. And his mom said a prayer. She said, 'I'm praying for Jacob and I'm praying for the policeman as well. I'm praying that things change.'"[122]

Sympathy for the Black Lives Matter movement had dipped since June, and Democrats worried that new wave of protest and urban disorder would work to Trump's benefit.[123] Reaction was indeed mixed: Ipsos found 43 percent supporting the demonstrations and 38 percent opposing. The partisan divide was stark, with 75 percent of Democrats in support, compared with just six percent of Republicans.[124] Some Republican activists openly praised the teenager who had killed protesters in Kenosha. The St. Louis couple who had pointed firearms at demonstrators got a phone call from Trump and an invitation to speak at the Republican convention. Biden began coming under pressure to denounce the violence coming from the left.

POLITICS GOES ON

During the season of disease and protest, the Biden and Trump campaigns prepared for the general election. Trump was eager to resume the massive rallies that he had enjoyed so much before the pandemic, and his aides chose Tulsa, Oklahoma, as the site of his comeback. They had originally set the date as June 19. African American critics took it as a double provocation, since June 19—Juneteenth—is a celebration of liberation at the end of the Civil War, and Tulsa was the site of a notorious 1921 massacre of Black residents. The campaign responded by moving the date one day, to June 20. On that night, he walked onto the stage at the city's BOK Center and looked out over a fiasco. Despite the Trump campaign's predictions of huge crowd, the venue was only one-third full. Trump gave a long, disjointed speech, referring to COVID-19 as "kung flu" and saying, "Here's the bad part. When you do testing to that extent, you're going to find more people, you're going to find more cases. So I said to my people slow the testing down, please."[125] (Aides tried to claim that he was just kidding, but three days later, he confirmed that he meant what he said: "I don't kid."[126]) When he returned to the White House after the event, cameras captured him exiting his Marine One helicopter looking weary and dejected.

Although the audience was embarrassingly small, its members sat indoors, close together, and barefaced—exactly what public health officials had asked people not to do during the pandemic. A few weeks later, the Tulsa area saw an unusually large increase in cases, and the city's health director suggested that the rally had "more than likely" contributed to the COVID spike.[127] Several campaign staffers at the rally subsequently tested positive for the disease, as did Trump surrogate Herman Cain, who had sought the Republican nomination in 2012. On July 30, Cain died. It is possible that he caught it somewhere else, but his death added to the Tulsa rally's lingering reputation as a cauldron of bad luck.

Tulsa also took a political casualty: Trump campaign manager Brad Parscale, who had made things worse by hyping expectations for the rally. It was not his first unfortunate boast. In May, he crowed about a record $61.7 million in contributions during the previous month. "Once again the Trump campaign's colossal fundraising haul reaffirms that President Trump will lead an unstoppable juggernaut this November."[128] He even issued a tweet comparing the Trump campaign to the Star Wars Death Star—which prompted Mark Hamill to reply that the Death Star blew up.[129] Parscale's critics said that he was the fatal flaw in the Trump Death Star. For months, he had been spending huge sums on items that promised little return on investment, such as television advertising during the Super Bowl. And a sizable chunk of the money was going into Parscale's own pockets.[130] Criticism mounted in Republican circles, and in mid-July, Trump replaced Parscale with Bill Stepien. By this time, the campaign and associated committees had burned through nearly three-quarters of the $1.1 billion they had raised since the start of 2019.[131]

In the meantime, Biden and the Democrats were doing surprisingly well on fundraising, despite lacking the advantages of incumbency.[132] Anger at Trump motivated small donors and developments in campaign finance rules had opened the door to big donors. Thanks to the 2014 *McCutcheon* decision, which removed aggregate limits on what any person could give during an election cycle, contributors could now write huge checks to joint fundraising committees, which could then split them among candidates and party committees. In May, the Biden Victory Fund filed an agreement letting donors give up to $620,000 each, with the funds going to the campaign, the Democratic National Committee and twenty-six state parties.[133] Virtual fundraising events proved successful, and Biden's "basement campaign" had the fortunate side effect of keeping campaign expenditures very low. By the end of August, the Democrats were in a position that they could not have imagined a year earlier: the Biden campaign and its associated committees had more cash on hand than their opponents.[134]

The Biden cause was also getting help from campaign operatives and former officials who had worked for the GOP but now opposed Trump. They formed several organizations that attacked Trump in television ads and social media posts. The most prominent was the Lincoln Project, a super PAC that received much of its funding from wealthy Democratic donors.[135] "Republicans are hierarchical," one leader of the Lincoln Project explained to the *Washington Monthly*. "So what's not getting a lot of attention right now is the structure we are building—the permission ramp for Republicans so that they will have some comfort that they are not alone in doing the right thing."[136] Another leader of the Lincoln Project told CBS reporter Lesley Stahl about the group's target voters, "So those independent-leaning men, those college-educated Republicans, the suburban Republican women. We understand where these voters are, we understand who they are and how they think. And Lesley, it's a game of small numbers. I mean, Donald Trump won this election by 77,000 votes in three states."[137] The Lincoln Project strategists wanted to provoke responses from Trump, because the resulting publicity would reach far more potential supporters than their tweets and television ads. Trump obliged them. Knowing that Trump would be watching, they ran a spot on Washington, DC's Fox News affiliate. "Mourning in America," a play on Reagan's 1984 ad "Morning in America," depicted a dystopian landscape under Trump's leadership. He answered with a tweetstorm that attacked the group's founders, including consultant Reed Galen, whom he called "Reed Galvin." Galen said, "It's one of these things where you work hard, and you have an idea, and sometimes it all comes to fruition. I would be lying if I said it does not seem surreal to be sitting in bed and watching the president of the United States trash you and your friends and spell your name wrong."[138] The ad cost just $10,000 to make and $5,000 to air, and within days it brought the Lincoln Project about $2 million from 25,000 new donors.[139]

In his episode, as in most of the interregnum's political events, Biden was on the sidelines. His biggest opportunity for the limelight came with the choice of a vice presidential candidate. As political scientists and savvy political operatives have always known, a running mate can help a little or hurt a lot. That is, a vice presidential candidate might add to a ticket's appeal among certain geographic regions, party factions, or demographic groups, though the effect is slight and evidence is scant.[140] A flawed choice can distract attention from the campaign's message and raise questions about the presidential candidate's judgment. Aides who vet vice presidential possibilities are painfully aware of Thomas Eagleton's mental health (1972), Geraldine Ferraro's finances (1984), Dan Quayle's avoidance of the Vietnam draft (1988), and Sarah Palin's lack of preparation on national issues (2008). Accordingly, Biden was looking for someone who obviously had the experience and knowledge to serve and who did not have any serious "baggage."

It often makes sense for presidential candidates to pick a running mate from among their rivals from the nomination. For instance, JFK picked LBJ in 1960, and Ronald Reagan turned to George H. W. Bush twenty years later. Not only can such a choice help unify the party after a tough nomination contest, but it can also reduce the risk that the vice presidential candidate suffers from hidden liabilities. A former contender for the nomination has already undergone a tryout on the national stage, and the presidential nominee has amassed a file of opposition research on that person. In 2020, the "last man standing" was Bernie Sanders. Despite the hopes of some hardcore progressives, a Biden-Sanders ticket was never going to happen. As an earlier chapter noted, the senator from Vermont was even older than Biden, had recently suffered a heart attack, and openly embraced the politically fraught label of "socialist."

The large 2020 Democratic field included other people who met the customary qualifications. Biden narrowed his choices in mid-March, when he committed to choosing a woman, and political considerations reduced the list even further. Senator Kirsten Gillibrand's ideological shifts had aroused suspicion among progressives and moderates alike. Representative Tulsi Gabbard was downright toxic, because of some of her positions and her failure to support the Trump impeachment. Senator Amy Klobuchar was a much more plausible alternative as a moderate liberal with potential appeal in the crucial Midwest, but the George Floyd protests drew attention to a potentially damaging aspect of her record as a local prosecutor: she had declined to bring charges against police officers involved in shootings.[141] Seeing the proverbial writing on the wall, she withdrew from consideration.

Two of Biden's nomination rivals made it to the finals. Senator Elizabeth Warren impressed the Biden vetting team with her command of the issues and her willingness to support Biden's issue agenda. Her staunchly progressive record was a mixed blessing: while it would surely please the Democratic left, it would also supply Republicans with ammunition for the fall campaign. And notwithstanding her discarded claim to Native American ancestry, Warren had another liability: she was white. Biden owed his nomination to African American Democrats, and the selection of a white running mate might have come across as a gesture of ingratitude.

The obvious choice, then, was Senator Kamala Harris. She had national experience as a senator and executive experience as a former district attorney and state attorney general. Not only was she African American, but her mother was an immigrant from India. Although the Indian American vote is quite small, it could potentially make a difference in closely contested key states. India is the second-most common country of origin among foreign-born residents in twenty-one states, including Texas, Georgia, North Carolina, and Pennsylvania.[142] One thing gave pause to Team Biden, however: the debate in which she had harshly attacked Biden's record on racial-balance busing. Chris Dodd, a former senator who took part in the vetting, reportedly expressed shock that she had no remorse for the ambush.[143]

And so Biden included others in the shortlist. Michigan was a crucial state that Trump had unexpectedly won in 2016, so Governor Gretchen Whitmer got a look. But she was white, had less than two years of statewide experience, and faced growing unrest because of her restrictive pandemic policy. Senator Tammy Duckworth of Illinois was an Asian American who had lost her legs in combat during the Iraq War. Her profile was potentially very appealing, but she was born in Bangkok to an American father and a Thai mother. Although there was no serious doubt about her citizenship—her ancestors on her father's side fought in the American Revolution—Biden lawyers worried that a partisan judge in a key state could twist the Constitution's "natural born citizen" clause to deny ballot access to the ticket.[144] Susan Rice, a former ambassador to the United Nations, was an African American with vast knowledge of foreign policy. She had never run for office, however, and no one could know how she would fare on the campaign trail. And Representative Karen Bass of California, also African American, had plenty of experience with practical politics, having built a reputation as a shrewd legislative leader when she served as speaker of the California State Assembly. Nevertheless, Bass's record of support for the Castro regime in Cuba proved to be politically disqualifying: her presence on the ticket would have killed any chance of carrying the key state of Florida, many of whose voters had escaped the Castro dictatorship.

By comparison, Harris's downside seemed manageable. She had previously said that she believed women who had accused Biden of inappropriate touching, but the media had moved on from the story by summer. The issue of busing had been legally moot for years, and Biden was the rare Irish American who did not hold grudges. He announced her selection several days before the Democratic convention.

Because of the pandemic, that convention would be like no other before it. The Democratic National Committee had originally planned to hold a traditional gathering in Milwaukee, hoping that it might help the ticket in a state that Trump had narrowly carried in 2016. In June, DNC bowed to the reality of COVID and announced that the convention would be a virtual affair, with speakers participating remotely from sites all over the country. In a way, this format was the culmination of a trend that had been under way for decades. Not since Ronald Reagan battled Gerald Ford for the 1976 GOP nomination had there been any suspense about a convention outcome. Now that the primary process decided the nominees months in advance, these events had become reality shows, with the delegates essentially serving as the studio audience. This time, the Democrats would have a four-day infomercial.

It served its purpose. Like vice presidential candidates, conventions can help a little or hurt a lot. Sometimes they had led to political trouble in the form of street violence (the Democrats in Chicago, 1968) or impolitic speeches (Pat Buchanan's GOP address in 1992). The virtual format left no room for disorder, and everything literally went according to script. The sessions were shorter than in the past, and the remarks were brief and pungent. Seeking to strengthen the "permission ramp" that the Lincoln Project had built, the Democrats featured several pro-Biden talks by prominent Republicans: former GOP governor John Kasich of Ohio, former New Jersey governor Christine Todd Whitman, 2010 California gubernatorial candidate Meg Whitman, and former representative Susan Molinari of New York, who had keynoted the 1996 GOP convention. Cindy McCain, who would later endorse the Democratic ticket, narrated a video about Biden's friendship with her husband, John McCain. The call of the states, usually the most tedious part of the proceedings, became a fast-paced travelogue. Party leaders and rank-and-file Democrats announced the delegate tallies from scenic locations in all the states and territories. And Biden, who had sometimes stumbled during the campaign, won praise for a forceful acceptance speech. *Politico*'s Tim Alberta tweeted, "we're watching an old ballplayer whose skills have diminished turn in a career-best performance in the biggest game of his life."[145]

Polls gave little evidence of a convention "bounce." At most, the television event may have shored up his existing support. That was good enough for the Democrats because Biden was already running ahead.

Like the Democrats, the Republicans had originally planned an in-person convention in a swing state. The site was to be the Spectrum Center in Charlotte, North Carolina, but in June the RNC pulled out after the state's Democratic governor rebuffed Trump's demand that the convention dispense with social distancing and other COVID safety measures. RNC then picked another swing-state site, in Jacksonville, Florida, but later had to cancel because of the summer COVID surge. By this point, GOP donors had laid out millions for preparations in both cities, which added to the campaign's financial woes.[146]

Thus the GOP ended up with a virtual convention whose format resembled that of its Democratic counterpart, though with more modest production values and less pre-recorded video. Just as the Democrats had sought a "permission ramp" for Republican-leaning moderates and suburbanites, the Republicans tried to build a couple of their own: one to keep these voters in the fold, and one for African Americans dissatisfied with the Democratic Party. The convention included speeches about Trump's personal empathy, and testimonials from African Americans such as former NFL star Herschel Walker, who said, "I take it as a personal insult that people would think I've had a 37-year friendship with a racist."[147] The convention also had plenty of red meat for the Trump base. Mark and Patricia McCloskey, the St. Louis couple who were facing charges for waving firearms at protesters in front of their house, spoke at the opening: "What you saw happen to us could just as easily happen to any of you who are watching from quiet neighborhoods around our country."[148]

During the convention, Trump used his incumbency in unprecedented ways. To demonstrate his commitment to criminal justice reform, the convention showed a video of him pardoning a felon who had helped rehabilitate former convicts. To show his support for lawful immigration, it featured a live broadcast of him hosting a naturalization ceremony at the White House. (The new citizens did not know ahead of time that they would be part of the convention.[149]) To drive home the administration's support for Israel, Secretary of State Mike Pompeo, who was on a taxpayer-funded official trip, spoke remotely from Jerusalem. All of these events raised questions about possible violations of federal law forbidding the use of federal employees and resources for explicit partisan purposes. Trump's acceptance speech on the White House lawn pushed the legal envelope even further, but his subordinates shrugged. "Nobody outside of the Beltway really cares," chief of staff Mark Meadows told *Politico*. "This is a lot of hoopla that is being made about things mainly because the convention has been so unbelievably successful."[150]

In fact, the Republicans got lower Nielsen ratings than the Democrats.[151] Trump's "convention bounce" was small and fleeting. As the Labor Day weekend approached, he was still running behind Biden in national surveys.[152]

THE INDECISIVE INTERREGNUM

The interregnum ended as it had begun, with a nation divided. Biden's lead was consistent, but hardly so overwhelming that a Trump victory was out of the question. On average, Biden barely cleared 50 percent of the vote.

COVID continued to dog the incumbent, with most polls showing strong disapproval of the way he had handled the crisis.[153] Yet the summer surge had ended, and some Americans were again hoping for a return to normal. In part because of the administration's "Operation Warp Speed," medical researchers were making impressive progress toward a vaccine. Saying the quiet part out loud, Trump suggested to Geraldo Rivera that the vaccine might even be ready by Election Day.[154]

The economic news gave material to both sides. In early September, the Bureau of Labor Statistics reported that unemployment in August was 8.4 percent, down sharply from the 10.2 percent level of the month before. A release from the White House proclaimed, "For perspective, following the Great Recession of 2008–09, it took nearly a decade for the unemployment rate to fall by 6.3 percentage points. President Trump's economy accomplished this in just four months."[155] At the same time, though, there was plenty of evidence of a "K-shaped recovery," with educated professional doing well while service workers faced ongoing job losses.[156]

Politically, each side had its strengths. Biden and the Democrats had a financial edge that they had not expected months earlier. Trump had the incumbency advantage, and as the convention showed, he was willing to press it as far as the law allowed, and then some. In August, he had issued an executive order allowing for deferral of payroll tax obligations, in the apparent hope that fatter paychecks would help him in November. But as employers and employees realized, the deferral merely meant a bigger tax bill later on, and few used it. This development hardly deterred Trump, who kept angling for an October surprise.

Scholars and media pundits alike were skittish about predicting how the fall campaign would turn out. On election night 2016, most of them had been shocked when Trump defied the odds and won an upset victory. It was a reminder that predicting presidential election outcomes is inherently a risky business. Between 1789 and 2016, there were only fifty-eight presidential races in all. For the first nine elections, reliable records of the popular vote are scarce and inconsistent, so we had tallies for just forty-nine. For forecasts relying on public opinion data, the number was smaller, because scientific national surveys dated back only to the 1930s. So with a starting point of 1936, when Gallup took its first presidential election poll, analysts had data on twenty-one elections. Many forecasting models involve post–World War II economic data, leaving a grand total of eighteen.[157] There is a good deal of uncertainty surrounding any prediction resting on so few cases. Social scientists call it a "small-n problem."

The 2020 race presented the ultimate small-n problem. We had never before held a presidential election in the midst of a pandemic that had killed hundreds of thousands of citizens, wounded the national economy, and forced massive changes in voting procedures. Moreover, polling results were more suspect than ever. Changes in living patterns and technology use had made American even more reluctant to answer surveys. Nobody could be sure what would happen in November because n equaled zero.

NOTES

1. James W. Ceaser and Andrew E. Busch, *The Perfect Tie: The True Story of the 2000 Presidential Election* (Lanham, MD: Rowman & Littlefield, 2001), 109.

2. James W. Ceaser and Andrew E. Busch, *Losing to Win: The 1996 Elections and American Politics* (Lanham, MD: Rowman & Littlefield, 1997), 89.

3. Roger Vincent, "Trump Seeks Trademark to Put 'You're Fired' to Work for Him," *Los Angeles Times*, March 19, 2004, https://www.latimes.com/archives/la-xpm-2004-mar-19-fi-donald19-story.html.

4. Franklin D. Roosevelt, Inaugural Address, March 4, 1933, American Presidency Project, https://www.presidency.ucsb.edu/node/208712.

5. Joe Biden, "Trump Is Worst Possible Leader to Deal with Coronavirus Outbreak," *USA Today*, January 27, 2020, https://www.usatoday.com/story/opinion/2020/01/27/coronavirus-donald-trump-made-us-less-prepared-joe-biden-column/4581710002.

6. Remarks by President Trump in State of the Union Address, February 4, 2020, https://www.whitehouse.gov/briefings-statements/remarks-president-trump-state-union-address-3.

7. Monmouth University Polling Institute, "Most Expect Trump Will Be Re-elected; Sanders Overtakes Biden Among Dem Voters," February 11, 2020, https://www.monmouth.edu/polling-institute/reports/monmouthpoll_US_021120/.

8. Remarks by President Trump in State of the Union Address.

9. Joe Ben, Twitter post, February 1, 2020, https://twitter.com/JoeBiden/status/1223727977361338370?s=20.

10. Jake Tapper, "Biden Campaign Says He Backs Trump's China Travel Ban," CNN, April 3, 2020, https://www.cnn.com/2020/04/03/politics/joe-biden-trump-china-coronavirus/index.html.

11. Interview: Sean Hannity Interviews Donald Trump at Mar-a-Lago—Part 1, February 2, 2020, https://factba.se/transcript/donald-trump-interview-sean-hannity-part-1-february-2-2020.

12. Donald J. Trump, Twitter post, February 7, 2020, https://twitter.com/realDonaldTrump/status/1225728756456808448?s=20.

13. Bob Woodward, *Rage* (New York: Simon and Schuster, 2020), xix.

14. Fred Imbert, "Larry Kudlow Says US Has Contained the Coronavirus and the Economy Is Holding Up Nicely," CNBC, February 25, 2020, https://www.cnbc.com/2020/02/25/larry-kudlow-says-us-has-contained-the-coronavirus-and-the-economy-is-holding-up-nicely.html.

15. Kate Kelly and Mark Mazzetti, "As Virus Spread, Reports of Trump Administration's Private Briefings Fueled Sell-Off," *New York Times*, October 17, 2020, https://www.nytimes.com/2020/10/14/us/politics/stock-market-coronavirus-trump.html.

16. Steve Eder et al., "430,000 People Have Traveled from China to U.S. Since Coronavirus Surfaced," *New York Times*, April 4, 2020, https://www.nytimes.com/2020/04/04/us/coronavirus-china-travel-restrictions.html.

17. Allyson Chiu and Allyson Chiu, "Autopsies Find First U.S. Coronavirus Death Occurred in Early February, Weeks Earlier Than Previously Thought," *Washington Post*, April 22, 2020, https://www.washingtonpost.com/nation/2020/04/22/death-coronavirus-first-california.

18. Transcript for the CDC Telebriefing Update on COVID-19, February 26, 2020, https://www.cdc.gov/media/releases/2020/t0225-cdc-telebriefing-covid-19.html.

19. Rebecca Ballhaus and Stephanie Armour, "Health Chief's Early Missteps Set Back Coronavirus Response," *Wall Street Journal*, April 22, 2020, https://www.wsj.com/articles/health-chiefs-early-missteps-set-back-coronavirus-response-11587570514.

20. Remarks by President Trump, Vice President Pence, and Members of the Coronavirus Task Force in Press Conference, February 27, 2020, https://www.whitehouse.gov/briefings-statements/remarks-president-trump-vice-president-pence-members-coronavirus-task-force-press-conference.

21. William Saletan, "The Trump Pandemic," *Slate*, August 9, 2020, https://slate.com/news-and-politics/2020/08/trump-coronavirus-deaths-timeline.html.

22. Daniel Joseph Finkenstadt, Robert Handfield, and Peter Guinto, "Why the U.S. Still Has a Severe Shortage of Medical Supplies," *Harvard Business Review*, September 17, 2020, https://hbr.org/2020/09/why-the-u-s-still-has-a-severe-shortage-of-medical-supplies.

23. Remarks by President Trump After Tour of the Centers for Disease Control and Prevention | Atlanta, GA, March 6, 2020, https://www.whitehouse.gov/briefings-statements/remarks-president-trump-tour-centers-disease-control-prevention-atlanta-ga.

24. Emily Baumgaertner and Soumya Karlamangla, "Chaos at Hospitals Due to Shortage of Coronavirus Testing," *Los Angeles Times*, March 6, 2020, https://www.latimes.com/science/story/2020-03-06/chaos-at-hospitals-due-to-shortage-of-coronavirus-tests.

25. J. David Goodman, "How Delays and Unheeded Warnings Hindered New York's Virus Fight," *New York Times*, April 8, 2020, https://www.nytimes.com/2020/04/08/nyregion/new-york-coronavirus-response-delays.html.

26. Fadel Allassan, "Surgeon general defends reversal on face mask policy," Axios News, July 12, 2020, https://www.axios.com/surgeon-general-reversal-face-mask-d385e2d5-42b7-433e-89a6-3584f3e61bf3.html.

27. Stephanie Watson, "Coronavirus on Surfaces: What's the Real Risk?" WebMD, September 3, 2020, https://www.webmd.com/lung/news/20200903/coronavirus-on-surfaces-whats-the-real-risk.

28. Justin Sink, "Trump's Error-Laden 'Foreign Virus' Speech Spooks Investors," *Bloomberg News*, March 12, 2020, https://www.bloomberg.com/news/articles/2020-03-12/trump-s-error-laden-foreign-virus-speech-has-investors-spooked.

29. Remarks by President Trump in Address to the Nation, March 11, 2020, https://www.whitehouse.gov/briefings-statements/remarks-president-trump-address-nation.

30. Remarks by President Trump, Vice President Pence, and Members of the Coronavirus Task Force in Press Briefing, March 18, 2020, https://www.whitehouse.gov/briefings-statements/remarks-president-trump-vice-president-pence-members-coronavirus-task-force-press-briefing-5.

31. Jeffrey M. Jones, "President Trump's Job Approval Rating Up to 49%," Gallup, March 24, 2020, https://news.gallup.com/poll/298313/president-trump-job-approval-rating.aspx.

32. Donald J. Trump, Twitter posts, March 18, 2020, https://twitter.com/rea lDonaldTrump/status/1240269231410774016.

33. Remarks by President Trump, Vice President Pence, and Members of the Coronavirus Task Force in Press Conference, March 13, 2020, https://www.white house.gov/briefings-statements/remarks-president-trump-vice-president-pence -members-coronavirus-task-force-press-conference-3.

34. Remarks by President Trump, Vice President Pence, and Members of the Coronavirus Task Force in Press Briefing, March 18, 2020.

35. Remarks by President Trump at a Turning Point Action Address to Young Americans, June 23, 2020, https://www.whitehouse.gov/briefings-statements/ remarks-president-trump-turning-point-action-address-young-americans.

36. Lauren Egan, "Trump Campaign Tells Surrogates to Paint Biden as 'The Opposition' in Coronavirus War," NBC News, April 1, 2020, https://www.nbcnews .com/politics/donald-trump/trump-campaign-tells-surrogates-paint-biden-opposition -coronavirus-war-n1174506.

37. Nick Corasaniti, Jeremy W. Peters, and Annie Karni, "New Trump Ad Suggests a Campaign Strategy Amid Crisis: Xenophobia," *New York Times*, April 10, 2020, https://www.nytimes.com/2020/04/10/us/politics/trump-ad-gary-locke.html.

38. Remarks by President Trump, Vice President Pence, and Members of the Coronavirus Task Force in a Fox News Virtual Town Hall, March 24, 2020, https:// www.whitehouse.gov/briefings-statements/remarks-president-trump-vice-president -pence-members-coronavirus-task-force-fox-news-virtual-town-hall.

39. Niall McCarthy, "COVID-19 Death Toll Surpasses Vietnam War," Statista, April 29, 2020, https://www.statista.com/chart/21545/deaths-from-the-coronavirus -and-vietnam-war.

40. "Unemployment Rate Rises to Record High 14.7 Percent in April 2020," U.S. Bureau of Labor Statistics, May 13, 2020, https://www.bls.gov/opub/ted/2020/ unemployment-rate-rises-to-record-high-14-point-7-percent-in-april-2020.htm.

41. Teresa Herbert, "National Survey on COVID-19 Pandemic Shows Significant Mental Health Impact," Beth Israel Deaconess Medical Center, July 1, 2020, https:// www.bidmc.org/about-bidmc/news/2020/07/covid-19-mental-health.

42. Liz Hamel et al., "KFF Health Tracking Poll—May 2020," Kaiser Family Foundation, May 27, 2020, https://www.kff.org/coronavirus-covid-19/report/kff -health-tracking-poll-may-2020/.

43. Remarks by President Trump at the White House Business Session with our Nation's Governors, February 10, 2020, https://www.whitehouse.gov/briefings-state ments/remarks-president-trump-white-house-business-session-nations-governors.

44. Ebony Bowden and Steven Nelson, "Blue-State Coronavirus Bailouts Are Unfair to Republicans, Trump Says," *New York Post*, May 5, 2020, https://nypost .com/2020/05/05/trump-blue-state-coronavirus-bailouts-are-unfair-to-republicans.

45. Bradley Jones, "Coronavirus Death Toll Is Heavily Concentrated in Democratic Congressional Districts," Pew Research Center, May 26, 2020, https://www .pewresearch.org/fact-tank/2020/05/26/coronavirus-death-toll-is-heavily-concentrated -in-democratic-congressional-districts.

46. William H. Frey, "Mapping COVID-19's Spread from Blue to Red America," Brookings Institution, June 3, 2020, https://www.brookings.edu/blog/the-avenue/2020/05/29/mapping-covid-19s-spread-from-blue-to-red-america.

47. Remarks by President Trump on Protecting Seniors with Diabetes, May 26, 2020, https://www.whitehouse.gov/briefings-statements/remarks-president-trump-protecting-seniors-diabetes. Issued on May 26, 2020.

48. Donald J. Trump, Twitter post, May 14, 2020, https://twitter.com/realdonaldtrump/status/1261117760962166786.

49. Michael C. Bender, "Americans Are More Troubled by Police Actions in Killing of George Floyd Than by Violence at Protests, Poll Finds," *Wall Street Journal*, June 7, 2020, https://www.wsj.com/articles/americans-are-more-troubled-by-police-actions-in-killing-of-george-floyd-than-by-violence-at-protests-poll-finds-11591534801.

50. Remarks by President Trump, Vice President Pence, and Members of the Coronavirus Task Force in Press Briefing, April 23, 2020, https://www.whitehouse.gov/briefings-statements/remarks-president-trump-vice-president-pence-members-coronavirus-task-force-press-briefing-31.

51. Diana Bradley, "Lysol and Clorox Respond to Trump Comment About Injecting Disinfectant," *PR Week*, April 24, 2020, https://www.prweek.com/article/1681380/lysol-clorox-respond-trump-comment-injecting-disinfectant.

52. U.S. Food and Drug Administration, "FDA Cautions Against Use of Hydroxychloroquine or Chloroquine for COVID-19 Outside of The Hospital Setting or a Clinical Trial due to Risk of Heart Rhythm Problems," June 15, 2020, https://www.fda.gov/drugs/drug-safety-and-availability/fda-cautions-against-use-hydroxychloroquine-or-chloroquine-covid-19-outside-hospital-setting-or.

53. Radhika Gharpure et al., "Knowledge and Practices Regarding Safe Household Cleaning and Disinfection for COVID-19 Prevention—United States, May 2020," *Morbidity and Mortality Weekly Report*, June 12, 2020, https://www.cdc.gov/mmwr/volumes/69/wr/mm6923e2.htm?s_cid=mm6923e2_w.

54. Robert Preidt, "Shortages of Hydroxychloroquine for Lupus Patients," *Health-Day News*, June 2, 2020, https://www.webmd.com/lung/news/20200602/shortages-of-hydroxychloroquine-for-lupus-patients.

55. Caitlin Oprysko, "Poll: Despite Trump's Endorsement, Few Voters Support Use of Hydroxycholoroquine," *Politico*, May 26, 2020, https://www.politico.com/news/2020/05/26/trump-hydroxychloroquine-poll-282426.

56. Remarks by President Trump After Senate GOP Policy Lunch, May 19, 2020, https://www.whitehouse.gov/briefings-statements/remarks-president-trump-senate-gop-policy-lunch-u-s-capitol.

57. Gabriela Schulte, "Poll: 59 Percent of Voters Disapprove of Trump's Decision to Share Videos Promoting Hydroxychloroquine," *The Hill*, August 7, 2020, https://thehill.com/hilltv/what-americas-thinking/511065-poll-59-percent-of-voters-disapprove-of-trumps-decision-to.

58. "Poll Finds Crime Top Fear at Home," *New York Times*, February 28, 1968, https://timesmachine.nytimes.com/timesmachine/1968/02/28/91222101.html?pageNumber=29.

59. Hazel Erskine, "The Polls: Causes of Crime," *Public Opinion Quarterly* 38 (Winter 1974–1975): 288–98.

60. Kathleen Weldon, "The Long Hot Summer: Riots in 1967," Roper Center for Public Opinion Research, August 28, 2017, https://ropercenter.cornell.edu/blog/long-hot-summer-riots-1967.

61. Carl Brown, "The Whole World Was Watching: Public Opinion in 1968," Roper Center for Public Opinion Research, June 30, 2016, https://ropercenter.cornell.edu/blog/whole-world-was-watching-public-opinion-1968.

62. George C. Wallace, Speech at Madison Square Garden, Oct 24, 1968, http://www-personal.umd.umich.edu/~ppennock/doc-Wallace.htm.

63. Richard Nixon, Address Accepting the Presidential Nomination at the Republican National Convention in Miami Beach, Florida, American Presidency Project, https://www.presidency.ucsb.edu/node/256650.

64. Museum Object 1970.2881.a-b; Hard Hat Presented to President Nixon after Kent State Riots; 5/8/1970; Collection RN-MUS: Richard Nixon Presidential Library Museum Collection; Richard Nixon Library, Yorba Linda, California. Online Version, https://www.docsteach.org/documents/document/hard-hat-president-nixon-kent-state-riots, October 20, 2020.

65. "Poll Finds Worry in Campus Unrest," *New York Times*, June 18, 1970, https://timesmachine.nytimes.com/timesmachine/1970/06/18/76769129.html?pageNumber=38.

66. Morris Kaplan, "Major Landlord Accused of Antiblack Bias in City," *New York Times*, October 16, 1973, https://www.nytimes.com/1973/10/16/archives/major-landlord-accused-of-antiblack-bias-in-city-us-accuses-major.html.

67. *New York Daily News*, May 1, 1989, at http://apps.frontline.org/clinton-trump-keys-to-their-characters/pdf/trump-newspaper.pdf.

68. Andrew Kaczynski and Jon Sarlin, "Trump in 1989 Central Park Five Interview: 'Maybe Hate Is What We Need,'" CNN, October 10, 2016, https://www.cnn.com/2016/10/07/politics/trump-larry-king-central-park-five/index.html.

69. Justin McCarthy, "Americans' Views Shift on Toughness of Justice System," Gallup, October 20, 2016, https://news.gallup.com/poll/196568/americans-views-shift-toughness-justice-system.aspx.

70. "Black, White, and Blue: Americans' Attitudes on Race and Police," Roper Center, September 22, 2015, https://ropercenter.cornell.edu/blog/black-white-and-blue-americans-attitudes-race-and-police.

71. John Gramlich, "5 facts about crime in the U.S.," Pew Research Center, October 17, 2019, https://www.pewresearch.org/fact-tank/2019/10/17/facts-about-crimt-in-the-u-s/.

72. Ford Fessenden and Lazaro Gamio, "The Relentless Shrinking of Trump's Base," *New York Times*, October 22, 2020, https://www.nytimes.com/interactive/2020/10/22/us/politics/trump-voters-demographics.html.

73. Philip Bump, "The Numbers Behind Trump's 'You Walk Down the Street, You Get Shot' Pitch to Black Voters," *Washington Post*, August 24, 2016, https://www.washingtonpost.com/news/the-fix/wp/2016/08/24/the-numbers-behind-trumps-you-walk-down-the-street-you-get-shot-pitch-to-black-voters.

74. Rebecca Morin, "'They Admitted Their Guilt': 30 Years of Trump's Comments about the Central Park Five," *USA Today*, June 19, 2019, https://www.usatoday.com/story/news/politics/2019/06/19/what-trump-has-said-central-park-five/1501321001.

75. Josh Penrod, C. J. Sinner, and MaryJo Webster, "Buildings damaged in Minneapolis, St. Paul after riots," *Minneapolis Star-Tribune*, July 13, 2020, https://www.startribune.com/minneapolis-st-paul-buildings-are-damaged-looted-after-george-floyd-protests-riots/569930671/.

76. Donald J. Trump, Twitter post, May 28, 2020, https://twitter.com/realDonaldTrump/status/1266231100172615680?s=20.

77. Bob Wilcox, "City Declares War on Crime," *Miami News*, December 26, 1967, https://www.newspapers.com/clip/52375853/miami-news-december-26-1967.

78. Joe Biden, Twitter post, May 29, 2020, https://twitter.com/JoeBiden/status/1266369893403770886?s=20.

79. Donald J. Trump, Twitter thread, May 30, 2020, https://twitter.com/realDonaldTrump/status/1266711221191020544?s=20.

80. J. Edward Moreno, "DC Mayor Blasts 'Gross' Trump Tweet Threatening 'Vicious Dogs' at White House," *The Hill*, May 30, 2020, https://thehill.com/homenews/news/500273-dc-mayor-blasts-gross-trump-tweet-warning-about-vicious-dogs-at-white-house.

81. Peter Baker, Maggie Haberman, Katie Rogers, Zolan Kanno-Youngs and Katie Benner, "How Trump's Idea for a Photo Op Led to Havoc in a Park," *New York Times*, June 2, 2020, https://www.nytimes.com/2020/06/02/us/politics/trump-walk-lafayette-square.html.

82. Statement by the President, June 1, 2020, https://www.whitehouse.gov/briefings-statements/statement-by-the-president-39.

83. Associated Press reviewed thousands of pages of court documents related to the unrest. References to "Antifa" or planned violence were rare. Alanna Durkin Richer, Colleen Long, and Michael Balsamo, "AP Finds Most Arrested in Protests Aren't Leftist Radicals," Associated Press, October 20, 2020, https://apnews.com/article/virus-outbreak-race-and-ethnicity-suburbs-health-racial-injustice-7edf9027af1878283f3818d96c54f748.

84. Jeffrey Goldberg, "James Mattis Denounces President Trump, Describes Him as a Threat to the Constitution," *The Atlantic*, June 3, 2020, https://www.theatlantic.com/politics/archive/2020/06/james-mattis-denounces-trump-protests-militarization/612640.

85. General Mark A. Milley, memorandum to the Joint Chiefs of Staff, June 2, 2020, https://www.jcs.mil/Portals/36/Documents/CJCS%20Memo%20to%20the%20Joint%20Force%20(02JUN2020).pdf.

86. Susan Page and Sarah Elbeshbishi, "USA TODAY Poll: Forceful Clearing of Lafayette Square Protest Was Defining Moment for President and Protests," *USA Today*, June 10, 2020, https://www.usatoday.com/story/news/politics/2020/06/10/trust-high-black-lives-matter-photo-op-defining-moment-trump/5317621002.

87. Scott Clement and Dan Balz, "Big Majorities Support Protests over Floyd Killing and Say Police Need to Change, Poll Finds," *Washington Post*, June 9, 2020, https://www.washingtonpost.com/politics/big-majorities-support-protests-over-floyd

-killing-and-say-police-need-to-change-poll-finds/2020/06/08/6742d52c-a9b9-11ea
-9063-e69bd6520940_story.html.

88. Kendall Karson, "Broad Disapproval for Trump's Handling of Coronavirus, Race Relations: POLL," ABC News, July 10, 2020, https://abcnews.go.com/
Politics/broad-disapproval-trumps-handling-coronavirus-race-relations-poll/story
?id=71704889.

89. Clement and Balz, "Big Majorities"; Gabriela Schulte, "Poll: 57 Percent of
Voters Support George Floyd Protests," *The Hill*, June 15, 2020, https://thehill.com/
hilltv/what-americas-thinking/502835-poll-57-percent-of-voters-support-george
-floyd-protests; Y Kim Parker, Juliana Horowitz and Monica Anderson, "Amid
Protests, Majorities Across Racial and Ethnic Groups Express Support for the Black
Lives Matter Movement," Pew Research Center, June 12, 2020, https://www.pew
socialtrends.org/2020/06/12/amid-protests-majorities-across-racial-and-ethnic
-groups-express-support-for-the-black-lives-matter-movement/.

90. Larry Buchanan, Quoctrung Bui and Jugal K. Patel, "Black Lives Matter May
Be the Largest Movement in U.S. History," *New York Times*, July 3, 2020, https://
www.nytimes.com/interactive/2020/07/03/us/george-floyd-protests-crowd-size.html.

91. "Protestors' Anger Justified Even If Actions May Not Be," Monmouth University Polling Institute, June 2, 2020, https://www.monmouth.edu/polling-institute/
reports/monmouthpoll_us_060220.

92. Donald J. Trump and Ben Carson, "We'll Protect America's Suburbs," *Wall
Street Journal*, August 16, 2020, https://www.wsj.com/articles/well-protect-americas
-suburbs-11597608133.

93. Donald J. Trump, Twitter post, August 12, 2020, https://twitter.com/real
DonaldTrump/status/1293517514798960640?s=20.

94. Cory Booker, Twitter post, August 12, 2020, https://twitter.com/CoryBooker/
status/1293587655079473164?s=20.

95. Emily Badger, "Women in Suburbia Don't Seem Too Worried about Its
Destruction," *New York Times*, September 18, 2020, https://www.nytimes.com/2020/
09/18/upshot/voters-suburbs-2020-election.html.

96. Frank Newport, "Affirmative Action and Public Opinion," Gallup, August
7, 2020, https://news.gallup.com/opinion/polling-matters/317006/affirmative-action
-public-opinion.aspx.

97. Jennifer A. Kingson, "Exclusive: $1 Billion-Plus Riot Damage Is Most Expensive in Insurance History," Axios, September 16, 2020, https://www.axios.com/
riots-cost-property-damage-276c9bcc-a455-4067-b06a-66f9db4cea9c.html.

98. Mariame Kaba, "Yes, We Mean Literally Abolish the Police," *New York
Times*, June 12, 2020, https://www.nytimes.com/2020/06/12/opinion/sunday/floyd
-abolish-defund-police.html.

99. Nathaniel Rakich, "How Americans Feel about 'Defunding the Police,'"
FiveThirtyEight, June 19, 2020, https://fivethirtyeight.com/features/americans-like
-the-ideas-behind-defunding-the-police-more-than-the-slogan-itself.

100. Lydia Saad, "Black Americans Want Police to Retain Local Presence," Gallup, August 5, 2020, https://news.gallup.com/poll/316571/black-americans-police
-retain-local-presence.aspx.

101. Donald J. Trump, Twitter post, June 8, 2020, https://twitter.com/realDonaldTrump/status/1269970808329437185?s=20.

102. Tim Hains, "Jim Jordan: It Is Pure Insanity to Abolish the Police, or ICE, or DHS," RealClearPolitics, June 10, 2020, https://www.realclearpolitics.com/video/2020/06/10/jim_jordan_it_is_pure_insanity_to_abolish_the_police_or_ice_or_dhs.html.

103. Jacqueline Alemany, "Power Up: Rep. Clyburn to Today's Activists: Don't Let 'Defund the Police' Hijack New Momentum for Reform," *Washington Post*, June 11, 2020, https://www.washingtonpost.com/news/powerpost/paloma/powerup/2020/06/11/powerup-rep-clyburn-to-today-s-activists-don-t-let-defund-the-police-hijack-new-momentum-for-reform/5ee145e1602ff12947e89a10.

104. Astead W. Herndon, "How a Pledge to Dismantle the Minneapolis Police Collapsed," *New York Times*, September 26, 2020, https://www.nytimes.com/2020/09/26/us/politics/minneapolis-defund-police.html.

105. U.S. Bureau of Labor Statistics, "The Employment Situation—May 2020," June 5, 2020, https://www.bls.gov/news.release/archives/empsit_06052020.pdf.

106. Donald J. Trump, Twitter post, July 13, 2020, https://twitter.com/realDonaldTrump/status/1282888821001072640?s=20.

107. Lydia Saad, "What Percentage of Americans Owns Stock?" Gallup, September 13, 2019, https://news.gallup.com/poll/266807/percentage-americans-owns-stock.aspx.

108. Board of Governors of the Federal Reserve System, "Report on the Economic Well-Being of U.S. Households in 2019—May 2020," May 2020, https://www.federalreserve.gov/publications/2020-economic-well-being-of-us-households-in-2019-financial-repercussions-from-covid-19.htm.

109. John Horgan, "Will COVID-19 Make Us More Socialist?" *Scientific American*, April 20, 2020, https://blogs.scientificamerican.com/cross-check/will-covid-19-make-us-more-socialist.

110. Laura Wronski, "NBC News|SurveyMonkey Poll: Coronavirus and Reopening," NBC News, July 12, 2020, https://www.surveymonkey.com/curiosity/nbc-poll-covid-july12.

111. Carroll Doherty et al., "In Changing U.S. Electorate, Race and Education Remain Stark Dividing Lines," Pew Research Center, June 2, 2020, https://www.pewresearch.org/politics/2020/06/02/in-changing-u-s-electorate-race-and-education-remain-stark-dividing-lines.

112. James Temple, "Yes, Climate Change Is Almost Certainly Fueling California's Massive Fires," *MIT Technology Review*, August 20, 2020, https://www.technologyreview.com/2020/08/20/1007478/california-wildfires-climate-change-heatwaves.

113. Brian Kennedy, "Most Americans Say Climate Change Affects Their Local Community, Including 70% Living Near Coast," Pew Research Center, June 29, 2020, https://www.pewresearch.org/fact-tank/2020/06/29/most-americans-say-climate-change-impacts-their-community-but-effects-vary-by-region-2.

114. Ray Sanchez, "Americans Made 'Tremendous Sacrifices': The Great Reopening of the Pandemic Summer Still Got Derailed," CNN, July 9, 2020, https://www.cnn.com/2020/07/09/us/us-coronavirus-summer-reopening/index.html.

115. William F. Frey, "COVID-19's Summer Surge into Red America Sets the Stage for November's Election," Brookings Institution, September 14, 2020, https://www.brookings.edu/blog/the-avenue/2020/09/11/covid-19s-summer-surge-into-red-america-sets-the-stage-for-novembers-election.

116. Rachel Meade, "The Movement Against Coronavirus Lockdowns Is Still Going—And Still Angry," *Washington Post*, August 10, 2020, https://www.washingtonpost.com/politics/2020/08/10/movement-against-coronavirus-lockdowns-is-still-going-still-angry.

117. Donald J. Trump, Twitter post, April 17, 2020, https://twitter.com/realDonaldTrump/status/1251169217531056130?s=20.

118. Donald J. Trump, Twitter post, May 1, 2020, https://twitter.com/realdonaldtrump/status/1256202305680158720.

119. Aaron C. Davis et al., "Alleged Michigan Plotters Attended Multiple Anti-Lockdown Protests, Photos and Videos Show," *Washington Post*, November 1, 2020, https://www.washingtonpost.com/investigations/2020/11/01/michigan-kidnapping-plot-coronavirus-lockdown-whitmer/?arc404=true.

120. Tobias Hoonhout, "Jacob Blake Himself Blows Up 'Unarmed' Media Narrative," *National Review*, January 14, 2021, https://www.nationalreview.com/news/jacob-blake-himself-blows-up-unarmed-media-narrative/.

121. Remarks by President Trump During a Wisconsin Community Safety Roundtable, Kenosha, Wisconsin, September 1, 2020, https://www.whitehouse.gov/briefings-statements/remarks-president-trump-wisconsin-community-safety-roundtable-kenosha-wi.

122. Eric Bradner, "Biden Speaks with Jacob Blake while Meeting with Family in Wisconsin," CNN, September 4, 2020, https://www.cnn.com/2020/09/03/politics/joe-biden-wisconsin-trip/index.html.

123. Laura Barrón-López, "Trump Attacks Take a Toll on Black Lives Matter Support," *Politico*, September 2, 2020, https://www.politico.com/news/2020/09/02/trump-black-lives-matter-poll-407227.

124. Mallory Newall, "Support for Protests After Jacob Blake Shooting Sharply Divided by Race, Partisanship," Ipsos, September 3, 2020, https://www.ipsos.com/en-us/news-polls/support-protests-Blake-shooting-divided.

125. Donald Trump Tulsa, Oklahoma Rally Speech Transcript, June 20, 2020, https://www.rev.com/blog/transcripts/donald-trump-tulsa-oklahoma-rally-speech-transcript.

126. Remarks by President Trump Before Marine One Departure, June 23, 2020, https://www.whitehouse.gov/briefings-statements/remarks-president-trump-marine-one-departure-95.

127. Maggie Astor and Noah Weiland, "Coronavirus Surge in Tulsa 'More Than Likely' Linked to Trump Rally," *New York Times*, July 8, 2020, https://www.nytimes.com/2020/07/08/us/politics/coronavirus-tulsa-trump-rally.html.

128. Republican National Committee, "Trump Campaign and RNC bring in $61.7M in April, Have $255M+ Cash on Hand," May 11, 2020, https://blog.4president.org/2020/2020/05/trump-campaign-and-rnc-bring-in-617m-in-april-have-255m-cash-on-hand.html.

129. Mark Hamill, Twitter post, May 7, 2020, https://twitter.com/HamillHimself/status/1258509463658434560?s=20.

130. Peter Elkind and Doris Burke, "The Myths of the 'Genius' behind Trump's Reelection Campaign," *ProPublica*, September 11, 2019, https://www.propublica.org/article/the-myths-of-the-genius-behind-trumps-reelection-campaign.

131. Shane Goldmacher and Maggie Haberman, "How Trump's Billion-Dollar Campaign Lost Its Cash Advantage," *New York Times*, September 7, 2020, https://www.nytimes.com/2020/09/07/us/politics/trump-election-campaign-fundraising.html.

132. Katie Glueck and Maggie Haberman, "Biden and Trump Teams Each Raised Over $60 Million in April," *New York Times*, May 11, 2020, https://www.nytimes.com/2020/05/11/us/politics/biden-trump-fundraising.html.

133. Michelle Ye Hee Lee, "Donors Can Now Give $620,600 to Biden and DNC, Expanding Democratic Big-Money Fundraising," *Washington Post*, May 16, 2020, https://www.washingtonpost.com/politics/donors-can-now-give-620600-to-biden-and-dnc-expanding-democratic-big-money-fundraising/2020/05/16/d2bf51cc-978a-11ea-82b4-c8db161ff6e5_story.html.

134. Ben Kamisar and Marianna Sotomayor, "Biden Has Big Cash on Hand Advantage Over Trump," NBC News, September 18, 2020, https://www.nbcnews.com/politics/meet-the-press/blog/meet-press-blog-latest-news-analysis-data-driving-political-discussion-n988541/ncrd1240614#blogHeader.

135. Karl Evers-Hillstrom, "Billionaire Democratic Donors Give Big to Anti-Trump Lincoln Project," *Open Secrets*, July 15, 2020, https://www.opensecrets.org/news/2020/07/billionaire-democrat-donors-lincoln-project. Note: Coauthor Pitney was a member of the Lincoln Project's California advisory board.

136. Nancy LeTourneau, "Can Anti-Trump Republican Groups Bring about a Biden Landslide?" *Washington Monthly*, July 8, 2020, https://washingtonmonthly.com/2020/07/08/can-anti-trump-republican-groups-usher-in-a-biden-landslide.

137. "The Lincoln Project: Career Republicans call on Americans to Vote out President Trump," *60 Minutes* transcript, October 11, 2020, https://www.cbsnews.com/news/the-lincoln-project-republican-strategists-super-pac-trump-60-minutes-2020-10-11/.

138. Seema Mehta, "Trump Lashes Out at GOP Critics, Exponentially Increasing Their Visibility," *Los Angeles Times*, May 10,2020, https://www.latimes.com/politics/story/2020-05-10/trump-gop-critics-lincoln-project-mourning-in-america.

139. Michelle Ye Hee Lee, "How George Conway's Super PAC Needled Trump with a Small-Budget Ad, Helping It Go Viral," *Washington Post*, May 8, 2020, https://www.washingtonpost.com/politics/how-george-conways-super-pac-needled-trump-with-a-small-budget-ad-helping-it-go-viral/2020/05/08/66cb7e1c-90a7-11ea-a0bc-4e9ad4866d21_story.html.

140. Christopher J. Devine and Kyle C. Kopko, *Do Running Mates Matter? The Influence of Vice Presidential Candidates in Presidential Elections* (Lawrence: University Press of Kansas, 2020).

141. Nick Corasaniti and Katie Glueck, "Protests in Minnesota Renew Scrutiny of Klobuchar's Record as Prosecutor," *New York Times*, May 29, 2020, https://www.nytimes.com/2020/05/29/us/politics/klobuchar-minneapolis-george-floyd.html.

142. Andy Kierz, "This Map Shows Where Each State's Largest Immigrant Group Comes From, Excluding Mexico," *Business Insider*, April 18, 2019, https://www.businessinsider.com/where-do-immigrants-come-from-map-most-common-countries-2019-4.

143. Natasha Korecki, Christopher Cadelago, and Marc Caputo, "'She had no remorse': Why Kamala Harris Isn't a Lock for VP," *Politico*, July 27, 2020, https://www.politico.com/news/2020/07/27/kamala-harris-biden-vp-381829.

144. Alexander Burns, Jonathan Martin and Katie Glueck, "How Biden Chose Harris: A Search That Forged New Stars, Friends and Rivalries," *New York Times*, August 13, 2020, https://www.nytimes.com/2020/08/13/us/politics/biden-harris.html.

145. Tim Alberta, Twitter post, August 20, 2020, https://twitter.com/TimAlberta/status/1296645100332777475?s=20.

146. Kristen Welker, Carol E. Lee, Shannon Pettypiece, and Monica Alba, "Trump's Convention Cancellation Is Costing GOP Donors Millions," NBC News, July 24, 2020, https://www.nbcnews.com/politics/2020-election/trump-s-convention-cancellation-costing-gop-donors-millions-n1234896.

147. Mike Allen and Treene, "Between the Lines of Trump's RNC Speech," Axios, August 28, 2020, https://www.axios.com/trump-rnc-speech-strategy-b2cbd308-6406-4308-a5d4-96c5a96dba49.html.

148. Caitlin Oprysko, "In Grievance-Filled Speech, St. Louis Couple Warn of Chaos in the Suburbs If Democrats Elected," *Politico*, August 24, 2020, https://www.politico.com/news/2020/08/24/mccloskey-convention-speech-guns-suburbs-401297.

149. Tarini Parti and Michael C. Bender, "Immigrants in Trump-Led Ceremony Didn't Know They Would Appear at RNC," *Wall Street Journal*, August 26, 2020, https://www.wsj.com/articles/immigrants-in-trump-led-ceremony-didnt-know-they-would-appear-at-rnc-11598481345.

150. Matthew Choi, "Meadows Dismisses Hatch Act Concerns at RNC: 'Nobody Outside of the Beltway Really Cares,'" *Politico*, August 26, 2020, https://www.politico.com/news/2020/08/26/mark-meadows-hatch-act-rnc-402194.

151. Eric Deggans, "Democrats Beat Republicans in Convention Television Ratings," National Public Radio, August 28, 2020, https://www.npr.org/2020/08/28/907289022/democrats-beat-republicans-in-convention-television-ratings.

152. Geoffrey Skelley, "Trump May Have Gotten a Convention Bounce. But It's Very Slight and May Already Be Fading," FiveThirtyEight, September 2, 2020, https://fivethirtyeight.com/features/trump-may-have-gotten-a-convention-bounce-but-its-very-slight-and-may-already-be-fading.

153. See compilation of 2020 surveys at https://www.pollingreport.com/corona virus.htm.

154. Brett Samuels, "Trump: COVID-19 Vaccine May Be Ready 'Right Around' Election Day," *The Hill*, August 6, 2020, https://thehill.com/homenews/administration/510853-trump-covid-19-vaccine-may-be-ready-right-around-election-day.

155. U.S. Council of Economic Advisers, "August Jobs Report: Economy Continues to Rebound as Unemployment Rate Drops," September 4, 2020, https://www.whitehouse.gov/articles/august-jobs-report-economy-continues-rebound-unemployment-rate-drops.

156. Curtis Dubay, "Latest Job Market Data Shows the Uneven Impacts of a K-Shaped Recovery on US Industries," U.S. Chamber of Commerce, September 30, 2020, https://www.uschamber.com/series/above-the-fold/latest-job-market-data-shows-the-uneven-impacts-of-k-shaped-recovery-us.

157. James W. Ceaser, Andrew E. Busch, and John J. Pitney Jr., *Defying the Odds: The 2016 Elections and American Politics, Post-2018 Election Update* (Lanham, MD: Rowman & Littlefield, 2019), 3.

Chapter Four

Blue over Red

The General Election

As the two candidates faced each other at the end of August, Joe Biden was holding the same roughly five-percentage-point lead he had maintained over Donald Trump since pollsters had begun regularly asking head-to-head questions a year earlier. That put him roughly in the same position as Hillary Clinton, who had also usually led Trump through 2016. (Her margin varied more than Biden's, and Trump had an occasional short-lived lead in the polls.[1]) The comparison gave hope to Trump's supporters and nightmares to Biden's, but the circumstances of the two elections were significantly different. In 2016, the fundamentals of the race were, if anything, tilted a bit in Trump's favor. In 2020, not so.

On one hand, where Clinton in 2016 was attempting the historically difficult task of winning a third consecutive term for her party, Trump in 2020 had the advantage of seeking a simple reelection. In the last century prior to 2020, only three incumbent presidents have been defeated for reelection: Herbert Hoover, Jimmy Carter, and George H. W. Bush. Twelve had succeeded in their quest to hold on to the White House. Additionally, as political scientist Helmut Norpoth has observed, incumbents who do not face serious intraparty competition for renomination almost always win their general elections, though there is debate over the direction of causation (perhaps presidents who are challenged in the primaries lose because the challenge divides their party, or perhaps they are already headed for defeat in November and their weakness invites a challenge).[2]

The economy worked in Trump's favor in 2016 and, before coronavirus hit, he had expected it to again. COVID largely vitiated that advantage. In 2016, nearly two-thirds of Americans saw the economy as poor or bad, which helped the outsider non-incumbent. After March 2020, the economy was again troubled, with high unemployment produced by COVID and (especially) the state and local economic shutdowns associated with COVID. More generally, the circumstances in the country roughly resembled other moments when incumbents had lost. Historically, beating an incumbent president has usually required a conflation of national difficulties that produce not just hardship but at least a vague sense of national unravelling. The most recent was Bush, who faced a recession, the Rodney King riots, and a mostly positive—but fatal to Bush—sense that the world had changed in ways that required adjustment.[3] Before that, Carter faced recession, inflation, high interest rates, riots in Miami, oil shortages, and simultaneous foreign crises. Then there was Herbert Hoover contending with the Great Depression and increasingly severe social unravelling, including the disorder surrounding the Bonus Army.[4]

For his part, Trump faced COVID, a deadly crisis of international scope that few democracies handled well; the depression-like economic plunge associated with the virus; and the most widespread, destructive, and costly civil disorder since the 1960s. Around Election Day, the percentage of Americans who said the country was on the wrong track outnumbered those who thought it was on the right track by a 61 to 32 percent margin. That, by the way, represented a modest recovery since August 3, when the margin was 71 to 23 percent.[5]

First and foremost, it is a truism of presidential elections that when an incumbent is running for reelection, the election becomes largely a referendum on the incumbent. As we have pointed out elsewhere, this incumbent was the most consistently unpopular president since polling began. According to presidential job approval surveys, his performance as president was approved by fewer than 40 percent of Americans for most of his first year in office, and by fewer than 45 percent for most of the remainder of his presidency. The RealClearPolitics approval average showed him reaching a high of 47 percent in late March 2020 after rallying the country to confront the coronavirus and falling again subsequently. He was "underwater," with more people disapproving than approving, continuously from January 27, 2017—one week after his inauguration—though Election Day 2020.[6]

The remarkable stability (at a relatively low level) of Trump's approval ratings was matched by a remarkable stability in Biden's lead over Trump since mid-2019 when pollsters began regularly asking head-to-head questions. For over a year, Biden led by about 5 percentage points, until building a larger lead in early October. Some of that lead was dubious at the end of the race and may have been before. But probably not all of it.

Finally, while party affiliation in the electorate can shift (and in fact did during the campaign) and is not a fixed "fundamental," it does set the parameters of the campaigns. In June, Democrats held a 33 percent to 26 percent lead over Republicans in self-reported party affiliation; counting "leaners"—people who say they are Independents but "lean" toward a major party—Democrats led by a 50 to 39 percent margin. The Democratic advantage had declined by mid-August, but it was still five points among affiliates and six including leaners.[7] Additionally, in 2016, third-party and Independent candidates gained unusually large support and scrambled the picture for a time; in 2020, there seemed to be much less appetite by voters for dabbling in exotic alternatives, a fact that some speculated would work to Biden's advantage.[8]

CONTINGENCIES

The first major contingency was the candidates. Donald Trump was a known quantity—bold (or disruptive), brash (or obnoxious), working to "drain the swamp" (or destroy key norms), authentic (or narcissistic), and outspoken (or dangerously unfiltered), depending on one's point of view. Joe Biden, unlike many challengers, was an equally well-known quantity. In Washington politics for almost forty-eight years, he was very nearly Trump's opposite in many respects. He was a conventional politician (or hack), a normal (or mediocre) figure, and an opponent of disruption (or a swamp creature), depending on one's point of view. Like Trump, Biden had serious shortcomings of verbal filtration, but they were in the style of a cranky grandpa rather than an aggressive radio talk-show host. For purposes of the election, the most important difference was that a majority or plurality of Americans saw Biden as more personally likeable than Trump. The president's favorability ratings consistently lagged below his job approval ratings, and stood at around 42 percent through the fall.[9] Biden's were consistently five to ten points higher.[10] The benefit Trump gained from running against the disliked Hillary Clinton in 2016 would not be there for him in 2020.

The candidates and their campaigns developed their own strategies to maximize their chances in the environment created by the fundamentals outlined above. In most respects, their approaches took shape in the interregnum and remained on the same trajectory. Biden exploited the disorder and disruption surrounding Trump to promise a sort of "return to normalcy," à la Warren Harding in 1920. Taking a cue from Napoleon, who was reported to have instructed "Never interfere with the enemy when he is in the process of destroying himself," he was content to allow Trump to be the center of attention, confident that the president would continue to alienate voters. During autumn, Biden continued to spend a large part of the campaign in his basement, venturing out occasionally to make statements, seldom answering questions from the media. Frequently, the campaign called "lids"—informing the media that campaigning was done for the day—early in the morning.[11] Rallies were few, small, and appropriately socially distanced. Altogether, Biden had positioned himself for over a year as the "boring" candidate, the "not Trump," and ran what was predominantly a negative campaign against Trump's character, temperament, and inadequacies in the fight against the coronavirus.[12] If it were not for the scant campaigning, it would have been a typical campaign by a challenger running against a vulnerable incumbent.

Trump took note of Biden's approach and tried to turn it against him, calling the former vice president "Sleepy Joe" or "Hidin' Biden." As usual, Trump took an energetic approach, holding large rallies. His campaign, unlike Biden's, also made major use of a "ground game"—volunteers going door-to-door.[13] His goal, as for all vulnerable incumbents, was to turn the election from a referendum into an even choice between two candidates. Biden was, Trump's campaign intimated, suffering from obvious cognitive decline, a case that Biden bolstered from time to time when he did venture out to campaign.

Though Biden mentioned issues such as global warming or race relations, his campaign was not primarily one of issues but of accountability for the incumbent. Indeed, he and Kamala Harris took pains to muddy issues like Supreme Court nominations, left-wing violence, and the environment, presumably in order to avoid either frightening moderate suburbanites or alienating their progressive base. For his part, to the extent he talked about issues, Trump focused on economic recovery and on "law and order," a theme with potential resonance given the ongoing riots and explosion of violent crime in many major cities but also one that had failed to get much traction over the summer. Where Biden collected celebrity endorsements, Trump collected endorsements from law enforcement officials and organizations. He attacked Biden's issue positions, or at any rate the farthest left versions of those positions. Gone as major themes were immigration, restoration of manufacturing, and other staples of the 2016 contest.

Another contingency was an offshoot from COVID. Over the summer, many states expanded voting by mail in order to accommodate voters who did not want to go to a crowded polling place on Election Day. In some states, every eligible voter was to be mailed a ballot. The parties were sharply divided over this development. Democrats, who had long wanted to expand mail-in voting, touted the change as an appropriate response to the virus. It would, they argued, prevent Election Day from becoming a "super spreader" event. Republicans from Trump down expressed grave concern that the innovation would open the door to massive fraud, and would at any rate inevitably lead to the random loss of a large number of ballots in the postal system.[14] There were, of course, partisan reasons for both sides to react as they did. It was broadly assumed that Democrats had more to gain from the maneuver, both because Democratic voters were, on average, more afraid of in-person voting this year and because Democrats rely more heavily on a support base (starting with young people) that is more likely to vote if one puts a ballot directly in their hands. (Some analysts dissented from this view, noting that senior citizens were both more likely to vote Republican and more likely to want to vote by mail than the average voter.) It was also true that if Trump was behind, as polls said he was, shifting voters from Election Day to days or weeks earlier would give him less time to catch up.

Without fanfare, Facebook mogul Mark Zuckerberg and his wife donated at least $400 million to the Chicago-based Center for Tech and Civic Life for grants to local election administrators. According to one post-election report, by Election Day, the Center had given money to 2,500 election administrations across the country that had been forced by the pandemic "to spend money on election workers, postage and printing for the increasing number of voters who wanted to vote by mail." When the extent of Zuckerberg's involvement in the election became known, it became the object of gratitude by some and concern by others. Bill Turner, the acting director of voting services in Chester County, Pennsylvania, said that "This grant really was a lifesaver in allowing us to do more, efficiently and expeditiously." At the same time, Rachael Cobb, political scientist at Suffolk University, contended that such extensive use of private money over time would be "in and of itself is corrosive" and "sullies [the election] in a way that we don't need it to be sullied at all."[15]

Finally, the two campaigns were in an uncertain competition for resources. Overall, Donald Trump and the Republican National Committee raised nearly $2 billion, while Joe Biden and the DNC raised about $1.7 billion; by themselves, Trump raised $800 million and Biden $1.06 billion—the first billion-dollar candidate in U.S. history.[16] Trump vastly outraised Biden in 2019 and early 2020, while Biden outraised the president in the crucial homestretch from August through October. Trump's "insurmountable" funding edge was not in fact insurmountable, as Biden received major infusions of donor cash following the announcement of Kamala Harris as his running mate and the first presidential debate. In addition, outside groups spent $582 million for Biden versus $320 million on behalf of Trump.[17]

EVENTS IN THE FALL

The final set of contingencies consisted of the events during the fall campaign. Some of them were as dramatic as one would expect, the year 2020 being what it was. The events consisted of five main sets: economic developments, media events, the death of Ruth Bader Ginsburg and resultant nomination battle over Amy Coney Barrett, presidential and vice-presidential debates, and a new surge of coronavirus (including Donald Trump's own brush with the disease).

Economic Developments

The steep economic decline related to COVID was sandwiched between a strong Trump economy before and a sharp recovery after midyear. Economic performance was Trump's best area in polls throughout his presidency and remained so in the fall. GDP bounced back, growing 33 percent on an annualized basis in the third quarter. Unemployment also continued to fall from its April peak of 14.7 percent and its August rate of 8.4 percent to 7.9 percent in September and 6.9 percent in October. Job growth was substantial, as many employees on COVID lockdown furloughs returned to work. Nevertheless, GDP was still 4 percent smaller than in the first quarter and there were 4.9 million more unemployed people in November than in February.[18]

Advantage: Trump, though not enough to make up for ground lost since February.

Media Events

Trump's defenders will argue that Biden owed much to the way the overwhelming majority of the national news media put its thumb on the scale for him, consistently painting the president in the worst light and his challenger in the best light. Since at least 2004, when CBS News featured an easily debunked forgery as part of its news campaign against George W. Bush, we have seen the return of the partisan press of the 1800s. In the 1800s there was a Republican and a Democratic newspaper in each city and town of a serious size. The return of the partisan press in our time has seen almost all major newspapers, all major networks but one, and all of the social media empires serving as adjuncts of the Democratic Party in lockstep. Trump critics will retort that the president had brought the negative coverage upon himself through his prodigious lying. The *Washington Post* counted 22,247 false or misleading Trump claims from his inauguration through late October 2020.[19] Whatever the case, things did not get any more balanced during the campaign. Examples:

- Coronavirus coverage was heavy, focusing on the failings of Trump and Republican governors while going easy on Andrew Cuomo, despite New York suffering a death rate more than twice that of Florida.
- On September 3, *The Atlantic* published a piece alleging that Trump had called dead American servicemen "suckers" and "losers" on a state visit to

France.[20] Some portions of the story were confirmed by other journalists such as Jennifer Griffin of Fox News.[21] Former Trump lawyer Michael Cohen had testified under oath that he had made similar comments in the past.[22] However, the *Atlantic* story was based on anonymous sources and the claim was disputed by several people who were there, some of whom (like John Bolton) had fallen out with Trump and had no reason to defend him.[23] Given the nearly instantaneous transformation of the *Atlantic* story into a Biden advertisement, some conservative commentators suspected that there had been some level of coordination between the publication and the campaign.

- On September 9, Bob Woodward (of Watergate fame) previewed revelations in his forthcoming book *Rage* that Trump had kept assessments of COVID from Americans early on to avoid panicking them. Woodward had been granted broad access to Trump in January through March, and he quoted the president as saying privately that the virus was "deadly stuff" and that he wanted to "play it down" to avoid a panic.[24] Woodward provided audio recordings of the conversations to the broadcast media, which played them frequently.
- On September 27, the *New York Times* published a piece claiming to show that Trump had paid only $750 in federal income tax in both 2016 and 2017.[25] Democrats jumped on the story as proof that Trump was a conniving plutocrat. Media skeptics pointed out that the information it was based on was almost certainly provided illegally.[26] They also argued that the story did not show that Trump had undisclosed income from Russia and contended that his low tax liability in some years was largely the result of provisions signed into law by Barack Obama, though he also avoided federal income tax in at least some years before Obama took office.[27]

This quick succession of high-profile negative stories set Trump back on his heels, forcing him onto the defensive. They did not, however, seem to affect the general outlines of the race. Biden maintained, but did not expand, his solid but modest lead in the polls. Perhaps worse from Trump's perspective was what got little coverage.

In mid-October, the *New York Post* broke an investigative story about Joe and Hunter Biden's foreign business dealings.[28] A large part of the story was based on emails supposedly retrieved from a laptop that Hunter had left unclaimed in a repair shop. The emails seemed to show that Joe Biden had known about Hunter's business dealings, had facilitated them, and may have profited from them as vice president—some of which would be deeply troubling ethically. Within days, a Biden business associate, Tony Bobulinski, came forward to support key aspects of the story, and Biden never asserted that the emails were false. The *Post* story amplified a report released three weeks earlier by Senate Homeland Security and Finance Committee Republicans on Hunter Biden's influence-peddling which stopped short of accusing him of criminal wrongdoing but alleged obvious ethical lapses and suggested criminal malfeasance was possible.[29] The story, which would likely have dominated the news for weeks had it been about Donald Trump Jr.'s laptop, was aggressively spiked by the social media giants, which prevented its sharing; Twitter even locked the *New York Post* out of its own Twitter account. Most of the rest of the national media complex followed suit.[30]

Trump critics, however, would note that the *Wall Street Journal* did dig into the story in some depth and found no smoking guns: "Text messages and emails related to the venture that were provided to the Journal by Mr. Bobulinski, mainly from the spring and summer of 2017, don't show either Hunter Biden or James Biden discussing a role for Joe Biden in the venture."[31]

Two news items also emerged bolstering Trump's contention that he was the victim of abusive behavior by the previous administration. The main source for the Steele Dossier was himself suspected of being a Russian spy, and U.S. intelligence sources in 2016 had picked up information that the Russians believed that Hillary Clinton had concocted the Trump-Russia collusion story in order to distract attention from her email server scandal.[32] The alleged Russian spy vehemently denied the accusation and accused Republicans of slandering him.[33] After a brief acknowledgment, these potential blockbuster stories were quickly dropped.

Similarly, the president's diplomatic victories in the Middle East, the big comeback in GDP in the third quarter, and Kamala Harris's Senate voting record (putting her by some reckonings to the left of Bernie Sanders) were likewise blacked out after a perfunctory acknowledgment, if any.

Advantage: Biden by a mile.

RBG/ACB

For nearly four years, liberals had feared the moment Ruth Bader Ginsburg's health would give way, allowing Donald Trump to nominate a conservative successor. After numerous cancer scares, on September 18, that day finally came.

Democrats immediately demanded that Trump refrain from nominating a replacement. They pointed out, correctly, that Republicans in 2016 had argued against filling Antonin Scalia's seat during a presidential election year so that voters could weigh in. The next president, so the argument went, should make the pick.[34] Republican Senate leader Mitch McConnell quickly responded: no, the president should make an appointment. He pointed out, just as correctly, that Democrats in 2016 had demanded a vote on Merrick Garland. Moreover, McConnell said, the key difference between 2016 and 2020 was that the president's party had a majority in the Senate.[35] Ten times in U.S. history, a president had nominated a new Supreme Court Justice prior to an election in an election year when his party had a majority in the Senate. In nine of those cases, the nomination was approved.[36]

Constitutionally, the situation was clear. When there is a Supreme Court vacancy, the president has the constitutional right (or, perhaps, duty) to make a nomination; the Senate has the right to either confirm it or not, using its best judgment. For half of the country that adored "the notorious RBG" and feared what might come in her place, constitutional clarity was cold comfort.

After a brief review, Trump announced that his nominee would by Amy Coney Barrett. Barrett was forty-eight years old and followed the mold of other Supreme Court justices in some respects. She had clerked for Antonin Scalia (whose philosophy she shared), taught law school, and sat as a judge on a federal appellate court. She was also unique. First in her class at Notre Dame law, she would be the only member of the Court not to receive her law degree from one of a handful of elite institutions such as Harvard, Yale, or the University of Chicago. She would also be the court's sole conservative woman, and unlike the other women on the court, she had embraced a large family, with seven children (two of whom she and her husband adopted from Haiti). Barrett was a devout Catholic, a fact that had disturbed some Democrats at her appellate court hearings in 2017. Dianne Feinstein, for example, had gravely intoned that "the dogma lives loudly within you, and that's a concern."[37]

Barrett won plaudits for her intelligence and decency. Liberal Harvard law professor Noah Feldman, who clerked with Barrett at the Supreme Court, wrote an op-ed acknowledging that "I disagree with Trump's judicial nominee on almost everything. But I still think she's brilliant" and deserved confirmation.[38] (Feldman was rewarded for his gracious gesture by being slammed from the left on Twitter.) Critics attacked Barrett's attachment to Scalia, scrutinized her participation in a religious community in Indiana several years before, and even questioned her decision as a white woman to adopt two Black children from Haiti. (The attack came from Ibram X. Kendi, whose purported expertise in "anti-racism" has made him a best-selling author.[39])

Nothing really stuck, and Democrats were left to fume. They boycotted the committee vote and then had to watch as Republicans nearly unanimously voted to approve the nomination on the floor. All Democrats voted against Barrett, including Joe Manchin of West Virginia, who was not caught in a tough reelection battle this year. All Republicans but Susan Collins—who was caught in a tough reelection battle in Maine—voted in favor.

Though it produced great heat, the political implications of the battle were not easy to discern. Both sides were mobilized, though Senate Democrats were more careful on the attack than they had been with Brett Kavanaugh, remembering the backlash they suffered in Senate races in 2018. By the time the Senate vote was held, Gallup polls showed a slim majority of Americans wanted Barrett confirmed, and Senate Republicans had an opportunity to burnish their credentials with social and constitutional conservatives, especially conservative Catholics.[40]

Advantage: Unclear. Possibly a slight Trump edge.

Debates

Since the 1990s, it has been the norm for there to be three presidential and one vice-presidential debates, and the same had been scheduled in 2020. One of the presidential debates has customarily been devoted to foreign policy. Debates have seldom, if ever, changed the overall outcome of a presidential contest, but they do often change the trajectory of a race for a time. They are one of the few opportunities that candidates have to get fresh traction in the national discussion. Trump signally failed to do so.

Trump scored a few hits in the first debate. Most notably, Biden refused to answer whether he would support packing the Supreme Court if he won. The idea had already been floated by a few legal scholars on the left even before the Barrett appointment, and the chorus had grown since then. It was, however, not a popular notion among ordinary Americans, who said they opposed it by as much as a 22-percentage-point margin.[41]

Whatever gains Trump may have made were counterbalanced by three things. One was the prominence of coronavirus in the debate, as the first topic of discussion. Another: when Chris Wallace asked Trump what he would say to the white supremacist group called the Proud Boys, Trump said "stand back and stand by." The next day, he said that he meant "stand down," but damage was done. The third was Trump's behavior. By one count, the president interrupted his challenger 128 times during the course of the debate.[42] To be clear, neither candidate covered himself in glory. Biden interrupted Trump dozens of times as well, and he resorted to calling Trump a "clown" and a "racist" who should "shut up, man"—breaches of etiquette that would once have been quite noticeable. (In fact, the main story of the 2012 vice presidential debate was Biden's constant interruption of Paul Ryan.[43]) But Trump made a worse impression, and post-debate polls deemed him the loser.[44] Most analysts argued that the debate would change nothing, holding that so few ideas from either candidate were able to escape the debate stage intact that voters learned little new. However, more than a few seemed to learn that they simply could not stomach another four years of a President Trump. Within a week, Biden's lead in polls had roughly doubled, to about ten percentage points.

The next debate was the vice-presidential debate. Again, the pandemic was the first item on the agenda, followed by other domestic issues. Here, most people saw what they wanted to see. Democrats were sure Kamala Harris had demonstrated her superiority, Republicans were sure Mike Pence had defended the Trump record and attacked the Biden alternative much more effectively than Trump himself. After the dumpster fire of the first presidential debate, more than a few observers wished that both tickets could be reversed top to bottom, and it is not inconceivable that the 2020 vice presidential debate previewed the 2024 presidential contest. A CNN poll of debate viewers found that Harris won, 59–38 percent.[45] For whatever it was worth, thirteen of fifteen members of Frank Luntz's focus group of undecided voters thought Pence had won.[46] At most, though, Pence may have stopped Trump's bleeding, as he did in the 2016 vice presidential debate.

The next debate would have been an important opportunity for Trump to right his own ship. Instead, the president contracted COVID and the second presidential debate was cancelled. Once he was sufficiently recovered, the third debate proceeded on October 22, after about 50 million Americans had already voted. Perhaps having learned his lesson in the first debate, Trump was more restrained, and he gained some ground when he pushed Biden into acknowledging that he intended to "end fossil fuels in the United States." Trump also tried to bring the Hunter Biden story to the forefront, bypassing the media gatekeepers who had tried to shut the story down. He succeeded in getting it in front of the public, but beyond that, the conflicting interpretations were hardly clarified.[47]

Overall, the debates were largely a missed opportunity for Trump, who could have benefited from Pence's more disciplined approach. The pandemic dominated the critical first twenty minutes in each of the three debates, and foreign policy—where Trump had some notable accomplishments—was almost entirely missing from the conversation. Moreover, the first debate seems to have reminded a non-trivial number of undecided voters what they didn't like about Trump, just as Al Gore's stalkerish behavior on the debate stage in 2000 moved the numbers noticeably toward George W. Bush. Not least, Biden held it together well enough to tamp down doubts about his capacities. *Advantage:* Biden, by a bit.

Coronavirus Developments

After an easing of COVID cases over the summer, a new surge began in the fall, as weather cooled and people moved indoors. Death rates remained flat through early November, indicating improved treatment strategies, but both cases reported and COVID hospitalizations surged, with daily cases roughly doubling from the lows of late summer.[48] Moreover, Congress deadlocked over a follow-up virus relief bill. As special unemployment benefits and small business support dried up, Republicans and Democrats blamed each other for lack of agreement and Trump appeared largely impotent.[49]

The crowning oddity to the presidential race appeared on the night of October 1, when President Trump announced that he himself had tested positive for COVID-19, as had First Lady Melania Trump. Speculation raged: Would the news help Trump by producing a wave of sympathy, or would it hurt him by bringing even more to the forefront the issue on which he seemed most vulnerable? Analysts leaned more heavily to the latter when the theory was advanced that the president and several members of his staff had been infected at a large, and largely maskless, gathering at the White House the previous Saturday to announce Amy Coney Barrett's Supreme Court nomination. Though Biden was circumspect, others were not. To them, Trump had demonstrated his irresponsibility and blasé attitude toward COVID and now was reaping the result. For some Americans, the whole episode was a morality tale indicting Trump and serving as a metaphorical illustration of his blame for the progress of the pandemic in the United States.[50]

The morbid question also began circulating: What if Trump dies? He was in his seventies and overweight. Not among the very most vulnerable, but also not the safest. The most likely answer was that Trump's name would remain on the ballot; in many states it was too late to take him off. The electors pledged to him would vote for someone else, presumably an alternative (possibly, but not necessarily, Mike Pence) nominated by an emergency meeting of the Republican National Committee. Unless, that was, they were from one of the two dozen states that require electors to vote for the candidate to whom they are pledged. Most of those state laws make no mention of what to do if that candidate dies. The trick for Republicans would be to get out their voters and prevent confusion.[51]

This conversation did not last long. No sooner had Trump been diagnosed and admitted to the legendary Walter Reed Hospital in Bethesda, Maryland, than he was released. His quick and complete recovery was followed by a tweeted declaration to Americans: "Don't fear COVID!" The divided nation, which was already looking at the virus through two very different sets of eyes, heard two very different things in the president's pronouncement. One side heard a reckless disregard for great risk, a diminishment of the deaths of 200,000 Americans; the other side heard fortitude and hope, a call to embrace living as well as life.[52]

Because Trump's COVID diagnosis came only a few days after the first debate, it is not entirely possible to separate out how much of Biden's expanded lead was associated with the debate and how much with the diagnosis. At the very least, it seems fair to conclude that sympathy was not the predominant effect. It seems likely that anything that heightened the profile of COVID in the race worked to Trump's detriment. And, of course, it led to cancellation of the second debate and hence an opportunity for Trump to make some gains.

Advantage: Biden.

FOREIGN INTERFERENCE?

In 2016, U.S. intelligence services believed that Russia had intervened in the presidential election, providing indirect assistance to a number of campaigns and movements that it concluded were disruptive of the American political order, including Donald Trump's. In 2018, the Justice Department filed a criminal complaint alleging a Russian conspiracy to interfere in the midterm election. "The conspirators' alleged activities did not exclusively adopt one ideological view; they wrote on topics from varied and sometimes opposing perspectives," the Department said. "Members of the conspiracy were directed, among other things, to create 'political intensity through supporting radical groups' and to 'aggravate the conflict between minorities and the rest of the population.'"[53]

In 2020, the question arose: Would foreign interference again rear its head? If so, in what form? In August, intelligence officials shared fears that Russia, China, and Iran might involve themselves in the U.S. election. Specific concerns included the potential for large-scale disinformation campaigns and electronic disruption of the election process. Most evidence indicates that actions taken by U.S. agencies and social media companies led to limited success by foreign actors.[54]

Observers were naturally attentive to the possibility that Russia might again seek to tip the scales in a U.S. election. A CIA analysis of foreign influence operations declared, "We assess that President Vladimir Putin and the senior most Russian officials are aware of and probably directing Russia's influence operations aimed at denigrating the former U.S. Vice President, supporting the U.S. president and fueling public discord ahead of the U.S. election in November."[55] In testimony before the House Homeland Security Committee, FBI Director Christopher Wray said that "we certainly have seen very active, very active efforts by the Russians to influence our election in 2020 through what I would call more the malign foreign influence side of things. Social media, use of proxies, state media, online journals, et cetera."[56] Specific verifiable examples, however, were hard to find in the public domain. When reports surfaced about the Hunter Biden laptop, a group of former intelligence officials blamed Russian disinformation, but their open letter admitted that they had no evidence for the charge and subsequent events seemed to refute the proposition, especially the post-election revelation that Hunter was actually under active federal investigation.[57] Concerns were also raised when it was revealed that Russia had obtained certain voter registration lists. In public, Putin played both sides. During the Trump impeachment, he said, "It's simply a continuation of internal political struggle. The party that lost the [2016] election, the Democratic Party, is trying to achieve results by other means."[58] Months later, he seemed to offer support to Joe Biden. Hunter's alleged malfeasance, Putin declared, did not seem criminal. Moreover, he said, he could easily work with Joe Biden, as his own ideology was quite compatible with the social democracy of Joe Biden's Democratic Party.[59]

In late October, a different adversary emerged. National security agencies traced messages sent by Iran to Democratic voters in four states, including Florida and Pennsylvania. The messages were designed to appear as threats from the ultra-right group the Proud Boys telling voters "we will come after you" if they did not vote for Trump.[60] Given Iran's antipathy to Trump, it is likely the Iranians were attempting to trigger a backlash against Trump in key states.

After the election, Director of National Intelligence John Ratcliffe shared his view that China, Russia, and Iran had all engaged in election interference. The official intelligence community report on election interference was delayed due to disagreements over the extent of Chinese activity.[61]

TWO BIG QUESTIONS

As Election Day approached, two important questions emerged. First, would Joe Biden and Democrats walk away with the election in a blowout? In mid- to late October, numerous national polls showed Biden with a double-digit lead. State polls showed him winning or potentially winning in all battleground states and some not usually thought of as battlegrounds, such as Texas. For most of October, Democrats worried that Biden, though apparently ahead of Trump, was actually lagging behind Hillary Clinton's 2016 numbers in battleground states at the same point in the race. In late October, Biden's showing in the key states overtook Clinton's.[62]

Biden's increasingly comfortable position was matched by Democrats' confidence in down-ballot races. As we will see in the next chapter, Democratic candidates seemed likely to sweep a number of hotly contested Senate races, and Nancy Pelosi's House Democratic majority was poised to grow by somewhere between five and fifteen seats. Many pundits held open the possibility of a big Democratic night across the board, perhaps akin to the success Republicans enjoyed in 1980 when Ronald Reagan won a presidential landslide, Republicans swept into a Senate majority, and big House gains allowed the GOP to form a working majority with conservative Democrats for the next two years.[63]

There were, however, good reasons to question whether this prospective blowout would actually come to pass. In a general sense, the picture did not match up well with the closely competitive character of contemporary U.S. politics. There were also specific caution flags that went up intermittently in October.

For example, a month before Election Day, Gallup released a survey indicating that 55 percent of Americans judged themselves to be better off than they had been four years before.[64] American elections have always been about more than individual economic assessments, but this data point alone should have forced pollsters and pundits to reexamine their confident predictions of a Biden blowout. The economy was important, but it cut in conflicting ways for different people—and sometimes for the same people.

Gallup party affiliation data released late in October also telegraphed to careful observers that no blowout was to be expected. In June, Democrats held a 33 percent to 26 percent lead over Republicans in self-reported party affiliation; in October, Republicans had drawn even, 31 to 31 percent. Counting "leaners," the 50–39 percent Democratic lead in June had been whittled down to 49–45 percent in October.[65] Yet another Gallup survey showed that voters preferred Trump over Biden on the issues most important to them by a 49–46 percent margin, though preferring Biden on personal attributes by a 49–44 percent gap.[66] All of these indicators flew in the face of polls showing a Biden landslide. In late October, the Biden campaign itself sent signals to the media that the race was closer than (Democratic) optimists believed.[67]

For those inclined to doubt the landslide, the second big pre-election question followed: If the presidential election results are close, will they trigger some sort of constitutional crisis, à la 1876? In that year, widespread fraud led to the appointment of two competing sets of electors in three Southern states (plus a single contested elector in Oregon). The extraconstitutional solution hit upon by Congress was to leave evaluation of the disputed electors in the hands of a special commission. By a one-vote margin, the commission awarded all disputed electors to Rutherford B. Hayes, the Republican nominee, whose election was accepted by Democrats only when he quietly agreed to end Reconstruction.

The potential for post-election crisis had been highlighted by the "Transition Integrity Project," a group of roughly 100 academics, journalists, and former government officials who role-played through a variety of electoral scenarios in June 2020.[68] The project was, strictly speaking, bipartisan, though the Republicans who were involved were anti-Trump. In both 2016 and 2020, Trump had refused to say that he would accept defeat, and the primary purpose of the project seemed to be to warn the nation against maneuvers that might be entertained by Trump to reverse an unfavorable outcome.

Those maneuvers ranged from asking Republican legislatures to appoint alternate electors to ordering the National Guard to seize disputed ballots to taking extraordinary measures to protect himself legally to brazenly declining to leave office at the appointed time on January 20, 2021.[69] On the other side of the ledger, though almost a side note in the project's report and subsequent journalistic portrayals of it, the project exposed another risk of constitutional meltdown, this time emanating from Democrats. In the scenario postulating a Trump win in the Electoral College combined with a Biden lead in the nationally aggregated popular vote, Team Biden, led by Democratic heavy-hitter John Podesta, refused to concede and solicited alternate electors while Biden states threatened secession. A couple of months later, Hillary Clinton publicly advised Biden that, if the election were close, he should not concede "under any circumstances."[70]

Naysayers argued that the country's legal and constitutional system could manage any conceivable dispute,[71] but many Americans on both sides could not escape a sense of dread at the impending election. *Alternate electors? Refusing to leave office? Secession?* The fact that such ideas were even being discussed seemed an ill omen.

The danger of a radical misfire was amplified by the mass use of mail ballots, whether because it would lead to mass fraud (the Republican fear), because engineered failures of postal delivery would amount to mass voter suppression (the Democratic fear), or because it would occasion so much confusion, so many delays in vote counting, and so many inadvertently lost ballots that it would compromise the legitimacy of the result.

Approaching the election, some election analysts began to warn of the "Red Mirage," a scenario in which Donald Trump would jump out to a big lead in Election Day votes, only to have Joe Biden come back to victory through the slow counting of mail ballots, which were likely to trend Democratic.[72] Trump announced that the winner should be known on Election Day, and Axios news service reported that he planned to declare victory early, a report the White House denied.[73] Analysts on the left accused Trump of plotting a coup.[74] Analysts on the right, such as Michael Anton, accused Democrats of plotting a coup.[75] Throughout the fall, signs of the radicalization of politics continued to burst out. In early October, a far-right (though not, apparently, pro-Trump) group calling itself the "Wolverine Watchmen" was arrested for planning to kidnap Michigan's controversial Democratic governor, Gretchen Whitmer.[76] In late October, a new round of left-wing riots rocked Philadelphia in the wake of a police shooting.[77]

The weekend before Election Day, businesses in major cities began boarding up their windows in anticipation of violence, depending on the results.[78]

RESULTS

It became obvious on the night of November 3 that the first question—would Biden win in a blowout?—was going to be answered in the negative. The first clue was that Florida came through for Trump by a bigger margin than four years earlier. Biden led in Texas for a short time, but he was overtaken by Trump—an example of a "Blue Mirage." It turned out that in Texas, mail ballots were counted first, followed by Election Day votes. Similarly, Biden's brief lead in Ohio vanished, and Trump again won the state comfortably. Iowa was the same. Some pre-election polls had shown all four leaning toward the challenger.

As votes dribbled in, Trump built up leads in Wisconsin, Michigan, Georgia, and North Carolina. In Pennsylvania, Trump was ahead by an impressive 600,000 votes. Many votes remained outstanding in each, however, and most of those were mail ballots. Trump was also in contention in Nevada and Arizona, where Fox News had controversially called the race for Biden but no one else had. When millions of Americans went to bed, Donald Trump seemed to be in the driver's seat, and betting markets shifted to predicting a Trump win.

At 2:30 a.m. Eastern time, Trump appeared on national television, claiming he had won and been the victim of fraud:

> This is a fraud on the American public. This is an embarrassment to our country. We were getting ready to win this election. Frankly, we did win this election. We did win this election. So our goal now is to ensure the integrity for the good of this nation. This is a very big moment. This is a major fraud in our nation.[79]

By midday on November 4, the picture had changed. First Michigan and then Wisconsin had flipped to a Biden lead. Trump's advantages in

Pennsylvania and Georgia had nearly disappeared, and he still trailed in Nevada and Arizona. By the end of the day Friday, Biden had moved into a comfortable lead in Pennsylvania and a narrow lead in Georgia. The former vice president likewise held on to narrow wins in Arizona and Nevada, while Trump maintained his modest lead in North Carolina. And that is where things remained when the last votes were tallied.

Biden had succeeded in his strategic goal of reversing Trump's 2016 Rust Belt wins and expanding into parts of the southwest and southeast that had experienced demographic change. Trump just had to hold on to what he won before, but he did not do so. Nevertheless, with a few exceptions, the key states that were close in 2016 remained close, just with a different outcome. Of the three Rust Belt "Blue Wall" states that Trump invaded in 2016 and lost in 2020—Michigan, Pennsylvania, and Wisconsin—Trump's percentages in 2020 were still higher than any other Republican candidate from 1992–2012 in Michigan and Pennsylvania, and compared favorably in Wisconsin.

Overall, turnout in the election was estimated at 67 percent of the voting eligible population, higher than in any election of the last century.[80] Both parties gained presidential votes relative to 2016, but Democrats more so. Biden won 51 percent of the nationally aggregated popular votes, a total of about 81 million, while Trump won about 47 percent of the vote, equating to 74 million votes. Biden's total vote was a massive 15 million higher than Hillary Clinton's, but Trump's total was also 11 million higher than he won in 2016. Unlike Al Gore and Hillary Clinton, whose national popular vote lead was entirely accounted for by their margins in California, Biden led outside

Table 4.1.   "Blue Wall" Republican Presidential Vote
Percentages 1992–2020

	MI	*PA*	*WI*
1992	−7.4	−9.0	−3.3
1996	−13.2	−9.2	−10.3
2000	−5.2	−4.2	−.2
2004	−3.4	−2.5	−.5
2008	−16.4	−10.3	−13.9
2012	−9.4	−5.4	−7.0
2016	+.2	+.7	+.7
2020	−2.8	−1.2	−.7
Avg 1992–2012	−9.2	−6.8	−5.9
Avg. 2016–2020	−1.3	−.3	0.0

Source: Dave Leip's Atlas of U.S. Elections, uselectionatlas.org; calculations by authors

Table 4.2. Democratic Reliance on California for Popular Vote Margins, 1992–2020

	California Margin	Rest of Country Margin	California as Percentage
Clinton 1992	1,490,751	4,314,505	25.7%
Clinton 1996	1,291,455	6,909,915	15.7%
Gore 2000	1,293,774	−746,376	236.3%
Obama 2008	3,262,692	6,286,413	34.2%
Obama 2012	3,014,327	1,969,773	60.5%
Clinton 2016	4,269,078	−1,401,454	148.9%
Biden 2020	5,103,821	1,956,456	72.3%

Source: Dave Leip's Atlas of U.S. Elections, uselectionatlas.org

of California, too. Nevertheless, nearly three-fourths of his national popular vote edge was owed to the Golden State.

The electoral vote total was 306 for Biden, 232 for Trump—an exact reversal of the distribution in 2016, before taking into account "faithless electors" who voted differently from their pledge. As widely expected, the third-party vote fell considerably from 2016, winning only about one-third the percentage of the vote as four years before. It also seems that most 2016 third-party voters cast their ballots for Biden in 2020.[81] In three battleground states—Arizona, Georgia, and Wisconsin—the Libertarian Party candidate, Jo Jorgensen, won significantly more votes than the margin between Biden

Table 4.3. Trump Margins in Key States, 2016 and 2020

	Trump Margin 2016	Trump Margin 2020
Arizona	+3.5%	−.3%
	+91,234	−10,457
Florida	+1.2%	+3.3%
	+112,911	+371,686
Georgia	+5.1%	−.2%
	+211,141	−11,779
Michigan	+.2%	−2.8%
	+10,704	−154,188
Nevada	−2.4%	−2.3%
	−27,202	−33,596
Ohio	+8.1%	+8.0%
	+446,837	+475,669
Pennsylvania	+.7%	−1.2%
	+44,284	−82,154
Wisconsin	+.7%	−.7%
	+22,748	+20,682

Source: Dave Leip's Atlas of U.S. Elections, www.uselectionatlas.org

and Trump. In two, Arizona and Georgia, she won at least five times more votes than the margin, and it is plausible to argue that she might have cost Trump those states.[82]

Though Biden's national vote margin was substantial, the election was a very close call where it counted—the Electoral College. If Trump had won Arizona (margin, 10,457), Georgia (margin, 11,779), and Wisconsin (margin, 20,682), he would have tied Biden in electoral votes, 269–269. The election would have gone into the House of Representatives, with each state getting one vote. Based on the party distribution of representatives in the new Congress, with Republicans controlling twenty-six state delegations, Trump would very probably have been reelected. In other words, the nation was 43,000 votes (out of 160 million cast) away from the third House contingency election in U.S. history and a second term for Donald Trump. Throw in another close state—say, Nevada, with a 33,596-vote margin—and Trump would have won outright. As we will explore in chapter 5, the expected Democratic blowout failed to materialize not only at the presidential level. Contingent on runoffs in Georgia, Democrats gained only one net Senate seat with Biden at the top of the ballot, not enough to win a majority, and they ended up losing House seats from Florida to California. Joe Biden had no national coattails.

There were a number of possibilities for why the national polls, which averaged a 7.2-percentage-point Biden lead on Election Day, underestimated Trump's performance.[83] One, which had been advanced even before the election by a few outlying pollsters who were finding greater Trump strength in the electorate, was that there was a significant contingent of "shy Trump voters" who supported Trump but would not admit it to a pollster. Given the exaggeration of Democratic strength in polls of congressional races, one might expand the hypothesis to suggest "shy Republican voters." Related is the thesis that Republicans simply had higher non-response rates, either because of the general distrust with which Republicans regard the media or because pro-Democratic demographic groups (especially people with college degrees) are more likely to answer a survey.

Another plausible explanation is that most pollsters simply were not working with valid turnout models. The unusual spike in turnout in 2020, this theory goes, made it more difficult to accurately predict the turnout levels of varying groups, a necessary ingredient to the weighting of responses that is frequently necessary. Some pollsters suggested that not enough survey firms used multiple methods, relying only on phone calls.

Finally, it could be that actual support for Trump was not hidden all along but experienced a real surge at the end of the campaign, which the polls only partially captured because it came too late. There is also evidence for this idea.

HOW BIDEN WON

Plainly speaking, Biden won by getting significantly more support than Trump. A close look at the exit polls shows that Trump's support had eroded across many key groups since 2016, in ways that were prefigured by House Republican losses in the midterm elections.[84]

On some dimensions, the distribution of votes hardly changed. For example, Trump won married voters and Biden won the unmarried by nearly identical margins as Trump and Clinton in 2016. The "gender gap" was also comparable, though Trump's margins deteriorated slightly among both men (a smaller Trump advantage) and women (a larger Trump deficit).

Given the level of partisan rancor over the past four years, it was perhaps unsurprising that both Republicans and Democrats were more wedded than ever to their party's nominee. A whopping 94 percent of Democrats reported voting for Biden and 94 percent of Republicans for Trump, a record in recent elections.

However, there were significant shifts that explain Biden's win.

Independents

One of the most important shifts occurred among Independents. In 2016, Trump won self-described Independent voters by a 46–42 percent margin. In 2020, Biden won them, by 54–41 percent.

Race

In comparison to 2016, Trump continued winning among white voters and losing among nonwhites. Biden cut Trump's margin among whites, who were two-thirds of the electorate, from 20 percentage points to 17. Trump partially compensated for those losses by increasing his vote share among every major group of nonwhites, cutting his 2016 margins by six percentage points among Blacks, five among Latinos, and 11 among Asians. Trump won nearly one in five votes of Black men and 36 percent of Latino men, and his supporters said that he won a larger share of his vote from nonwhite voters than any Republican candidate since Nixon in 1960.[85] One major reason for that showing, however, is that nonwhites made up a larger share of the total population than ever before. Between 2000 and 2018, they accounted for 76 percent of the growth in the electorate.[86] Trump did improve upon GOP performance, but he was starting from a very low base. In any case, George W. Bush won larger percentages among nonwhites in 2004.[87]

Religion

Joe Biden, running to be only the second Roman Catholic president in U.S. history, turned a four-point Trump win among Catholics in 2016 into a five-point edge for himself. The shift took place largely among white Catholics, with Hispanic Catholics voting Democratic at the same rate as 2016.[88] At the same time, Biden shaved twelve points off of Trump's lead among white evangelical Protestants.

Age

In a contest between the two oldest major party nominees in U.S. history, Trump held on to his 2016 lead among voters aged fifty and older, though at slightly reduced margins. Speculation that Trump might lose the senior vote due to COVID, endangering his position in Florida, did not pan out. He lost the youngest cohort (aged eighteen to twenty-four) by half again larger a margin than in 2016 and turned a three-percentage-point lead among voters age forty to forty-nine into a ten-point deficit.

Type of Community

Trump lost ground among voters in rural communities, though he retained a solid lead. However, connected with his improved performance among nonwhite voters, he improved his showing a bit in urban areas, though still losing badly. As always, the suburbs were the crucial battleground, and here Biden turned a four-point Republican edge in 2016 into a two-point Democratic edge in 2020. Analysts argued that suburbanites had become both more racially diverse and more likely to be college educated, contributing to a long-term trend toward Democrats.[89]

Education and Income

Interestingly, given the attention paid by analysts to the turn away from Trump by affluent, college-educated voters, it seems to have been the shift from non-college graduates and voters making less than $100,000 a year that hurt Trump most. While he lost among college grads by slightly more than in 2016, his seven-point lead among non-college grads collapsed to two points. At the same time, Trump's narrow 2016 loss among voters making $100,000 or less turned into a thirteen-percentage-point drubbing by Biden. According to exit polls, the president actually won the over $100,000 vote decisively.

Military Veterans

This group, which represented 15 percent of the electorate in 2020, moved away from Trump in substantial numbers. In 2016, Trump held a 26-percentage-point lead here. Four years later, his edge had fallen to ten points. Perhaps the September 3 *Atlantic* story had an impact. Perhaps, also, there was an accumulated impact of many respected former military leaders such as James Mattis and John Kelly distancing themselves from the president, as well as Trump's well-publicized spats with war hero John McCain. (Though speculation, the latter may also have contributed to Trump's razor-thin loss of Arizona.)

Aside from his improvement in urban areas and among nonwhite voters, Trump benefited from a couple of bright spots that have gone largely un-noticed in post-election analyses. One is that Trump won among voters who decided in October. Hunter Biden may have broken through to some voters despite the best efforts of Jack Dorsey and the national media, as may have Joe Biden's admission in the second debate that he intended to end fossil fuels in America.

The other is that Trump ended up breaking even among those who had voted before. Biden's entire popular vote margin was accounted for by first-time voters.

Both of these exit poll results repeated results in 2016, when Trump won October despite the *Access Hollywood* tape and lost among first-time voters while breaking even among all others. One implication of these figures is that the first-time voters in 2016 who swung heavily against Trump had become assimilated into a 50–50 country by the time they voted again. One should not assume that this year's first-time voters are irretrievably lost to Republicans.

Otherwise, it was Biden who made gains where he needed to.

Surveys showed a significant gulf between Biden and Trump voters in the issues that motivated them. When asked which of a battery of twenty issues were "very important" to their vote choice, most Trump and Biden voters named controlling the spread of COVID, unifying the country, lowering health costs, lowering unemployment, economic recovery, and protecting the United States from terrorism. A majority of Biden voters called "very important" another seven issues, particularly having to do with health care, global warming, and social issues, that most Republicans did not mention. A majority of Republicans named four fiscal and immigration issues as "very important," though only a minority of Democrats did so.

Table 4.4. Vote Distribution by Groups, 2016 vs. 2020

	Clinton	Trump	Biden	Trump
R	8	88	6	94
D	89	8	94	5
I	42	46	54	41
White	37	57	41	58
Black	89	8	87	12
Latino	66	28	65	32
Asian	65	27	61	34
Catholic	46	50	52	47
Protestant	39	56	39	60
Evangelical	16	80	24	76
Female	54	41	57	42
Male	41	52	45	53
Married	44	52	46	53
Unmarried	55	37	58	40
Urban	60	34	60	38
Suburban	45	49	50	48
Rural	34	61	42	57
<$100,000	49	45	56	43
>$100,000	47	47	42	54
College Grad	52	42	55	43
No Coll. Degree	44	54	48	50
Veterans	34	60	44	54
Nonveterans	50	44	53	45
1st time voters	57	38	64	32
Not 1st time	47	47	49	49
Decide last month	40	48	46	51
Decided earlier	51	45	51	47

Source: CNN Presidential Exit Polls 2016 and 2020

INTERPRETATIONS

In the wake of the presidential election, a divided nation asked one of two questions. One half asked, incredulously, "Why did Donald Trump lose?" The other half, equally incredulously, "How could he almost win?"

Why Trump Lost

Trump's defeat was consistent with a referendum model of presidential elections. His job approval ratings had been "underwater" his entire presidency,

Table 4.5. Issues Called "Very Important" by a Majority of Biden and/or Trump Voters (and Gap between Biden and Trump Voters)

Majority of Biden Voters and Trump Voters
Controlling spread of COVID (Biden+34)
Unifying the country (Biden+24)
Lowering health care costs (Biden+15)
Economic recovery (Trump+5)
Lowering unemployment (Trump+5)
Protecting United States from terrorism (Trump+23)

Majority of Biden Voters, Minority of Trump Voters
Protecting Obamacare (Biden+61)
Addressing climate change (Biden+59)
Protecting abortion rights (Biden+47)
Reducing racial inequality in justice system (Biden+41)
Raising taxes on wealthy (Biden+41)
Universal health care (Biden+40)
Balancing SCOTUS (Biden+26)

Majority of Trump Voters, Minority of Biden Voters
Lowering deficit (Trump+11)
Lowering taxes for most (Trump+12)
Reducing immigration (Trump+40)
Building border wall (Trump+45)

Minority of Biden Voters and Trump Voters
Increase government spending (Biden+2)
Eliminate Obamacare (Trump+22)
Overturn *Roe v. Wade* (Trump+22)

Source: *Morning Consult,* "2020 Exit Polling Live Updates: COVID-19, Economy and Health Care Are 2020's Dominant Voting Issues," November 3, 2020, https://morningconsult.com/exit-polling-live-updates/#section -100; calculations by authors

two-thirds of Americans thought the country was on the "wrong track," and the nation was mired in a pandemic and recession that many blamed on the president. The fundamentals were against him.

Trump was never able to turn the crises to his advantage in a sustained way. Instead, his reality-TV persona and endless Twitter bombardment proved unequal to the tasks at hand—to calm the nation, embrace the presidential role of head of state, administer the executive branch competently, and make a careful, reasoned argument in his defense.

In the end, too many Americans simply stopped listening to Trump. It is entirely possible that a majority had stopped listening long before the year 2020 began. Given the overall performance of the election polls underestimating the Trump vote, it is possible (though not certain) that job approval polls similarly underestimated Trump support throughout his presidency. It is important, however, not to exaggerate such an effect. The RealClearPolitics election polling averaged a Biden lead of 7.2 percent on Election Day. The end result was a Biden lead of 4.5 percent nationally. If one adds two percentage points to Trump's approval ratings from the beginning of his presidency to today, he would still be the most consistently unpopular president since polling began. Most presidents have experienced lows, and some (including Truman, Nixon, Carter, and George W. Bush) have briefly experienced lower lows. Many have been in the low 40 percent range a year before being reelected. None have spent their entire presidencies there.

Clearly, part of the referendum did not have to do with issues or even the state of the country, but Trump's conduct as president. His most fervent supporters tended to dismiss the importance of his comportment, but it is undeniable that voters have some vague standard of what is "presidential," and Trump too often failed to meet it. CNN exit polls showed that Trump narrowly won among the three-fourths of voters who said issues were most important, while Biden had a 2–1 margin among the quarter of voters who said the personal qualities of the candidates were most important. Among voters, 54 percent thought Biden had the temperament to be president, while only 44 percent said Trump did. It was also probably not a coincidence that the president's boorish behavior in the first debate was followed immediately by a doubling of Biden's lead, though it is hard to untangle the debate and the president's contraction of COVID days later. Biden also won overwhelmingly among voters who said the candidate's most important quality was to "unite the country" and those who said it was to exercise "good judgment," additional slaps at Trump's temperament and conduct. Overall, CNN exit polls indicated one of four voters said their votes were cast mainly against their candidate's opponent, rather than for their candidate, and Biden won 68 percent of those. A separate pre-election survey by Pew Research, worded slightly differently, found that 63 percent of Biden's supporters said their vote was more a vote against Trump than for Biden.[90]

Another element of the referendum had to do with COVID, and the virus's effect was multifaceted. Biden won a solid majority among the 55 percent of voters who said the virus had caused them financial hardship. He also won 68 percent among voters—about a quarter of the total—who said the recent surge in coronavirus cases was the most important factor to their vote for president, while Trump led among the rest. To the chagrin of many commentators, 51 percent of voters judged that the fight against coronavirus was going well, and Trump won those voters handily. However, 47 percent said the fight was going badly, and they leaned toward Biden by an even greater margin. Overall, the virus was only the third most important issue identified by voters, but they gave Biden 81 percent of their votes. The bottom line was that Biden held a ten-percentage-point lead on the question of who would better handle the coronavirus pandemic.

What about the effects of mail-ballot voting—another product of COVID? Leaving aside the disputed potential for fraud, there were two effects. The first was to boost voter turnout overall, disproportionately on the Democratic side. The second was more random and may accidentally have either reinforced or undercut the pro-Democratic effect. When all is said and done, a nontrivial number of ballots will have gone missing, either on their way to voters or from them. The U.S. Postal Service estimated that 150,000 ballots were delivered nationwide the day after the election, too late to be counted in most jurisdictions, and over four thousand were lost in North Carolina and Pennsylvania alone.[91] How those random misfires affected vote totals may never be unwound. Coronavirus may thus be said to have hurt Trump in three ways: by darkening the national mood, by throwing the nation into a recession, and by expanding a voting system that (probably) advantaged Democrats. However, the voting system also had the effect of producing results confirming what the job approval data and head-to-head polls had been saying all along.

The president's supporters did not hesitate to lay blame for their man's defeat at the feet of the media. And, indeed, a survey of Biden voters commissioned after the election by the Media Research Center showed that in six crucial states, nearly one-half of Biden voters had never heard about Hunter's laptop. Around five percent of his voters said they would have switched their votes had they known, enough to swing those states.[92] Nevertheless, it is too easy to assign responsibility to the media. Trump did, after all, give them plenty of material to work with. Moreover, a large part of the public already had low levels of trust in the media and adjusted their thoughts accordingly. In any case, when Trump had the opportunity to connect with Americans unfiltered by the media—tweets, debates—he often did not look any better than when the media controlled the narrative.

Given the realities under which the election was taking place, any incumbent in Trump's position would have faced an uphill climb. Of eight notable election models fashioned by political scientists and historians, most based on the "fundamentals" of the election, six predicted a Biden win.[93]

Why Was It Close?

While half of the country wondered what went wrong, the other half also wondered what went wrong. Why did they have to go to bed fearing they lost and then sweat for days waiting to find out whether Biden's small, early-morning margins in a tassel of key states would hold up?

First, neither the strong economy of February nor the steep plunge of second quarter dominated voting. Instead, a robust but incomplete recovery combined with continued uncertainty to produce a mixed economic picture for voters. Voters were evenly split on the question of whether the nation's economy was "excellent" or "good" (49 percent) or "not so good" or "poor" (50 percent). Unsurprisingly, Trump won big among the former, Biden among the latter. Likewise, voters were split 49–49 percent on which candidate would do a better job handling the economy. Of the 35 percent who declared that the economy was their number one issue, Trump won overwhelmingly.

Second, the narrowing of the partisan affiliation gap since summer may have resulted from the perceived radicalism of the Democratic Party, manifest most clearly in Democrats' embrace of the Black Lives Matter movement and their refusal to even acknowledge the existence of Antifa while it was assaulting a federal courthouse in Portland on a nightly basis. These movements were openly revolutionary. A BLM leader in New York promised that if BLM's demands were not met, "we will burn down this system. . . . And I could be speaking figuratively. I could be speaking literally."[94] Another in Chicago defended rampant looting as a form of reparations.[95] Some Democratic members of Congress agreed; Alexandria Ocasio-Cortez endorsed the BLM Chicago interpretation of looting,[96] while Ilhan Omar declared that police reform was not enough: "We must begin the work of dismantling the whole system of oppression," which she had just defined as the U.S. political and economic system.[97] With few criticisms by prominent Democrats, rioters tore down or defaced statues of, among others, George Washington, Abraham Lincoln, a Wisconsin abolitionist who died in battle at Gettysburg, and the 54th Massachusetts regiment, the second unit of colored troops in the Union Army. The impression of a Democratic Party that was comfortable, if not complicit, with the radical unrest of 2020 was bolstered by Democratic mayors in Chicago, Portland, Seattle, and Washington, DC, where Mayor Muriel Bowser touted recommendations by a hand-picked task force that the city "remove, relocate, or contextualize" dozens of "problematic" remembrances, including the Washington Monument and Jefferson Memorial.[98]

Antifa was quite real, and so was the damage that it did in Portland and other places. But if Democrats averted their eyes from Antifa, Republicans may have exaggerated its impact. Nobody charged with serious federal crimes during the initial riots in late May and early June had any documented links to the diffuse movement, and the FBI indicated that no Antifa fingerprints were found in the Minneapolis riots that got things going.[99] The Department of Homeland's Security's 2020 domestic threat assessment did not even mention Antifa, reporting that white supremacists "will remain the most persistent and lethal threat in the Homeland" among domestic violent extremists.[100]

In whatever proportions they were responsible, the combination of Antifa, BLM, and inchoate radicalism created a toxic stew. On a more pedestrian level, the metaphorical (and sometimes literal) assault on the police coincided with a dramatic surge in homicides in American cities.[101] The statements of some political leaders—and the silence of others—enabled Republicans to depict the Democratic Party as a safe haven for dangerous radicals. Add this to calls by progressive Democrats to "defund the police," end fossil fuels, pack the Supreme Court, enact large tax increases, and reform health care in a way that might ultimately destroy private insurance, and the result was a message at cross-purposes with Biden's attempt to "return to normalcy." Tied with health care for the fourth most important issue to voters, the one in ten who identified "law and order" gave Trump 71 percent of their votes. The effect down-ballot was probably greater. Law and order was not the silver bullet Trump had hoped, but it made a difference.

Just as Trump had given Democrats plenty of ammunition to run a campaign against his character and temperament, Democrats gave Trump abundant material to try to turn his campaign into an existential fight for America. It was not enough to overcome the referendum dynamic and win, but it was enough to narrow the gap. And it was enough to give Republicans a chance to turn the tide in the congressional elections, where they held Senate losses well below expectations and actually gained seats in the House, putting them within striking distance of a majority in 2022.

Not least, with all the focus of political scientists on the fundamentals of the race, it is easy to forget that campaigns and candidates can matter, at least at the margins. Donald Trump was an exceptionally polarizing figure who mobilized a record number of voters both for and against himself. Biden won by playing it safe. But whether its source was Napoleonic brilliance or physical and mental exhaustion, Biden's low-key strategy also gave Trump the opportunity to make it close by energetically mobilizing his enthusiastic supporters. In 1948, Tom Dewey found out the hard way that Americans like candidates who scrap and are hesitant to give their votes to candidates who take victory for granted. In 2020, Joe Biden nearly learned the same lesson. Trump was a live candidate, running a real campaign. At times, Biden seemed a cardboard cutout. When he did appear, he steadfastly refused to say anything (except sometimes by accident) that would clarify the deliberately muddy picture the campaign had created. It is hardly surprising that a certain subset of voters rebelled, choosing the candidate who was clearly alive and whose views were not difficult to parse. Trump won decisively among voters who said they most wanted a "strong leader."

Not least, underneath Biden's apparent lead in likeability lay the fact that, for many voters, as in 2016, the choice was not a good one. When asked whether Biden had the physical and mental health to serve effectively as president, 49 percent said yes, 49 percent no. The same question asked about Trump led to the same response: 49 percent yes, 49 percent no. Though Biden led Trump in personal approval, Gallup polls showed both candidates below 50 percent. If Trump had won in 2016 by being the anti-Hillary, Biden won in 2020 simply by being the anti-Trump.

At the end of the story, Democrats won but with less room to spare in the states that put them over the top than Trump had enjoyed in 2016. The nation remained deeply divided. And the presidential vote was just the beginning.

NOTES

1. Dante Chinni, "Why Biden's Poll Lead Is Different from Hillary Clinton's," NBS News, October 18, 2020, https://www.nbcnews.com/politics/meet-the-press/why-biden-s-poll-lead-different-hillary-clinton-s-n1243837.

2. Before the full impact of the pandemic was evident, Norpoth gave Trump a 91 percent chance of winning. Helmut Norpoth, "Trump Not a Bad Bet to Win Re-election," *Newsday*, April 17, 2020, https://www.newsday.com/opinion/commentary/donald-trump-2020-election-joe-biden-norpoth-prediction-1.43910576.

3. John J. Pitney Jr., *After Reagan: Bush, Dukakis, and the 1988 Election* (Lawrence: University Press of Kansas, 2019), 185–86.

4. Here and some other portions of chapter 4 and chapter 6 are adapted from Andrew E. Busch, "Why Trump Lost, but Almost Won," *Claremont Review of Books* XXI, no. 1 (Winter 2020/2021).

5. "Direction of Country," RealClearPolitics, https://www.realclearpolitics.com/epolls/other/direction_of_country-902.html.

6. "President Trump Job Approval," RealClearPolitics, https://www.realclearpolitics.com/epolls/other/president_trump_job_approval-6179.html.

7. "Party Affiliation," Gallup, https://news.gallup.com/poll/15370/party-affiliation.aspx.

8. Allan Smith, "'Nothing happening': Third-party candidacies appear less a factor in 2020," NBC News, October 10, 2020, https://www.nbcnews.com/politics/2020-election/nothing-happening-third-party-candidacies-appear-less-factor-2020-n1240433; Jane Coaston, "Why third parties likely won't be a big deal this year," *Vox*, November 3, 2020, https://www.vox.com/2020/11/3/21535058/third-party-vote-2020-trump.

9. "Favorability Ratings: Political Leaders," RealClearPolitics, https://www.realclearpolitics.com/epolls/other/other/FavorabilityRatingsPoliticalLeaders.htmls.

10. On September 18, for example, Gallup reported that Trump was viewed favorably by 41 percent of Americans, Biden by 46 percent. Lydia Saad, "Trump, Biden Favorable Ratings Both Below 50%," Gallup, September 18, 2020, https://news.gallup.com/poll/320411/trump-biden-favorable-ratings-below.aspx.

11. Christopher Cadelago and Marc Caputo, "When Biden calls a 'lid,' Democrats wet the bed—and Trump starts mocking," *Politico*, September 25, 2020, https://www .politico.com/news/2020/09/25/biden-campaign-lid-trump-421824.

12. Carlo Invernizzi-Accetti, "Joe Biden is a boring candidate. That's why he is doing well," *The Guardian*, August 19, 2019, https://www.theguardian.com/ commentisfree/2019/aug/19/joe-biden-exciting-candidate.

13. Brian Bennett and Tessa Berenson, "An Election Day Upset Hangs on Donald Trump's Formidable Ground Game," *Time*, November 2, 2020, https://time .com/5906581/donald-trump-campaign-ground-game/.

14. See "Changes to absentee/mail-in voting procedures in response to the coronavirus (COVID-19) pandemic, 2020: Debate," Ballotpedia, https://ballotpedia.org/ Changes_to_absentee/mail-in_voting_procedures_in_response_to_the_coronavirus_ (COVID-19)_pandemic,_2020#Debate.

15. Tom Scheck, "How Private Money from Facebook's CEO Saved the 2020 Election," NPR, December 8, 2020, https://www.npr.org/2020/12/08/943242106/ how-private-money-from-facebooks-ceo-saved-the-2020-election.

16. Sean McMinn, "Money Tracker: How Much Trump and Biden Have Raised in the 2020 Election," NPR, December 4, 2020, https://www.npr.org/ 2020/05/20/858347477/money-tracker-how-much-trump-and-biden-have-raised-in -the-2020-election.

17. "2020 Presidential Race," *Open Secrets*, accessed December 23, 2020, https:// www.opensecrets.org/2020-presidential-race.

18. Kimberly Amadeo, "What Is the Current U.S. Unemployment Rate?" *The Balance*, December 4, 2020, https://www.thebalance.com/current-u-s-unemployment -rate-statistics-and-news-3305733; "U.S. economy grew at an unrevised 33.1% rate in the third quarter," CNBC, November 25, 2020, https://www.cnbc.com/2020/11/25/ us-gdp-q3-2020-second-reading.html; Jay Shambaugh, "Don't let flashy 3rd quarter GDP growth fool you, the economy is still in a big hole," Brookings Institution, https://www.brookings.edu/blog/up-front/2020/10/26/dont-let-flashy-3rd-quarter -gdp-growth-fool-you-the-economy-is-still-in-a-big-hole/.

19. Glenn Kessler, Salvador Rizzo, and Meg Kelly, "Trump Is Averaging More Than 50 False or Misleading Claims a Day," *Washington Post*, October 22, 2020, https://www.washingtonpost.com/politics/2020/10/22/president-trump-is-averaging -more-than-50-false-or-misleading-claims-day.

20. Jeffrey Goldberg, "Trump: Americans Who Died in War Are 'Losers' and 'Suckers,'" *The Atlantic*, September 3, 2020, https://www.theatlantic.com/politics/ archive/2020/09/trump-americans-who-died-at-war-are-losers-and-suckers/615997/.

21. Jeremy Barr, "Jennifer Griffin Defended by Fox News Colleagues After Trump Twitter Attack Over Confirmation of Atlantic Reporting," *Washington Post*, September 5, 2020, https://www.washingtonpost.com/media/2020/09/05/jen-nifer-griffin-defended-by-fox-news-colleagues-after-trump-twitter-attack-over-her -confirmation-atlantic-reporting/.

22. Leo Shane "Trump Made Up Injury to Dodge Vietnam Service, His Former Lawyer Testifies," *Military Times*, February 27, 2019, https://www.militarytimes

.com/news/pentagon-congress/2019/02/27/trumps-lawyer-no-basis-for-presidents
-medical-deferment-from-vietnam.

23. Evan Semones, "Trump furiously denies report he disparaged military service, insulted dead and disabled troops," *Politico*, September 4, 2020, https://www
.politico.com/news/2020/09/04/trump-responds-to-insults-us-service-members
-408750; https://www.washingtonpost.com/politics/2020/09/15/trump-says-there-are
-25-witnesses-disputing-atlantic-nope/; Alex Ward, "Did Trump call US war dead
'losers' and 'suckers'? The controversy, explained," *Vox*, September 4, 2020, https://
www.vox.com/2020/9/4/21422733/atlantic-trump-military-suckers-losers-explained.

24. Jamie Gangel, Jeremy Herb, and Elizabeth Stuart, "'Play it down': Trump admits to concealing the true threat of coronavirus in new Woodward book," CNN, September 9, 2020, https://www.cnn.com/2020/09/09/politics/bob-woodward-rage-book
-trump-coronavirus/index.html. For Trump's response, see Quint Forgey and Matthew
Choi, "Trump rushes to contain fallout from his interviews with Woodward," *Politico*, September 10, 2020, https://www.politico.com/news/2020/09/10/trump-counter
attack-against-bob-woodward-411625.

25. See https://www.nytimes.com/interactive/2020/09/27/us/donald-trump-taxes
.html; https://www.nytimes.com/2020/09/27/us/trump-taxes-takeaways.html; https://
www.nytimes.com/2020/09/29/us/trump-750-taxes.html.

26. Jim Geraghty, "Taxing *Times*," *National Review*, September 28, 2020, https://
www.nationalreview.com/the-morning-jolt/taxing-times/.

27. Ken Tarbous, "Donald Trump Took Advantage of Barack Obama-Era Laws to
Avoid Paying Taxes," *Newsweek*, September 29, 2020, https://www.newsweek.com/
donald-trump-took-advantage-barack-obama-era-laws-avoid-paying-taxes-1535070.

28. Emma-Jo Morris and Gabrielle Fonrouge, "Smoking-gun email reveals how
Hunter Biden introduced Ukrainian businessman to VP dad," *New York Post*, October
14, 2020, https://nypost.com/2020/10/14/email-reveals-how-hunter-biden-introduced
-ukrainian-biz-man-to-dad/.

29. Tia Sewell, "Senate Committees Release Two Different Reports on Bidens,"
Lawfare, September 23, 2020, https://www.lawfareblog.com/senate-committees
-release-two-different-reports-bidens.

30. Brian Flood, "Liberal media 'snuffed out' Hunter Biden coverage until after
election to help defeat Trump: critics," *New York Post*, December 10, 2020, https://
nypost.com/2020/12/10/liberal-media-ignored-hunter-biden-until-after-election-to
-defeat-trump/.

31. Andrew Duehren and James T. Areddy, "Hunter Biden's Ex-Business Partner
Alleges Father Knew about Venture," *Wall Street Journal*, October 23, 2020, https://
www.wsj.com/articles/hunter-bidens-ex-business-partner-alleges-father-knew-about
-venture-11603421247.

32. "Chairman Graham Releases Newly Declassified Summary Indicating FBI
Knew Steele Dossier Source Was Likely a Russian Agent, Had Been Under U.S.
Counterintelligence Investigation," Senate Judiciary Committee, September 24,
2020, https://www.judiciary.senate.gov/press/rep/releases/chairman-graham-releases
-newly-declassified-summary-indicating-fbi-knew-steele-dossier-source-was-likely

-a-russian-agent-had-been-under-us-counterintelligence-investigation; Sam Dorman, "Obama admin briefed on claims Hillary Clinton drummed up Russia controversy to vilify Trump, distract from emails," Fox News, September 29, 2020, https://www .foxnews.com/politics/obama-briefed-clinton-russia-vilify-trump-distract.

33. Charlie Savage, Adam Goldman, and Jonah M. Kessel, "Analyst Who Reported the Infamous Trump Tape Rumor Wants to Clear His Name," *New York Times*, October 21, 2020, https://www.nytimes.com/2020/10/21/us/politics/igor-danchenko -steele-dossier.html.

34. Lisa Desjardins, "What every Democratic senator has said about filling a Supreme Court vacancy in an election year," PBS, September 24, 2020, https://www .pbs.org/newshour/politics/what-every-democratic-senator-has-said-about-filling-a -supreme-court-vacancy-in-an-election-year.

35. Rebecca Shabad and Julie Tsirkin, "McConnell: I will fill Ginsburg's seat with Trump's nominee. Schumer says don't dare," NBC News, September 19, 2020, https://www.nbcnews.com/politics/congress/schumer-senate-must-not-fill-ginsburg -vacancy-until-we-have-n1240505.

36. Dan McLaughlin, "History Is on the Side of Republicans Filling a Supreme Court Vacancy in 2020," August 7, 2020, https://www.nationalreview.com/2020/08/ history-is-on-the-side-of-republicans-filling-a-supreme-court-vacancy-in-2020/.

37. "Feinstein: 'The dogma lives loudly within you, and that's a concern,'" *Washington Post*, September 7, 2017, https://www.washingtonpost.com/video/politics/ feinstein-the-dogma-lives-loudly-within-you-and-thats-a-concern/2017/09/07/ 04303fda-93cb-11e7-8482-8dc9a7af29f9_video.html.

38. Noah Feldman, "Amy Coney Barrett Deserves to Be on the Supreme Court," *Bloomberg Opinion*, September 26, 2020, https://www.bloomberg.com/opinion/ articles/2020-09-26/amy-coney-barrett-deserves-to-be-on-the-supreme-court.

39. Jason Lemon, "Why Ibram Kendi Is Facing a Backlash Over a Tweet about Amy Coney Barrett's Adopted Haitian Children," *Newsweek*, September 27, 2020, https://www.newsweek.com/why-ibram-kendi-facing-backlash-over-tweet-about -amy-coney-barretts-adopted-haitian-children-1534507.

40. Megan Brenan, "51% in U.S. Want Amy Coney Barrett Seated on Supreme Court," Gallup, https://news.gallup.com/poll/322232/amy-coney-barrett-seated -supreme-court.aspx.

41. Linley Sanders, "Washington Examiner/YouGov Poll: By 47% to 34% voters oppose court packing," YouGov, October 7, 2020, https://today.yougov.com/topics/ politics/articles-reports/2020/10/07/supreme-cort-packing-poll; Thomas Barrabi, "Majority of Americans oppose court-packing, new poll finds," Fox News, October 20, 2020, https://www.foxnews.com/politics/majority-americans-oppose-court-packing -poll; Gary Langer, "Most say wait on Ginsburg seat, while opposing packing the court: Poll," ABC News, September 25, 2020, https://abcnews.go.com/Politics/wait -ginsburg-seat-opposing-packing-court/story?id=73239784.

42. Jeremy Stahl, "We Counted Every Single Time Trump Interrupted During the First Presidential Debate," *Slate*, September 30, 2020, https://slate.com/news -and-politics/2020/09/trump-interruptions-first-presidential-debate-biden.html. The

BBC had a more modest count of 73 presidential interruptions: "Presidential debate: Trump and Biden trade insults in chaotic debate," September 30, 2020, https://www.bbc.com/news/election-us-2020-54350538.

43. Alexander Burns, "Biden goes after Ryan in VP debate," *Politico*, October 11, 2012, https://www.politico.com/story/2012/10/biden-ryan-to-clash-in-only-vp-debate-082309.

44. Jennifer de Pinto, Anthony Salvanto, Fred Backus, Kabir Khanna, and Elena Cox, "Debate-watchers say Biden won first debate, but most felt 'annoyed'—CBS News poll," September 30, 2020, https://www.cbsnews.com/news/who-won-debate-first-presidential-biden-trump/; Laura Bronner, Aaron Bycoffe, Elena Mejía, and Julia Wolfe, "Who Won The First 2020 Presidential Debate?" FiveThirtyEight, September 30, 2020, https://projects.fivethirtyeight.com/trump-biden-debate-poll/.

45. Jennifer Agiesta, "Post-debate CNN Poll: Harris Seen as Winner in a Contest That Matched Expectations," CNN, October 8, 2020, https://www.cnn.com/2020/10/07/politics/mike-pence-kamala-harris-vice-presidential-debate-poll/index.html.

46. Kevin Stankiewicz, "GOP pollster: Pence beat Harris in debate not for what he said but how he said it," CNBC, October 8, 2020, https://www.cnbc.com/2020/10/08/gop-pollster-mike-pence-beat-harris-in-vice-presidential-debate.html.

47. Doug Schoen, "Trump vs. Biden—Here's who won the debate and what it means for the 2020 election," Fox News, October 23, 2020, https://www.foxnews.com/opinion/trump-biden-who-won-the-debate-2020-election-doug-schoen.

48. Jason Hanna and Daniel Wolfe, "These charts show how serious this fall's Covid-19 surge is in the US," CNN, November 13, 2020, https://www.cnn.com/2020/11/12/health/coronavirus-fall-surge-statistics/index.html.

49. Jacob Pramuk, "Senate Republicans fail to advance coronavirus stimulus bill as stalemate drags on," CNBC, September 10, 2020, https://www.cnbc.com/2020/09/10/coronavirus-stimulus-update-senate-relief-bill-fails.html.

50. See, for example, Jerry Davich, "Column: President Trump deserves the unmasked backlash from critics over his COVID-19 diagnosis," *Chicago Tribune*, October 5, 2020, https://www.chicagotribune.com/suburbs/post-tribune/opinion/ct-ptb-davich-trump-covid-diagnosis-backlash-dilemma-st-1006-20201005-r7fpw4rluzdv7h6il3xnfg4rla-story.html.

51. Joseph Ax and Jan Wolfe, "What happens to the U.S. presidential election if a candidate dies or becomes incapacitated?" Reuters, October 2, 2020, https://www.reuters.com/article/us-health-coronavirus-usa-trump-election/what-happens-to-the-u-s-presidential-election-if-a-candidate-dies-or-becomes-incapacitated-idUKKBN26N347.

52. "Trump's 'don't fear COVID' tweet angers pandemic survivors, relatives of the dead," CBC, October 6, 2020, https://www.cbc.ca/news/world/trump-covid-tweet-reaction-1.5751806; Glenn Beck, "Trump is right—Don't Fear COVID-19," Facebook, October 6, 2020, https://www.facebook.com/GlennBeck/videos/trump-is-right-dont-fear-covid-19/275045583551042/.

53. U.S. Department of Justice, "Russian National Charged with Interfering in U.S. Political System," October 19, 2018, https://www.justice.gov/opa/pr/russian-national-charged-interfering-us-political-system.

54. Scott Jasper, "Why foreign election interference fizzled in 2020," Atlantic Council, November 23, 2020, https://www.atlanticcouncil.org/blogs/new-atlanticist/why-foreign-election-interference-fizzled-in-2020/.

55. Josh Rogin, "Secret CIA Assessment: Putin 'Probably Directing' Influence Operation To Denigrate Biden," *Washington Post*, September 22, 2020, https://www.washingtonpost.com/opinions/2020/09/22/secret-cia-assessment-putin-probably-directing-influence-operation-denigrate-biden.

56. House Homeland Security Hearing Chris Wray Testimony Transcript September 17: FBI Director Testifies, https://www.rev.com/blog/transcripts/house-homeland-security-hearing-transcript-september-17-fbi-director-testifies.

57. Natasha Bertrand, "Hunter Biden story is Russian disinfo, dozens of former intel officials say," *Politico*, October 19, 2020, https://www.politico.com/news/2020/10/19/hunter-biden-story-russian-disinfo-430276; Rich Lowry, "The Embarrassing Russian Disinformation Canard," *National Review*, December 15, 2020, https://www.nationalreview.com/2020/12/the-embarrassing-russian-disinformation-canard/.

58. Vladimir Isachenkov and Harriet Morris, "Putin says Trump Was Impeached for 'Far-Fetched' Reasons," Associated Press, December 19, 2019, https://apnews.com/article/0530c2e93d9d5186d0a807888c1c0bb0.

59. Andrew Osborn, "Putin rejects Donald Trump's criticism of Biden family business," Reuters, October 25, 2020, https://www.reuters.com/article/us-usa-election-putin/putin-rejects-donald-trumps-criticism-of-biden-family-business-idUSKBN27A0TA; David Brennan, "Putin Says He Wants to Work with Biden, Claims 'Shared Values' Between Democrats and Communism," *Newsweek*, October 8, 2020, https://www.newsweek.com/vladimir-putin-says-wants-work-joe-biden-claims-shared-values-between-democrats-communism-1537501.

60. Eric Tucker and Frank Bajak, "US officials link Iran to emails meant to intimidate voters," AP, October 21, 2020, https://apnews.com/article/donald-trump-florida-elections-voting-2020-voting-2124f257f89649630e123952df34b186.

61. Jennifer Jacobs, "Trump Spy Chief Stirs Dispute Over China Election-Meddling Views," *Bloomberg News*, December 16, 2020, https://www.bloomberg.com/news/articles/2020-12-16/trump-spy-chief-stirs-dispute-over-china-election-meddling-views.

62. "Top Battlegrounds (2020 vs. 2016)," RealClearPolitics, https://www.realclearpolitics.com/epolls/2020/president/us/trump-vs-biden-top-battleground-states-2020-vs-2016/.

63. See https://projects.economist.com/us-2020-forecast/president; https://harvardpolitics.com/hpr-2020-presidential-election-forecast/; https://projects.economist.com/us-2020-forecast/senate.

64. Lydia Saad, "Americans' Economic Attitudes and the Election," Gallup, October 14, 2020, https://news.gallup.com/opinion/gallup/321992/americans-economic-attitudes-election.aspx.

65. "Party Affiliation," Gallup, https://news.gallup.com/poll/15370/party-affiliation.aspx.

66. Gallup September 14–28 survey; Byron York, "What are Trump's chances?" *Star Herald*, October 18, 2020, https://starherald.com/opinion/columnists/syndicated/

byron-york-what-are-trump-s-chances/article_f83d745c-f211-5b30-b12f
-016335c4f0c2.html.

67. Barbara Sprunt, "Biden Campaign Warns Supporters: 'Donald Trump Can Still Win This Race,'" NPR, October 18, 2020, https://www.npr.org/2020/10/18/925102703/biden-campaign-warns-supporters-donald-trump-can-still-win-this-race.

68. Transition Integrity Project, http://transitionintegrityproject.net/.

69. Indeed, by Election Day a veritable cottage industry of observers had asked whether Trump would actually leave office if he lost the election. Rex Huppke, "Column: Trump's upcoming coup: A formal invitation from a cowardly president who knows he might lose," *Chicago Tribune*, September 25, 2020, https://www.chicagotribune.com/columns/rex-huppke/ct-trump-coup-transition-power-biden-election-supreme-court-gop-huppke-20200925-j2nso6hufrfvzhn5oyb4mddyta-story.html.

70. Matthew Choi, "Hillary Clinton to Biden: Don't concede if the election is close," *Politico*, August 25, 2020, https://www.politico.com/news/2020/08/25/hillary-clinton-joe-biden-election-advice-401641.

71. John Yoo and Robert Delahunty, "What Happens if No One Wins?" *The American Mind*, October 19, 2020, https://americanmind.org/salvo/what-happens-if-no-one-wins/.

72. David Wasserman, "Beware the 'blue mirage' and the 'red mirage' on election night," NBC News, November 3, 2020, https://www.nbcnews.com/politics/2020-election/beware-blue-mirage-red-mirage-election-night-n1245925.

73. Jonathan Swan, "Scoop: Trump's plan to declare premature victory," Axios, November 1, 2020, https://www.axios.com/trump-claim-election-victory-ballots-97eb12b9-5e35-402f-9ea3-0ccfb47f613f.html.

74. Rex Huppke, "Column: Trump's upcoming coup: A formal invitation from a cowardly president who knows he might lose," *Chicago Tribune*, September 25, 2020, https://www.chicagotribune.com/columns/rex-huppke/ct-trump-coup-transition-power-biden-election-supreme-court-gop-huppke-20200925-j2nso6hufrfvzhn5oyb4mddyta-story.html.

75. Michael Anton, "The Coming Coup?" *The American Mind*, September 7, 2020, https://www.realclearpolicy.com/ 2020/09/07/the_coming_coup_576551.html.

76. Christina Carrega, Veronica Stracqualursi, and Josh Campbell, "13 charged in plot to kidnap Michigan Gov. Gretchen Whitmer," CNN, October 8, 2020, https://www.cnn.com/2020/10/08/politics/fbi-plot-michigan-governor-gretchen-whitmer/index.html.

77. David Chang, Dan Stamm, and Joe Brandt, "Violence Tears Through W. Philly After Police Shoot, Kill Man; 30 Officers Hurt," 10 Philadelphia, October 27, 2020, https://www.nbcphiladelphia.com/news/local/crowds-protest-violence-west-philly-after-deadly-police-shooting/2574729/.

78. Alissa Wilkinson, "Boarded-up stores are another sign of election anxiety," *Vox*, November 2, 2020, https://www.vox.com/policy-and-politics/2020/11/2/21546327/boarded-up-business-election-day-protests.

79. "Donald Trump 2020 Election Night Speech Transcript," *Rev*, https://www.rev.com/blog/transcripts/donald-trump-2020-election-night-speech-transcript.

80. See https://www.statista.com/statistics/1184621/presidential-election-voter-turnout-rate-state/.

81. https://morningconsult.com/2020/10/22/trump-biden-third-party-voters -polling/.

82. In Arizona, the margin was about 10,000 and Jorgensen won 51,000; in Georgia the margin was about 12,000, and Jorgensen won 62,000; and in Wisconsin, the margin was about 21,000 and the Libertarian won about 38,000.

83. Danielle Kurtzleben, "Why Were the Polls Off? Pollsters Have Some Early Theories," NPR, November 19, 2020, https://www.npr.org/2020/11/19/936317341/ why-were-the-polls-off-pollsters-have-some-early-theories; Alex Roarty and David Catanese, "2020's polling miss? These Republicans say they saw it coming," *McClatchy Newspapers*, November 4, 2020.

84. For data here and following, see "Exit Polls—President," CNN, https://www .cnn.com/election/2020/exit-polls/president/national-results.

85. Josh Hammer, "Despite 'racist' charges, Trump did better with minorities than any GOP candidate in 60 years," *New York Post*, November 4, 2020, https://nypost .com/2020/11/04/despite-racist-charges-trump-did-better-with-minorities-than-any -gop-candidate-in-60-years/.

86. Ruth Igielnik and Abby Budiman, "The Changing Racial and Ethnic Composition of the U.S. Electorate," Pew Research Center, September 23, 2020, https://www .pewresearch.org/2020/09/23/the-changing-racial-and-ethnic-composition-of-the-u.s -electorate.

87. Avik Roy, "No, Trump Didn't Win 'The Largest Share of Non-White Voters of Any Republican in 60 Years,'" *Forbes*, November 9, 2020, https://www.forbes .com/sites/theapothecary/2020/11/09/no-trump-didnt-win-the-largest-share-of-non -white-voters-of-any-republican-in-60-years/?sh=1497c18a4a09.

88. Chris Alcantara et al., "How Independents, Latino Voters and Catholics Shifted from 2016 and Swung States for Biden and Trump," *Washington Post*, November 12, 2020, https://www.washingtonpost.com/graphics/2020/elections/exit -polls-changes-2016-2020/#noop.

89. Geoffrey Skelley, Elena Mejía, Amelia Thomson-DeVeaux, and Laura Bronner, "Why the Suburbs Have Shifted Blue," FiveThirtyEight, December 16, 2020, https://fivethirtyeight.com/features/why-the-suburbs-have-shifted-blue/.

90. "The Trump-Biden presidential contest," Pew Research Center, October 9, 2020, https://www.pewresearch.org/politics/2020/10/09/the-trump-biden-presidential -contest/.

91. "USPS Says Thousands of Mail-In Ballots May Have Gone Missing," *Transport Topics*, November 6, 2020, https://www.ttnews.com/articles/usps-says -thousands-mail-ballots-may-have-gone-missing.

92. Overall, testing knowledge of three issues that reflected negatively on Biden and five issues that reflected positively on Trump, the survey found that Biden voters in key swing states were unaware of the issue 25 to 51 percent of the time, and the shift of votes that would have occurred with awareness of the issues would have left Trump with 311 electoral votes. Paul Bedard, "Trump would have won 311 Electoral College votes if media weren't biased: Survey," *Washington Examiner*, November 24, 2020, https://www.washingtonexaminer.com/washington-secrets/trump-would -have-won-311-electoral-votes-if-media-wasnt-biased-survey.

93. See https://www.cambridge.org/core/journals/ps-political-science-and -politics/2020-presidential-election-forecasting-symposium; Allan Lichtman, "The Keys to the White House: Forecast for 2020," *HDSR*, October 27, 2020, https://hdsr .mitpress.mit.edu/pub/xhgpcyoa/release/2.

94. Michael Faulkner, "Radicals are hijacking the black dignity movement," *New York Daily News*, August 22, 2020, https://www.nydailynews.com/opinion/ny -oped-radicals-are-hijacking-the-black-dignity-movement-20200822-k2e6xwijrbcnzj cla2hpsbyz6u-story.html.

95. Khaleda Rahman, "Black Lives Matter Chicago Organizer Defends Looting: 'That's Reparations,'" *Newsweek*, August 12, 2020, https://www.newsweek.com/ black-lives-matter-chicago-defends-looting-reparations-1524502. For a more general discussion of the radicalism of BLM, see Mike Gonzalez and Andrew Olivastro, "The Agenda of Black Lives Matter Is Far Different from the Slogan," Heritage Foundation, July 3, 2020, https://www.heritage.org/progressivism/commentary/the-agenda -black-lives-matter-far-different-the-slogan.

96. David Goldiner, "AOC blames NYC crime spike on parents shoplifting food for their hungry families," *New York Daily News*, July 12, 2020, https://www.ny dailynews.com/news/politics/ny-ocasio-cortez-crime-nyc-shoplifting-bread-hungry -20200712-4ga4tm6vzze7ricmk2o2er4iwa-story.html.

97. Becket Adams, "Why is the *Washington Post* so eager to rescue Ilhan Omar from herself?" *Washington Examiner*, July 10, 2020, https://www.washington examiner.com/opinion/why-is-the-washington-post-so-eager-to-rescue-ilhan-omar -from-herself.

98. "Bowser task force targets Washington Monument, Jefferson Memorial, doz-ens more," NBC News, September 2, 2020, https://www.nbcnews.com/politics/2020 -election/bowser-task-force-targets-washington-monument-jefferson-memorial -dozens-more-n1239051.

99. Neil MacFarquhar, Alan Feuer, and Adam Goldman, "Federal Arrests Show No Sign That Antifa Plotted Protests," *New York Times*, June 11, 2020, https:// www.nytimes.com/2020/06/11/us/antifa-protests-george-floyd.html; Andy Mannix, "Court records, FBI Contradict Trump's Claims Of Organized 'Antifa-Led' Riots in Minneapolis After George Floyd's Death," *Minneapolis Star-Tribune*, December 20, 2020, https://www.startribune.com/court-records-fbi-contradict-trump-s-claims -of-organized-antifa-led-riots-in-minneapolis-after-georg/573438811/. See also Al-anna Durkin Richer, Colleen Long, and Michael Balsamo, "AP Finds Most Arrested in Protests Aren't Leftist Radicals," Associated Press, October 20, 2020, https:// apnews.com/article/virus-outbreak-race-and-ethnicity-suburbs-health-racial-injustice -7edf9027af1878283f3818d96c54f748.

100. Department of Homeland Security, "Homeland Threat Assessment, Octo-ber 2020," p. 18, https://www.dhs.gov/sites/default/files/publications/2020_10_06_ homeland-threat-assessment.pdf.

101. Stephen Loiaconi, "Homicides spike in dozens of major cities in 2020 as other violent crimes fall," ABC6 News, August 4, 2020, https://abc6onyourside .com/news/nation-world/homicides-spiked-in-dozens-of-major-cities-in-2020-as -other-violent-crimes-fell.

Chapter Five

The Imperfect Tie
Congressional and State Elections

The most consequential congressional races of the 2020 cycle concluded early in 2021. Runoffs for two Senate seats from Georgia resulted in the election of Democrats Jon Ossoff and Raphael Warnock. Together with a net Democratic gain of one seat on Election Day, their victories created a 50–50 split in the Senate. (Angus King of Maine and Bernie Sanders of Vermont, who ran as Independents, caucused with the Democrats.) In 2001, the last time the Senate was evenly divided, the Senate set a precedent for such cases: majority status would go to the party of the vice president, who casts tie-breaking votes.[1] With Kamala Harris in that role, Democrats would now gain control of the Senate for the first time since 2014. Joe Biden would take office with unified Democratic control of the elected branches.

Notwithstanding this triumph, Democrats had expected more. Before the November election, there was widespread talk of a "blue wave." Democrats assumed that they would score a substantial net gain of House seats, and they also hoped for a decisive, clear-cut majority in the Senate. Activists on both sides of the partisan divide speculated that unified deep-blue government could open the way for enactment of a far-reaching progressive agenda. And at the state level, Democrats strove to win enough state legislative chambers to blunt the redistricting advantage that the GOP had enjoyed since the 2010 midterm.

It did not work out that way. Republicans defied expectations by gaining seats in the House, just a few short of a majority. In the Senate, the even division meant that a single moderate Democrat—particularly Joe Manchin of West Virginia—could thwart the ambitions of party progressives. At the state level, the balance of power changed little, leaving the GOP in a strong position for the redrawing of district lines after the 2020 census. Americans had ousted Trump from the White House but denied Democrats the sweeping control that conservatives had worried about and liberals longed for.

There was no guarantee the Democrats' tenuous grip on Congress would endure for long. The last extended span of unified partisan control of government had occurred during the Kennedy-Johnson years of 1961–1969. Divided control prevailed most of the time between 1969 and 2021. Of the nine presidents who served during this period, only Jimmy Carter (1977–1981) enjoyed congressional majorities throughout an entire four-year term. An influential 1990 scholarly book tried to explain divided government by suggesting that voters preferred Republicans on "presidential" issues such as national security while favoring Democrats on health care and other distributional issues in the congressional wheelhouse.[2] This idea seemed plausible at the time. Republicans had won five out of six presidential elections between 1968 and 1988, while Democrats held an unbroken grip on the House of Representatives. (The GOP controlled the Senate between 1980 and 1986, but its majorities seemed to be a fluke stemming from a string of good luck in small states.[3]) But then the pattern flipped. Democrats won the aggregated popular vote in six of the seven presidential elections between 1992 and 2016, while Republicans controlled the House since 1994 except for the four years between 2006 and 2010.

So were voters de facto Madisonians all along, bolstering checks and balances by scrambling patterns of congressional party balance? The answer is a firm "maybe, for a small share of the electorate." There was some modest evidence for this phenomenon in the 1990s.[4] In the first two decades of the twenty-first century, however, polls usually showed increasing support for unified government, at least as an abstract proposition.[5] When partisans said that they favored divided government, they meant that their party should control Congress when the other party controlled the presidency.

The South's partisan realignment mattered more than conscious party balancing. Although Southern states had been trending Republican in presidential elections since Eisenhower, Democrats long held the residual loyalty of Southern voters in other races. For instance, the 1992 election left them with a majority of Southern seats in both chambers of Congress and control of every state legislative chamber in the region except for the Florida Senate. Together with their dominance in metropolitan areas elsewhere in the country, their Southern stronghold made it tough for Republicans to reach national parity down the ballot. Except for brief periods in the Truman and Eisenhower administrations, Democratic presidents could count on unified government, and Republican presidents had to expect divided government. In 1994, Southern breakthroughs helped Republicans take control of both chambers for the first time in forty years. In subsequent elections, Republicans would grow even stronger in the region, winning posts from sheriff to U.S. senator. The new Republican South, however, was less monolithic than old Democratic South. Amid GOP gains, Democrats retained significant pockets of support, especially in areas with large numbers of African Americans and (in Texas) Hispanics. By the second decade of the twenty-first century, moreover, they were expanding their Southern beachheads. Economic change in the region brought immigrants and college-educated professionals, who tended to have more liberal attitudes on politics. These groups helped tip the balance in the 2021 Georgia runoffs.

Meanwhile, Democrats partially offset their losses in the South with gains in other regions, particularly the Northeast and Pacific Coast, which had become party bastions in presidential elections. The result was that fewer and fewer constituencies split their vote. In 1988, 24 percent of House districts backed a presidential candidate of one party and a congressional candidate of the other.[6] In the thirty-three Senate races that year, a *majority* of states (seventeen) did so. For instance, incumbent Democrat Jim Sasser won the Bush state of Tennessee while incumbent Republican John Chafee won the Dukakis state of Rhode Island. By 2016, however, only 8 percent of House districts had split outcomes. Senate races had none at all. Trump carried every state that elected a Republican, and Clinton carried every state that elected a Democrat.

The United States was well sorted and closely divided. After 1994, congressional majorities tended to be slim, with control changing hands several times.[7] A 2001 party switch by a Vermont senator gave control of the Senate to the Democrats, who then lost it in the 2002 midterm. Democrats took both chambers four years later, only to lose the House in 2010 and the Senate in 2014. And they would regain the House in the 2018 Trump midterm.

Majority parties could not take their power for granted, and minority parties did not consider their status a life sentence. Control of both chambers was often in play, a development that reshaped congressional party politics. Parties often staged floor votes less to influence policy than to send messages to the electorate.[8] Bipartisan cooperation became more complicated, as members on each side were leery of yielding electoral advantages to their opponents. More than ever before, party leaders on Capitol Hill and the congressional campaign committees focused their efforts on the struggle for chamber control. After a 2002 law ended huge "soft money" giving, congressional parties got their members to step up their contributions to the campaign committees. In the wake of the *Citizens United* decision, outside spending groups laid out millions of dollars, focusing on races that could tip the partisan balance. All of this campaign finance activity made congressional elections more expensive than ever before. It also ensured that the congressional parties would enjoy ample support even when their presidential candidates were having problems.

For much of the 2016 campaign, as in 2020, it seemed possible that Trump would drag the congressional GOP down to defeat. He did lose the aggregated popular tally nationwide, but the party's House and Senate candidates generally did better than Trump on their own turf. In seven of the ten Senate races that RealClearPolitics listed as "toss-ups" or "leans," the GOP candidate got a larger share of the vote than Trump.[9] Among the handful of House districts with split outcomes, twenty-three voted for a Republican House candidate and Clinton, while only twelve voted for a Democrat and Trump. Republicans figured that they and their party were more popular than Trump, and relatively few campaigned with him. For his part, Trump did not supply other Republicans with much material support. When journalist Robert Draper asked whether he cared if Republican kept control of the Senate, he answered, "Well, I'd like them to do that. But I don't mind being a free agent, either."[10]

Congressional Republicans were on their own in 2016, which worked out for them. In addition to the National Republican Senatorial Committee (NRSC) and the National Republican Congressional Committee (NRCC), GOP campaigns benefited from outside money. Tapping generous contributions by wealthy donors, the Congressional Leadership Fund spent lavishly to help the party's House candidates, and the Senate Leadership Fund did the same for its Senate candidates. Though nominally independent, these super PACs were unofficially aligned with their party leadership, as were their counterpart organizations on the Democratic side. Other super PACs and "dark money" organizations arose to support specific candidates. In some races, outside spending exceeded candidate spending.[11] All told, the Republican congressional "team" (candidates, party organizations, and outside groups) outspent the Democratic team by more than $100 million.[12]

In previous cycles, Republicans had yielded ground when incumbents and strong open-seat candidates lost their primaries to rivals from the hard right. By 2016, the national parties were taking proactive measures to prevent such losses. In Kansas, Representative Mike Pompeo, a hardline conservative, considered a primary race against Senator Jerry Moran. NRSC discouraged conservative groups from backing Pompeo, and it sent opposition researchers to Wichita. Reid Wilson reported at *The Hill*, "And the retired FBI agents didn't bother to cover their tracks; it would help the NRSC's cause if Pompeo knew the campaign arm was preparing a thick binder of opposition research."[13] Pompeo declined to run against Moran, which proved to be a wise choice. Had he lost the primary, he would have retreated to obscurity. Instead, he won reelection to the House and then accepted Trump's offer to become CIA director. He ended up as secretary of state.

Thanks to robust fundraising and providential recruitment, congressional Republicans survived the 2016 elections mostly unscathed, with a net loss of just two Senate seats and six House seats. (Although no one could have known it at the time, one narrow defeat had huge long-term consequences. In New Hampshire, Democrat Maggie Hassan beat incumbent Republican Kelly Ayotte by just 1,017 votes. If a minimum of 509 votes had switched from one to the other in 2016, the GOP would have retained its Senate majority in 2021.) A puzzle thus arises: When Congress convened in 2017, few (if any) Republicans owed their election to Trump. He had gotten only 46 percent of the popular vote, and during his first 100 days in office, he had the lowest approval rating of any president since Gallup started tracking the first months of presidential terms in 1953.[14] Yet when CQ measured how often his position prevailed in congressional roll calls, it found that he scored a record-high 98.7 percent in 2017 and a near-record 93.4 percent in 2018.[15] According to popular wisdom, unloved presidents without electoral mandates should not have that much success. So how did Trump get his way?

A large part of the answer is that he often gave congressional Republicans their way, rather than the reverse. He hardly had to bully his party into supporting tax cuts, which had been GOP doctrine for decades. The pressure to move fast and big on the issue came from the contributor class. Representative Chris Collins of New York admitted to reporters in 2017, "My donors are basically saying, 'Get it done or don't ever call me again.'"[16] On health care, Republicans had unanimously opposed the Affordable Care Act and backed its repeal long before Trump headed the party. To the delight of social conservatives on Capitol Hill, he essentially subcontracted judicial selection to the Federalist Society and the Heritage Foundation. On issues ranging from agriculture to education, his knowledge and interest were minimal, and he was content to sign whatever the congressional Republicans sent to the Resolute Desk. As for matters on which he did take a general position, he avoided most details and let his party fill in the blanks.

Trump's attitude toward politics was transactional, and he offered the congressional GOP an implicit bargain: He would agree to their preferences on most issues, and in return, they could do him a couple of favors. First, they would bow to the few policy positions he did care about, such as trade protectionism and stringent immigration limits. Second, they would have his back when Democrats attacked him. For Republicans, it seemed like a sweet deal. On trade and immigration, the party's rank and file had always been skeptical of the "globalist" policies that George W. Bush had espoused in the previous decade. They held "Trumpian" attitudes long before Trump came along, so they would applaud GOP members for standing with him.[17]

Similarly, the base would cheer congressional Republicans for rejecting attacks on Trump's character. In 2016, *New York Times* columnist Frank Bruni wrote, "Conservative commentators and die-hard Republicans often brush off denunciations of Donald Trump as an unprincipled hatemonger by saying: Yeah, yeah, that's what Democrats wail about every Republican they're trying to take down. Sing me a song I haven't heard so many times before." Bruni quoted veteran Democratic operative Howard Wolfson, who admitted that he and his colleagues had cried wolf: "I'm quite confident I employed language that, in retrospect, was hyperbolic and inaccurate, language that cheapened my ability—our ability—to talk about this moment with accuracy and credibility."[18]

If the incentives for supporting Trump were not enough, Republicans had to ponder the penalties for criticizing him. Despite his low national approval ratings, he had a fervent following in Red America. To stray from the Trump line was to invite hellfire from the GOP base, and Trump was ready to call out his Republican critics by name. One was Senator Jeff Flake of Arizona, who had split with Trump on immigration. In the summer of 2017, Trump tweeted, "Phoenix crowd last night was amazing—a packed house. I love the Great State of Arizona. Not a fan of Jeff Flake, weak on crime & border!"[19] Flake soon announced that he was not running for reelection. On NBC, he explained, "The bottom line is if I were to run a campaign that I could be proud of, and where I didn't have to cozy up to the president and his positions or his behavior, I could not win in a Republican primary."[20] After Senator Bob Corker (R-TN) criticized Trump's reaction to the Charlottesville melee, he tweeted, "Strange statement by Bob Corker considering that he is constantly asking me whether or not he should run again in '18. Tennessee not happy!"[21] Corker then decided not to run again.

Most significant was the fate of Representative Mark Sanford of South Carolina. When he was governor of the state, he declined to run for reelection in 2010 in the wake of a sex scandal. (While he was visiting his paramour in Argentina and statehouse reporters asked about his absence, his staff claimed that he had been "hiking the Appalachian Trail." After the truth came out, that phrase instantly became a smirking euphemism for adultery.) He made a comeback in a 2013 special election for the House. In 2016, he had earned Trump's enmity with an op-ed titled "I Support You, Donald Trump. Now Release Your Tax Returns."[22] In 2017, he said that Trump had "fanned the flames of intolerance."[23] Even though he voted with the administration most of the time, he faced a strong 2018 primary challenge from an opponent who accused him of being insufficiently pro-Trump. On the day of the primary,

Trump tweeted, "Mark Sanford has been very unhelpful to me in my campaign to MAGA. He is MIA and nothing but trouble. He is better off in Argentina. I fully endorse Katie Arrington for Congress in SC, a state I love. She is tough on crime and will continue our fight to lower taxes. VOTE Katie!"[24] It is not clear that the last-minute tweet changed any votes, but Sanford lost.

Correctly or incorrectly, the GOP political community drew a lesson from Flake, Corker, and Sanford: defying Trump was a one-way ticket to Loserville. As 2018 approached, however, congressional Republicans faced an uncomfortable question: Did satisfying the base mean alienating the general electorate?

Some states hold elections in odd-numbered years, and these off-year elections sometimes foreshadow midterm results: for instance, GOP successes in 1993 preceded the historic victory of 1994. In the fall of 2017, Democrats swept state elections in Virginia and New Jersey. Notwithstanding Republican Chris Christie's governorship, New Jersey had long favored Democrats in state elections, so the outcome was no surprise. Virginia was more telling. Republicans had high hopes for their candidate Ed Gillespie, a former national party chair who had nearly defeated incumbent Democrat Mark Warner in a 2014 race for the U.S. Senate. But Democrat Ralph Northam beat Gillespie by nine percentage points, and the GOP lost ground in the state legislature. Decades earlier, Virginia had been at the leading edge of the Republican realignment of the South, and these results suggested that parts of the South—at least those with large metropolitan areas—might be shifting back to the Democrats. More generally, the state results gave national Democrats hope for 2018.

MIDTERM

Midterm elections are the political equivalent of Festivus: an occasion for the airing of grievances. Two years into a presidential term, voters usually have a long list. Accordingly, the president's party had lost House seats in eighteen of the twenty midterm elections between 1938 and 2014. In 1994, 2006, and 2010, midterms had flipped control of the chamber. In 2018, House Democrats would only need to flip twenty-three seats to get a majority. And twenty-five Republicans represented districts that voted for Hillary Clinton in 2016. Perhaps anticipating a harsh electoral environment, thirty-eight Republican House incumbents retired in 2018, a large number. Together with two who lost primaries, there were forty open Republican seats. Democrats only had to defend twenty open seats. Moreover, the Democratic Congressional Campaign Committee had recruited strong candidates, including many women and military veterans. The DCCC also culled the candidate herd in several California races, while establishing an unprecedented early organizational presence in usually Republican Orange County.[25]

The president took a special interest in two incumbents: Duncan Hunter (R-CA) and Chris Collins (R-NY), the first two House members who had endorsed him in 2016. Both were under federal indictment: Collins for insider trading and Hunter for illegally using campaign funds for extramarital affairs and other personal uses. "Two long running, Obama era, investigations of two very popular Republican Congressmen were brought to a well publicized charge, just ahead of the Mid-Terms, by the Jeff Sessions Justice Department," he tweeted. "Two easy wins now in doubt because there is not enough time. Good job Jeff . . ."[26] Both would win reelection in their heavily Republican districts, only to resign in disgrace after plea deals. In December 2020, Trump pardoned them.

As chapter 1 explained, the controversy over the Kavanaugh nomination probably helped Senate Republicans score a net gain of two seats. On other fronts, however, the GOP faced setbacks. A blue wave hit the House, as undecided races broke heavily toward the Democrats. Their net gain of forty seats was well below Republican gains in 1994 or 2010, but above the twenty-nine-seat average since 1938. One respected analyst ranked 2018 as seventh of the nineteen midterms since World War II in the magnitude of the voter shift.[27] Overall, Democrats won about 53 percent of the national House vote and about 54 percent of the House seats. Democrats gained seven governorships, while Republicans lost six (in Alaska, a Republican replaced an Independent). California Democrats swept all statewide offices, as they had four years before. Democrats also gained a new majority in several state chambers, but these wins did not make up for gains by Republicans at the state level through the Obama years. Indeed, the GOP still held unified control of more state governments after their 2018 losses (twenty-three) than they held immediately following their big 2010 gains (twenty-one).[28]

Midterm results are not a reliable guidepost to the presidential election that follows. In 1982 as in 2018, Republicans suffered hefty losses in the House and held onto the Senate. Two years later, President Reagan carried forty-nine states. President Obama acknowledged a "shellacking" in 2010 and went on to win in 2012, albeit with a shrunken margin. Nevertheless, midterms do offer clues about political trends. In 2018, one such trend was a boom in political participation. About 50 percent of the voter-eligible population cast ballots, the highest midterm turnout since 1914 and the biggest-ever increase from a previous midterm.[29] Strong feelings about the Trump presidency were at work, of course, but so were election procedures. More states had liberalized their laws on registration and early voting. Among the ten states with the highest turnout, seven had same-day registration, and three sent all registered voters their ballots, which they could mail in or drop off at secure sites.[30] Forty percent of the midterm electorate either used early-voting sites or cast their ballots by mail.[31] In some states, the result was a slow count of ballots that ended in the defeat of candidates who had led on election night. Some Republicans smelled fraud. Trump tweeted, "An honest vote count is no longer possible—ballots massively infected. Must go with Election night!"[32]

Another trend was a massive increase in campaign spending. With more than $5.7 billion in outlays by candidates, parties, committees, PACs, and outside groups, the 2018 midterm was by far the most expensive in history, even after inflation.[33] Large donors were giving more to outside spending groups and victory funds, but small donors were also stepping up. "Although a small group of wealthy individuals continue to drive the cost of elections ever higher by donating millions to outside groups, candidates are countering their influence by relying more and more on small donations," said Sarah Bryner, research director at the Center for Responsive Politics. "Elections may be more expensive, but in 2018 we saw that candidates are able to convert small dollars into wins, and we suspect that this trend will continue into the presidential cycle."[34] The Democrats' not-so-secret weapon was ActBlue, an online fundraising platform that brought nearly $1.6 billion to Democratic candidates and causes—an increase of more than an 80 percent from the previous midterm.[35]

Politicians study midterms to learn how they can do better next time. In a post-election interview, House Republican leader Kevin McCarthy (R-CA) expressed grudging admiration for Democratic fundraising: "We have to combat ActBlue. It's a new era . . . that made a difference in races."[36] Senate majority leader Mitch McConnell made similar comments in a meeting with party donors, and one of his advisers lamented the fragmented structure of GOP fundraising. "I think everybody acknowledges we have a helluva problem," said Josh Holmes. "The question is whether we can get everybody to set egos and business considerations aside to solve it. I'd certainly like to try."[37] Try they did, and in 2018, the GOP set up a doppelganger organization dubbed WinRed.

Republicans also reflected on recruitment. News organizations tweaked the House GOP with photos contrasting the diverse Democratic freshman class with their mostly male and monochrome Republican counterparts. Former NRCC chair Tom Cole (R-OK) said, "This is something we've got to come to grips with." Cole, himself a Native American, added, "We're maximizing rural voters, we're maximizing white male voters, particularly white males without a college education. Those are all great to have, but they're not enough to be a majority in the House."[38] Elise Stefanik (R-NY), who headed recruitment during the 2018 cycle, refocused her political action committee on recruiting, funding, and mentoring high-quality female Republican candidates. "Women bring a unique perspective," Stefanik said. "I think having more at the table makes us more effective policymakers."[39]

Midterm elections can produce a new crop of future leaders for the out-party.[40] The 1978 midterm gave the House a conservative Republican gadfly from Georgia named Newt Gingrich, who immediately took the spotlight with his attacks on Democrats and creative use of C-SPAN coverage.[41] Forty years later, the midterm gave the House a Democratic socialist gadfly from New York named Alexandria Ocasio-Cortez. Even before taking office, she had made the news by upsetting a member of the Democratic leadership in a primary. Once in Washington, she made creative use of social media to attack Trump and raise her public profile. Just as Gingrich had a set of like-minded colleagues (the nucleus of what would become the Conservative Opportunity Society), Ocasio-Cortez had "the Squad." And both became polarizing figures in national campaigns. Because of the velocity of news in the Trump era, Ocasio-Cortez rose even faster than Gingrich had. (Both would probably object to any comparison between them.)

The most obvious effect of a midterm is to change the composition and party balance of Congress. The gain of two seats gave Senate Republicans some leeway on close votes and made it less likely that one or two GOP senators could thwart presidential priorities. (Trump would always remember John McCain's dramatic "thumbs-down" vote that tanked the party's health care legislation.) With typical bravado, Trump said that the 2018 midterm "was very close to complete victory."[42] From the standpoint of securing Senate approval of nominations for the executive and judicial branches, the result was a success. But split-party control of Congress would make it harder to enact controversial bills. Most important, control of the House would enable Democrats to conduct investigations of the Trump administration.

THE 116TH CONGRESS

Things did not get off to a good start. Even before the new session began, Trump had a televised confrontation with Senate Democratic Leader Charles Schumer (D-NY) and incoming Speaker Nancy Pelosi (D-CA). The issue was the continuing resolution that kept the government running, and Trump insisted on border security measures that the Democrats opposed. Trump openly said that he would let government funding lapse to get his way. "So I will take the mantle. I will be the one to shut it down. I'm not going to blame you for it. The last time you shut it down, it didn't work. I will take the mantle of shutting down."[43] Bill Clinton and Barack Obama had managed to shift blame for government shutdowns to their political opponents in Congress, but Trump's statement ensured that the blame would fall on the White House. After weeks of negotiation, including a short-term continuing resolution and a delay in the State of the Union Address, Trump and Congress reached an agreement that kept the government open while failing to meet his demands on border security. If simply keeping the lights on was going to be this hard, then the 116th Congress seemed unlikely to produce much landmark legislation.

On the House side, the focus was on hearings. In February, former Trump lawyer Michael Cohen testified about the president's financial activity. Cohen literally brought receipts, including a check from Trump reimbursing him for illegal hush-money payments to a porn star. This testimony implicated Trump in a felony, but the House did not follow up with any official action. Cohen had previously lied to Congress, so despite his documentary evidence, his credibility was in question. And remembering the backlash against the Clinton impeachment, senior Democrats were leery of getting into a fight with a president over sex.

Then came the Mueller report. Although it contained disturbing information about Trump's willingness to accept help from Russia and his efforts to avoid accountability for his actions, the report did not directly recommend indictment or impeachment. Mueller had worked under serious constraints. As mentioned earlier, one was a longstanding Justice Department policy against the prosecution of a sitting president. Another was an unusual degree of noncooperation from witnesses. Why did they expose themselves to legal liability? The report noted that "the President's acts directed at witnesses, including discouragement of cooperation with the government and suggestions of possible future pardons."[44] (In December 2020, Trump did pardon key figures in the Mueller investigation, including campaign chair Paul Manafort.) Whatever the legal truth may have been, the report was a political dud. It was also a backhanded vindication for Speaker Pelosi, who had warned her members against betting their political future on impeachment. "I think her instincts were correct, that we're putting way too much into the Mueller report, and what if it disappoints?" said Gerry Connolly (D-VA). "What did we really think Mueller was going to do?"[45]

Attacks on Trump continued to come from House Democrats, including the chair of the Oversight Committee, Elijah Cummings (D-MD). After the committee probed the treatment of migrant children at the border with Mexico, Trump struck back on Twitter:

Rep, Elijah Cummings has been a brutal bully, shouting and screaming at the great men & women of Border Patrol about conditions at the Southern Border, when actually his Baltimore district is FAR WORSE and more dangerous. His district is considered the Worst in the USA. . . . As proven last week during a Congressional tour, the Border is clean, efficient & well run, just very crowded. Cumming [sic] District is a disgusting, rat and rodent infested mess. If he spent more time in Baltimore, maybe he could help clean up this very dangerous & filthy place.[46]

Democrats heard a racist undertone in Trump's attack on Cummings, an African American representing a majority-Black district. Trump's defenders said that he was just being an effective counterpuncher. Cummings—who died suddenly in the autumn—was a senior lawmaker and committee chair, so Trump was not punching down. Quite different was his Twitter attack on "the Squad," four members who had been serving for only a few months.

So interesting to see "Progressive" Democrat Congresswomen, who originally came from countries whose governments are a complete and total catastrophe, the worst, most corrupt and inept anywhere in the world (if they even have a functioning government at all), now loudly and viciously telling the people of the United States, the greatest and most powerful Nation on earth, how our government is to be run. Why don't they go back and help fix the totally broken and crime infested places from which they came.[47]

The tweet erred on facts. Three of the Squad members were natural-born citizens: Rashida Tlaib (D-MI), a Palestinian American born in Detroit; Alexandria Ocasio-Cortez (D-NY), a Hispanic American born in New York; and Ayanna Pressley (D-MA), an African American born in Cincinnati. The fourth, Ilhan Omar (D-MN), was a naturalized citizen who had come as a refugee from Somalia at the age of twelve.

Leave aside questions of accuracy: what was the point of attacking four junior lawmakers who did not yet wield significant power within the House? Democrats said that Trump was merely stoking prejudice against minority women with names that sounded exotic to many Americans. But another agenda was at play, since all four had taken positions that were well to the left of the American mainstream. Tlaib and Omar supported a boycott of Israel, which they criticized in terms that struck many observers as anti-Semitic.[48] Ocasio-Cortez embraced the label of "socialist" as Pressley did with "radical." The day after the "go back" comment, Trump issued another tweet that revealed his purpose: "The Dems were trying to distance themselves from the four 'progressives,' but now they are forced to embrace them. That means they are endorsing Socialism, hate of Israel and the USA! Not good for the Democrats!"[49] Throughout the campaign, Trump and congressional Republicans would keep going after the Squad—especially the mediagenic Ocasio-Cortez—in an attempt to make them the face of the other party. It was a new riff on an old tactic. During the 1996 campaign, Democrats ran against "Dole-Gingrich," linking the respected Kansas senator to the unpopular House speaker.

During the fall of 2019, impeachment eclipsed other political stories. Democrats hoped that many voters would turn against the GOP over Trump's effort to squeeze opposition research from the government of Ukraine. As the first chapter explained, it did not happen. Polls indicated that the impeachment controversy served mostly to drive voters deeper into their partisan camps.[50] In an NPR/*PBS NewsHour*/Marist poll, most respondents in both parties openly said nothing in the hearings would change their minds on impeachment.[51] Surveys on the congressional generic ballot changed very little, except for a short-lived narrowing of the Democratic advantage during the Senate trial. Some individual House members gained national followings among their partisans, but it was unclear whether they would reap any lasting political benefit.

By Election Day, impeachment felt like ancient history. The triple crises of the pandemic, the recession, and the outbreak of civil disorders had pushed it far down the memory hole. The year's events shocked everyone, and the congressional elections had their share of surprises, too.

THE HOUSE

Upending the conventional wisdom, Republicans gained ground in the 2020 House elections. Democrats took only three GOP seats while Republicans won fourteen Democratic seats. (The final Republican victory came on February 8, 2021, when incumbent Anthony Brindisi (D-New York) conceded an extremely close race to challenger Claudia Tenney.) The GOP also regained the Michigan seat of Justin Amash, who had switched from Republican to Libertarian before deciding not to seek reelection. In all, the Democrats had won 222 seats to Republicans' 213. They held a majority, but it was their smallest in more than a century. According to election analyst David Wasserman, they would fallen back into the minority if not for court cases that had overturned GOP redistricting plans prior to 2016 (Florida and Virginia), 2018 (Pennsylvania), and 2020 (North Carolina). The court-ordered maps enabled Democrats to win about ten more seats than under the earlier GOP plans.[52]

The 2018 midterm had resulted in thirty-five crossover House districts: thirty-one Trump districts with a Democrat and four Clinton districts with a Republican. (One of the Democrats in the former group, Jeff Van Drew of New Jersey, switched to the GOP in 2019.) After the 2020 election, there were only sixteen crossover districts, the fewest in a century. This shift worked against the Democrats, as there were now only seven Democratic

House members in districts that Trump won in 2020, compared with nine Republicans in districts that voted for Biden.[53]

House Democrats had expected triumph, not a setback. Perhaps they had failed to consider that the peculiar circumstances of the 2018 midterm had given them an artificially large bump and that the 2020 results were a more "normal" outcome for a closely divided electorate. If so, the misperception was understandable: a successful midterm can give a congressional party a sense of momentum.[54] The 2018 elections encouraged House Democrats to believe that demographic and ideological trends would be on their side next time. Early signs seemed to bear out their confidence. Although impeachment was not the boost that some were expecting, Democrats held a consistent lead in the congressional generic ballot throughout 2019 and into early 2020. The Democratic Congressional Campaign Committee raised more in 2019 than it had two years earlier, building a substantial financial edge over its GOP counterpart.[55]

Many congressional Republicans acted as if they agreed with the Democratic assessment. Voluntary departures are often a good sign of how House members think that the coming election will turn out. If they believe that their party will gain or keep the majority, most will probably stick around to enjoy the benefits. If they see minority status in the future, they are more likely to seek other office or return to private life.[56] Moreover, exits can be a self-fulfilling prophecy since an open seat is harder to defend than one in which the party's candidate has the advantages of incumbency. In the 116th Congress, twenty-seven House Republicans called it quits, compared with just nine Democrats.[57]

The advent of the pandemic appeared to bolster Democratic congressional prospects even further. It would naturally focus voter attention on health care issues, where Democrats had a massive advantage in public opinion.[58] The subsequent recession was another challenge for their GOP opponents, since past economic downturns had costs seats for the party holding the White House. And public disapproval of Trump's handling of the pandemic convinced many observers that a "blue wave" would augment Democratic numbers in the House.

In hindsight, the blue wave was not so inevitable.

A decade earlier, the 2010 midterm had resulted in historic Republican gains in state legislatures, and the party used its newfound legislative strength to draw favorable district lines. As mentioned, Democratic lawsuits blunted some of this advantage, but GOP gerrymanders persisted in states such as Texas. Democrats also grappled with "unintentional gerrymandering." Much of their support clustered in urban areas where landslides for their candidates resulted in many "wasted" votes, whereas GOP support had a more efficient distribution.

In 2018, House Democrats could overcome these problems because dissatisfaction with the Trump administration powered fundraising and voter turnout. If voters disliked the way things were going, the most direct way to express themselves was to support Democratic congressional candidates. Except in states where backlash to the Kavanaugh hearings pumped up GOP challenges to incumbent Democratic senators, there was not a similar motive for Republicans to join the fray. California was especially dispiriting for the party's identifiers and leaners. Their candidate for governor was an obscure eccentric who lost by a record margin. In the Senate race, the state's top-two primary system landed two Democrats on the November ballot, with no option for a write-in. Against this backdrop, California Republicans lost seven House seats.

Things would be different in 2020. Republicans and Democrats had a strong motive to participate because they perceived high stakes in the election. Pew reported that 90 percent of Biden supporters and 89 percent of Trump supporters said that a victory by the other candidate would do "lasting harm" to the country.[59] Compared with 2018, there was a voter surge for both sides—but more for the GOP. Political scientist William Galston reckons that Democrats increased their aggregate vote for the House by about 16.8 million while Republicans gained 21.9 million. The House Democrats' overall vote margin dropped from 8.6 percent to roughly 3 percent.[60] The House GOP aggregate vote was 1.4 million less than for Trump, while the Democratic House vote lagged Biden's total by 3.9 million. These differences hindered Democratic House candidates in close races. The GOP did well in these districts, another example of the efficient distribution of their vote. As in the past, a chunk of Democratic support consisted of wasted votes in uncontested races.

The Democrats had campaign problems. An influential academic study has confirmed one bit of practical wisdom about campaigning: "Door-to-door canvassing by enthusiastic volunteers is the gold-standard mobilization tactic."[61] During the pandemic, however, national Democratic leaders discouraged congressional candidates and volunteers from adopting the gold standard. Republicans were less likely to observe such constraints. Whatever the health effects may have been, the party reaped a political advantage. In his concession speech, incumbent California Democrat T. J. Cox spoke for other defeated colleagues when he said, "Unfortunately, this year due to the coronavirus, we weren't able to engage in door-to-door personal canvassing and the election results reflected that."[62]

Party moderates also blamed the growing prominence of the party's left wing. During the primary season, the progressives sought to oust several mainstream Democratic incumbents. They fell short in some cases, but they also had notable victories. In Missouri, Black Lives Matter activist Cori Bush defeated ten-term incumbent William Lacy Clay. In New York City, Jamaal Bowman beat Eliot Engel, the long-serving chair of the House Foreign Affairs Committee. And in a suburban Chicago district, moderate Dan Lipinski—one of the party's last remaining opponents of abortion—fell to Marie Newman. Media coverage emphasized the progressives' growing power, and Republicans were happy to reinforce that message, with particular emphasis on "the Squad." As noted before, Ilhan Omar and others talked about "defunding the police"—a gift to GOP opposition researchers.

In the fall campaign, Republicans aired about 70 different broadcast ads that mentioned "defund the police."[63] "Republicans hung around Democrats' necks that we are all socialist or communist and we all wanted to defund the police," said Harley Rouda, a first-term Democrat from California who lost his seat. "In my opinion, we as a party did a less than adequate job in refuting that narrative. We won in 2018 and took the House back because of people like me—moderates—flipping radical Republican seats."[64] Abigail Spanberger (D-VA), who barely won reelection, angrily told a post-election conference call of House Democrats, "We need to not ever use the word 'socialist' or 'socialism' ever again. ... We lost good members because of that. If we are classifying Tuesday as a success ... we will get f—ing torn apart in 2022."[65]

The socialist label was toxic with voters who had fled left-wing dictatorships. "Socialism broadly speaking in the United States is a bad brand. In Florida, it is a horrific brand," said Florida-based consultant Rick Wilson, a leader of the Lincoln Project. To people who had escaped places such as Cuba and Venezuela, he explained, "socialism isn't universal health care and day care, socialism was secret police knocking at their door and shooting a family member in the head."[66] Republican Carlos Giménez defeated incumbent Debbie Mucarsel-Powell in Florida's majority-Hispanic 26th District, attacking her for supporting the Squad. In a post-election interview, he said, "We didn't have to call them socialist, they called themselves socialists."[67]

The House Republicans applied the harsh lessons that they had learned from their defeat in 2018. First, they improved their fundraising. Whereas the DCCC outraised NRCC by 44 percent in 2018, NRCC narrowed that gap to 25 percent in 2020.[68] Thanks in part to the WinRed, the average fundraising total for individual GOP candidates was close to that Democratic average.[69]

The second lesson literally involved the face that the party showed the electorate. Susan Brooks (R-IN), the NRCC recruitment chair, told *Roll Call* in 2019, "It's important that we, as a conference, do a better job of looking like America, and better representing the very diverse country that we have."[70] In February 2020, she explained how NRCC was following through: "With help from my fellow Members of Congress serving as Recruitment Captains, we went out looking for candidates who uniquely fit their district, reflect the diversity of America, and can win competitive races. We didn't stop because one person announced they were running. We kept looking for the best candidates in these districts to win in November."[71] Alongside NRCC's efforts, Elise Stefanik's PAC added support for Republican women candidates.

Notwithstanding the GOP's professed disdain for "identity politics," the emphasis on demographic diversity paid off. An early indicator was a special election for a Southern California House seat. Democrat Katie Hill, who had defeated a GOP incumbent in 2018, resigned after a bizarre sex scandal. To run for the vacated seat, Republicans recruited Raytheon executive Mike Garcia. As a Hispanic and a former Navy fighter pilot, Garcia fit the perfect profile for a constituency that includes many Hispanic voters, as well as veterans and military personnel. (Edwards Air Force Base is in the district.) Garcia narrowly defeated a Democratic assemblywoman in both the springtime special election and the fall general election. A remarkable feature of the general election is that *every* Republican who flipped party control of a House district was a woman or a member of a racial or ethnic minority group:

- California 21: David Valadao, Portuguese American
- California 39: Young Kim, Korean American woman
- California 48: Michelle Park Steel, Korean American woman
- Florida 26: Carlos Gimenez, Cuban American
- Florida 27: Maria Elvira Salazar, Cuban American woman
- Iowa 1: Ashley Hinson, woman
- Iowa 2: Mariannette Miller-Meeks, woman
- Minnesota 7: Michelle Fischbach, woman
- New Mexico 2: Yvette Herrell, Native American woman
- New York 11: Nicole Malliotakis, Cuban American woman
- New York 22: Claudia Tenney, woman
- Oklahoma 5: Stephanie Bice, Iranian American woman
- South Carolina 1: Nancy Mace, woman
- Utah 4: Burgess Owens, African American

The California victories were especially significant in such a heavily Democratic state. The three winners were all well-experienced "quality candidates": Valadao had held the seat before, Kim had served in the State Assembly, and Steel was a member of the Orange County Board of Supervisors. All three benefited from "ballot harvesting," the practice by which political operatives gather mail ballots from voters and drop them off at an election office or polling place. At the national level, Republicans denounced the practice, with Trump tweeting, "GET RID OF BALLOT HARVESTING, IT IS RAMPANT WITH FRAUD. THE USA MUST HAVE VOTER I.D.,

THE ONLY WAY TO GET AN HONEST COUNT."[72] But after seeing how effectively Democrats had harvested ballots two years earlier, California Republicans chose not to lose a political arms race. "The issue of ballot harvesting is we don't like it. We don't agree with it," California RNC committeewoman Harmeet Dhillon told *National Review*. "However, it'd be political malpractice not to do it where the other side is doing it, and the other side has done it effectively."[73]

THE SENATE: REGULATION TIME

The party composition of the Senate was not certain on the night of the election, or even in the days after. Their 2018 disappointment had left Democrats with forty-seven seats. So if Trump won reelection, they would need a net gain of four. If Biden won, they would need only three, as Vice President Harris's tie-breaking vote would give control to her party, as Vice President Cheney had done after the 2000 election resulted in a 50–50 Senate. On election night, Democrats won two seats and lost one, for a disappointing net gain of one. But the contest for control was not over during regulation time, because two Republican seats in Georgia were heading to a January 5 runoff. If Democrats could win both, they could still score a victory in overtime.

In the two races in which Democrats gained seats, they benefited from changing demographics and smart recruitment. In Arizona, their candidate was Mark Kelly, whose biography generated admiration and sympathy. A former navy captain and astronaut, Kelly was married to former representative Gabrielle Giffords, who had suffered disabling injuries during a mass shooting in 2011. He ran as a practical problem-solver, the formula that had helped Democrat Kyrsten Sinema defeat Representative Martha McSally in a 2018 race for the state's other Senate seat. After that election, Governor Doug Ducey appointed McSally to fill the seat of deceased Senator John McCain. By 2020, McSally had statewide name identification from her earlier campaign and two years of Senate service, but Arizona's growing Hispanic population was becoming a challenge for Republican candidates. Together with Kelly's appealing profile, it was too much for McSally to overcome, though she did manage to hold Kelly to just 51.2 percent of the vote.

In Colorado, another Western state with a burgeoning Hispanic population, incumbent Republican Cory Gardner was already vulnerable. Then Democrats got their strongest possible candidate. Popular former governor John Hickenlooper had made a quixotic race for the Democratic presidential nomination and dropped out early. Though he had denied interest in seeking any other office, Senate Democratic Leader Charles Schumer persuaded him to run. Polls consistently showed him ahead of Gardner, who did not help himself by clutching the Trump banner. The Democratic-trending state voted for Biden by a double-digit margin, and Hickenlooper won by nine.

Republicans partially offset the two Democratic election-night gains by winning the Alabama seat of Democrat Doug Jones. In the 2017 special election that brought him to the Senate, Jones defeated the scandal-scarred Roy Moore, who was just about the only Republican who could have lost. In the 2020 GOP primary, former attorney general Jeff Sessions sought to reclaim the seat that he had once held. But Trump despised Sessions for recusing himself from the Russia investigation, so he endorsed former football coach Tommy Tuberville. In Alabama, it is difficult to beat a Trump-endorsed football legend. Tuberville crushed Sessions in the primary and went on to another romp in the general election.

On their tally sheets, national Democrats took it for granted that Jones would lose. They also worried about Michigan, where incumbent Gary Peters faced a strong challenge from Republican John James, a charismatic African American businessman and former Army Ranger. In another electoral setting, James probably would have won, but strong Democratic turnout carried the state for Biden and barely pushed Peters over the finish line.

With these results, and with the Georgia races stretching to January 5, Democrats needed two more seats to win control on election night. Unfortunately for them, the GOP held on to every other Republican seat that RealClearPolitics rated as a "toss-up" or "lean." In a post-election Tweet, Trump took credit for the wins and scolded Senate Republicans for their ingratitude.[74] A glance at the results (table 5.1) casts doubt on the idea that Trump had coattails. In three of the races, Trump got a smaller percentage of the vote than the GOP winner. (In Georgia, he also underperformed David

Table 5.1. Percentage of the Vote for Winning Republican Senate Candidate and President Trump in Key States

		Senate Winner Percentage	Trump Percentage
Alaska	Sullivan	53.9	53.1
Iowa	Ernst	51.8	53.2
Maine	Collins	51.0	44.0
Mississippi	Hyde-Smith	54.1	57.6
Montana	Daines	55.0	56.9
North Carolina	Tillis	48.7	50.1
South Carolina	Graham	54.5	55.1
Texas	Cornyn	53.5	52.1

Source: www.realclearpolitics.com

Perdue.) In the rest, Trump did a little better than his party's Senate candidate, but not by more than 3.5 percent.

GOP retentions were less a Trump phenomenon than the alignment of Senate and presidential races. On election night of 2020, only one state split its Senate and presidential vote. In Maine, Susan Collins hung onto her seat by a substantial margin despite running behind Democrat Sara Gideon in every public poll.[75] In a race where nearly all politics was national, Collins kept it local by emphasizing her Maine roots and criticizing the outside money pouring in for her opponent. She also straddled the Trump line. She had earned Democratic contempt by voting for the Supreme Court nomination of Brett Kavanaugh. She went the other way just weeks before the election, becoming the only Republican to oppose Amy Coney Barrett. Even though Democrats spent enormous sums to link her to Trump, Mainers saw her as an independent voice, enabling her to run far ahead of Trump.

Maine was hardly the only state with an influx of money. The most expensive Senate contest in American history—until overtime—was the North Carolina race between incumbent Republican Thom Tillis and Democratic challenger Cal Cunningham. The spending by candidates was impressive enough—$51 million for Cunningham, $25 million for Tillis—but these sums paled in comparison with a record-breaking $220.6 million in outside spending. Many groups across the country saw the race as crucial to control of the Senate. The McConnell-aligned Senate Leadership Fund put $47.1 million into the race while the Democratic Senate Majority PAC spent $35.8 million.[76] The race was close, but a "sexting" scandal probably hurt Cunningham just enough to cost him a narrow victory.

The second-most-expensive race took place in neighboring South Carolina. In his quest to defeat incumbent Republican Lindsey Graham, Democrat Jamie Harrison spent $129.8 million. Harrison had the background to be a prodigious fundraiser, as he had worked as a lobbyist and had served as the first African American chair of the state's Democratic Party. But the real financial fuel came from the Democrats' loathing of Graham. His abrupt transformation from a fierce Trump critic to an equally fierce Trump supporter struck them as rank hypocrisy, even by the loose standards of national politics. Graham relied on his alliance with the Trump wing to raise $97.6 million. Polls showed a close race, which turbocharged fundraising on both sides. But the home state of Strom Thurmond and Lee Atwater was not ready to ditch the GOP in federal races, and Graham won by a comfortable margin.

Ragefunding also boosted Democrat Amy McGrath in her doomed race against Senate Majority Leader Mitch McConnell of Kentucky. Despite her slim chances, she outraised him by $30 million. The Democrats' bill of particulars against McConnell included his 2016 scuttling of President Obama's Supreme Court nominee, his use of the "nuclear option" to ensure approval of Trump's judicial nominees, and his defense of Trump during the Russia investigation. The latter gave rise to the hashtag #MoscowMitch. In the end, all of this activity had little effect on Kentucky voters, and McConnell defeated McGrath by nearly twenty points.

After the election, some Democrats complained that the passion-powered flow of money into South Carolina and Kentucky only served to divert Democratic resources from more winnable Senate races. But Democratic Senate candidates spend a total of $1.2 billion.[77] Outside groups spent hundreds of millions more. The party's candidates did not starve. Their problem was not a lack of funding but the predispositions of the voters.

Take Montana, for instance. Like John Hickenlooper of Colorado, term-limited Governor Steve Bullock ran for the Democratic presidential nomination but pulled out when his campaign did not get enough traction. Also like Hickenlooper, he was reluctant to run for the Senate but changed his mind after fervent appeals from Charles Schumer and other party leaders. No wonder top Democrats wanted him to run: in normally Republican Montana, he had won three successive statewide races (once for attorney general and twice for governor). With his emphasis on bipartisan bridge building, Bullock was well liked and had received high marks for his skillful leadership during the pandemic. In a state with a small population, he spent more than $48 million, which came to about $175 for every vote that he earned. Nevertheless, he lost to incumbent Steve Daines by ten points. Unlike Hickenlooper, he ran in a state that tended to favor Republicans in federal elections. The state's other senator, Jon Tester, was a Democrat, but he had twice won because of Libertarian spoilers who siphoned votes from GOP candidates. In his most recent race, Tester benefited from a favorable midterm environment for Democrats. Bullock had no such luck.

But fellow Democrats were about to have some luck in the Peachtree State.

THE SENATE: OVERTIME IN GEORGIA

In 2020, Georgia had two incumbent Republican senators on the ballot. Running for reelection to a full term was David Perdue, the cousin of Sonny Perdue, the state's first Republican governor since Reconstruction and later Trump's secretary of agriculture. A management consultant and former CEO of a Fortune 500 company, Perdue won the 2014 race to fill the open seat of retiring Republican Saxby Chambliss. In the Senate, he established a voting record as a hardline conservative and Trump ally. He also got media attention for undertaking more stock transactions than any other senator. His 2,596 trades in stocks, bonds, and funds exposed him to criticism about potential conflicts of interest.[78]

His November opponent was Jon Ossoff, a thirty-three-year-old film producer who had previously run a surprisingly close race for a longtime Republican House seat in the Atlanta suburbs. In November, Perdue received 49.7 percent to Ossoff's 47.9 percent. Anywhere else, that outcome would have meant a Perdue victory. But Georgia is the only state that requires runoffs in general elections when no candidate wins an absolute majority, so Perdue and Ossoff would face off on January 5. This race illustrates the role of contingency: had Libertarian candidate Shane Hazel not pulled quite as many Republican votes, Perdue would have topped 50 percent and the GOP would have had a lock on a Senate majority.

Incumbent Johnny Isakson had resigned from the state's other Senate seat in 2019 because of ill health. Republican Governor Brian Kemp then got to pick an interim successor, who would then face a special election for the remainder of the term, through 2022. Trump pressed him to choose conservative House member Doug Collins, who was zealously defending him during impeachment proceedings. Kemp instead opted for financial executive Kelly Loeffler, a woman with a reputation as a moderate. Kemp reportedly thought that Loeffler's profile would be a good fit for the state's changing electorate. Moreover, she could put a great deal of her own money into a campaign. Like Perdue, Kelly Loeffler had been a career executive and corporate CEO. Her household was even wealthier than Perdue's, as her husband was chairman of the New York Stock Exchange.

Collins announced that he would run against her, and that National Republican Senatorial Committee was displeased. "With this emotional, ill-informed decision, Doug Collins has united conservatives in opposition to his candidacy, and Senator Loeffler has quickly assembled more Republican support in Georgia than Collins ever knew existed," said NRSC spokesman Jesse Hunt, who called Collins "a swamp creature."[79] With national support, personal wealth, and the power of incumbency, Loeffler vastly outspent Collins. But she had liabilities. Like Perdue, she faced questions about stock transactions, specifically as to whether she traded on inside information at the start of the pandemic. Though the Senate Ethics Committee dropped its investigation of the trades, the issue would continue to dog her. She differed from Perdue in one important way: she was not a native Georgian. The efforts of the Illinois-bred Loeffler to come across as Southern seemed artificial, especially when she addressed audiences as "y'all." More significantly, she tacked hard to the right to fend off the Collins challenge and keep Trump's support. The right turn helped her with conservative GOP voters but limited her appeal outside the party base, thus defeating the purpose for which Kemp had chosen her.

Under Georgia law, all contenders for the seat appeared on the same ballot in November, and if no one got a majority, the top two candidates would face a runoff. Collins ran a tough, divisive race against Loeffler but finished third. With a split in the Republican vote, Loeffler got only 25.9 percent for second place. The leading candidate was Raphael Warnock, the African American pastor of Ebenezer Baptist Church, famous as the home base of Martin Luther King.

With the November election over and control of the Senate in the balance, the two Georgia runoffs obsessed political activists across the country. The state practically groaned under the weight of volunteers, politicians, and celebrities campaigning for their party champions. And the money poured in. Even before the final campaign finance reports, the Georgia runoffs surpassed the 2020 North Carolina Senate contest as the most expensive congressional races in history. In the Perdue-Ossoff election, candidates and outside groups spent at least $470 million. The Loeffler-Warnock special election drew at least $363 million.[80] Public surveys showed both contests to be close, but many observers expected the Republicans to win. The state had been deep-red turf for years: no Democrat had won a Georgia Senate election since Zell Miller in 2000. Biden's upset victory in the state provided only modest comfort to the Democrats because runoff turnout tended to lag far behind November totals.

In the end, though, Democrats won both seats by similar margins of about 51–49 percent, with Warnock doing slightly better than Ossoff. There were several reasons for the result.

First was the makeup of the electorate (see table 5.2). Black turnout was extraordinarily high for a runoff, thanks in part to the mobilization efforts of Stacey Abrams, who had nearly defeated Kemp for the governorship two years earlier. The chance to elect the state's first African American senator for Georgia motivated turnout for Warnock. In the other race, Perdue may

Table 5.2. Democratic Vote in the Georgia Senate Runoffs

	Ossoff	*Warnock*
Black (30% of electorate)	92%	93%
Hispanic (5%)	64%	64%
Asian (2%)	59%	60%
College Educated (38%)	54%	55%

Source: CNN exit polls, https://www.cnn.com/election/2020/exit-polls/senate-runoff/georgia and https://www.cnn.com/election/2020/exit-polls/senate-special-election-runoff/georgia

have inadvertently fired up Black Democrats by mocking Kamala Harris's name at a Trump rally.[81] Hispanics and college graduates also favored the Democrats. Asian voters made up a small slice of the voting population, but their numbers had increased over the years, which helped Ossoff and Warnock at the margins.[82]

Second, Democrats made shrewd tactical decisions. They dropped their ban on door knocking, which had hampered get-out-the-vote efforts in the fall campaign.[83] Ossoff and Warnock ran as a ticket, and their strengths—Ossoff in the suburbs, Warnock in Black communities—reinforced each other. Perdue and Loeffler also ran as a ticket, but that approach only reminded people that they were both multimillionaires who had made controversial financial dealings. And both tied themselves to Trump, the first Republican presidential candidate in twenty-eight years who had lost Georgia.

Third, in the weeks before the runoff, Trump proved to be an even bigger problem for the Republicans. In a tweet, he repeated his claims about fraud in the state, arguing that Georgia's elections were "therefore both illegal and invalid, and that would include the two current Senatorial Elections."[84] Telling Republicans that an election is illegal is not a good way to encourage them to cast ballots. He attacked Governor Kemp and Secretary of State Brad Raffensperger for not helping him overturn the presidential results in the state, thus deepening the intraparty divisions that stemmed from the fight between Collins and Loeffler. Shortly before the runoff, Raffensperger leaked a recording of a phone call in which Trump urged him to "find" enough votes for him to edge out Biden in the state.[85] The call, which may have violated state and federal law, probably did further damage to the GOP's image in the state.

With the victories of Warnock and Ossoff, Maine stood as the only state to vote for a presidential candidate of one party and a Senate candidate of the other. This outcome reflected the pattern of recent years, and it left only six states sending one Republican and one Democrat to the Senate. The others were:

- Maine (Independent Angus King caucused with Democrats)
- Montana
- Ohio
- Pennsylvania
- West Virginia
- Wisconsin

That is the lowest number since the direct election of U.S. senators. During the late 1970s and early 1980s, about half of the states had split delegations.[86]

In the 2020 Senate elections, the red states were red, the blue states were blue, and the country was divided.

STATE ELECTIONS

A few states hold elections in odd-numbered years, and the 2019 results heartened the Democrats. In Mitch McConnell's home state of Kentucky, Democrat Andy Beshear narrowly defeated Republican incumbent Matt Bevin. (McConnell had a fraught relationship with Bevin, who had once challenged him in a primary, so he was probably not heartbroken.) In Virginia, Democrats took control of the state's General Assembly, giving them unified control of the state's government for the first time in twenty-six years. And whereas Virginia Democrats of the past tended to be conservative white men, the new crop was as diverse and progressive as their counterparts in other Eastern states.

But as with the House, the 2020 results at the state level proved to be a letdown for the Democratic Party. Eleven states held gubernatorial elections, which produced little change. Incumbents won nine of the races. In Utah, where the incumbent Republican governor chose not to run, Republican Spencer Cox and Democrat Chris Peterson appeared together in a remarkable series of public service ads, where they spoke of the need for civility and a peaceful transition of power. "We can debate issues without degrading each other's character," Peterson said. "We can disagree without hating each other," Cox added.[87] Deep-red Utah voted for Cox. In the only state where the governorship changed hands, the winner had a different approach to politics. Republican House member Greg Gianforte succeeded Bullock. In 2017, he had pleaded guilty to misdemeanor assault for body-slamming a reporter during his congressional campaign.

One retention was a positive sign for Democrats. In North Carolina, Roy Cooper held on with 51 percent of the vote even as the state voted Republican for president and Senate. Cooper benefited from his high profile during the pandemic. His televised press briefings gave him a level of visibility that his opponent, the state's Republican lieutenant governor, could not match. Overall, Republicans would hold twenty-seven governorships to the Democrats' twenty-three, a net gain of one.

There was little change in state legislatures, which was bad news for Democrats as they looked ahead to redistricting after the 2020 census. They had targeted the Arizona House and Senate, Iowa House, Minnesota Senate, North Carolina House and Senate, Pennsylvania House and Senate, and the Texas House. Republicans successfully defended each chamber while gaining the New Hampshire House and Senate. Kansas Republicans kept supermajorities that would enable them to pass redistricting plans over the Democratic governor's veto. And just a year after Virginia Democrats assumed unified control, the state's voters approved a ballot measure removing the legislature's power to draw the lines and giving it to an independent commission. After the election, FiveThirtyEight estimated that Republicans could draw 188 congressional districts while Democrats would control no more than 73.[88]

The Democrats' statehouse frustrations mirrored those at the national level. Emily Skopov, a candidate for a state legislative seat in Pennsylvania, told the *New York Times* that she tried to reassure voters, "I'm a fan of our police. I'm not looking to defund police." It did not work. Republicans hammered the message, and she lost. "A lot of the suburban districts that you're trying to flip, you can't win by just turning out your base," her campaign manager added. "We could get every Democratic vote in those districts and you're still not going to win. You have to be able to turn out independents and Republican voters for your message."[89] Biden's talk about transitioning away from fossil fuels may or may not have been defensible as policy, but it probably repelled voters in Texas and other oil-dependent states. And the party's adherence to pandemic guidelines may have hurt it most at the state legislative level. "The candidate that knocks on more doors in a state legislative race is going to outperform the district," Daniel Squadron, a former Democratic state senator from New York, told Russell Berman of *The Atlantic*. "We've never before had a scenario where one party did it and the other party didn't."[90]

As for state ballot measures, drugs were a big winner. Voters in Arizona, Montana, New Jersey, and South Dakota approved the legalization of recreational marijuana, while Mississippians and North Dakotans approved medical marijuana. Oregon voters decriminalized possession of small amounts of heroin and cocaine. They also legalized psilocybin—the active ingredient in "magic mushrooms"—making Oregon the first state to do so.[91] These results indicated a liberalization of attitudes toward drugs. In a Gallup survey, 68 percent backed legalization of marijuana, compared with just 12 percent in 1969.[92]

Results in California should encourage political observers to rethink stereotypes about the state. In 1978, state voters had passed Proposition 13, a measure that limited property taxes and helped launch the national tax revolt. By 2020, state Democrats and their allies reasoned that the California electorate had become much more liberal and so would approve a revision of the law. They proposed Proposition 15, which would have raised billions in revenue by stripping Prop 13 protections from many business properties. Opponents and proponents each spent more than $50 million, and in the end, it lost 48–52 percent.

Perhaps the most under-reported political story of the year was the defeat of California's Proposition 16. The measure was to be a repeal of Proposition 209, a 1996 ballot initiative that generally banned the consideration of race, sex, color, ethnicity, or national origin in public employment, public education, and public contracting. Progressives argued that this law hamstrung efforts to diversify public workforces and student bodies at state institutions of higher education. In June 2020, the Democratic supermajorities in the state legislature voted to put repeal on the November ballot. Democrats thought that Proposition 209 could not survive in a state that had become majority-minority and during a year when revulsion against Trump was likely to boost Democratic turnout in California. Yet voters rejected it, 43–57 percent.

Proposition 16 had every advantage. Proponents outspent opponents by a margin of 14 to 1.[93] It had the backing of the high-ranking state officials, all of whom were Democrats.[94] (No Republican had held statewide office in a decade.) Attorney General Xavier Becerra wrote favorable ballot language, with the headline "ALLOWS DIVERSITY AS A FACTOR IN PUBLIC EMPLOYMENT, EDUCATION, AND CONTRACTING DECISIONS."[95] But according to a pre-election poll, African Americans were the only major ethnic group to give it clear support. It split Hispanics (40 percent for, 42 percent against) and got substantial approval from non-Hispanic whites (53–35 percent) and Asia/Pacific Islanders (50–39 percent).[96]

A television spot by supporters said it was "opposed by those who have always opposed equality," as footage from the white supremacist march on Charlottesville played on screen. Wenyuan Wu, the executive director of the leading opposition group, told the *San Francisco Chronicle*, "I remember thinking to myself and talking to our chief consultant that this is a colossal strategic error on their part of painting us with a broad stroke as white nationalists and Trump supporters, because it's simply not true. . . . And I think strategically they lost partly because of that ad and that attitude, that arrogance."[97] More generally, people simply opposed racial or ethnic preferences—and not just in California. In a 2019 Pew survey, 73 percent said that colleges and universities should not consider race or ethnicity when making decisions about student admissions.[98]

Curiously, the issue has largely been absent from partisan politics at the national level. No one even mentioned the term "affirmative action" during the 2016 or 2020 presidential debates. It remains to be seen whether the California result will inject the issue into congressional or presidential politics in the future. Nevertheless, California elections and national surveys should cause us to ask whether political scientists and journalists have missed important undercurrents of public opinion. Just as the 1978 tax revolt shocked the national political community, the voters may have other surprises in store.

As the following chapter explains, the defeat of Donald Trump does not mean the end of disruption.

NOTES

1. "The Senate Powersharing Agreement of the 107th Congress (2001–2003): Key Features," Congressional Research Service, December 27, 2006, https://www.everycrsreport.com/files/20061227_RS20785_c2a33ed96b4cd522a2130c1b25f2bf 6b7661eeab.pdf.

2. Gary C. Jacobson, *The Electoral Origins of Divided Government* (Boulder, CO: Westview Press, 1990), 112–20.

3. John T. Pothier, "The Partisan Bias in Senate Elections," *American Politics Quarterly* 12 (January 1984): 89–100.

4. Michael S. Lewis-Becl and Richard Nadeau, "Split-Ticket Voting: The Effects of Cognitive Madisonianism," *Journal of Politics* 66 (February 2004): 97–112, at https://core.ac.uk/download/pdf/192654891.pdf.

5. Jeffrey M. Jones, "New High Favors One-Party Control of U.S. Federal Government," Gallup, October 2, 2020, https://news.gallup.com/poll/321158/new-high -favors-one-party-control-federal-government.aspx.

6. Molly E. Reynolds, *Vital Statistics on Congress* (Washington: Brookings Institution, 2020), https://www.brookings.edu/multi-chapter-report/vital-statistics-on -congress.

7. Katherine Schaeffer, "Slim Majorities Have Become More Common in the U.S. Senate and House," Pew Research Center, December 1, 2020, https://www .pewresearch.org/fact-tank/2020/12/01/slim-majorities-have-become-more-common -in-the-u-s-senate-and-house.

8. Frances Lee, *Insecure Majorities: Congress and the Perpetual Campaign* (Chicago: University of Chicago Press, 2016), ch. 6.

9. James W. Ceaser, Andrew E. Busch, and John J. Pitney Jr., *Defying the Odds: The 2016 Elections and American Politics* (Lanham, MD: Rowman & Littlefield, 2017), 149.

10. Robert Draper, "Can the G.O.P. Senate Majority Survive Donald Trump?" *New York Times Magazine*, July 17, 2016, https://www.nytimes.com/2016/07/17/ magazine/can-the-gop-senate-majority-survive-donald-trump.html.

11. Niv M. Sultan, "Outside Groups Spent More Than Candidates in 27 Races, Often by Huge Amounts," *Open Secrets*, February 24, 2017, https://www.opensecrets .org/news/2017/02/outside-groups-spent-more-than-candidates-in-27-races-often-by -huge-amounts.

12. David B. Magleby, "Change and Continuity in the Financing of the 2016 U.S. Federal Election," in *Financing the 2016 Election*, ed. David B. Magleby (Washington, DC: Brookings Institution Press, 2019), 34.

13. Reid Wilson, "The Untold Stories of the 2016 Battle for the Senate," *The Hill*, November 15, 2016, https://thehill.com/homenews/senate/306002-2016s-battle-for -senate-crushing-the-tea-party.

14. Karen Yourish and Paul Murray, "President Trump's 100 Days of Record-Low Approval Ratings," *New York Times*, May 1, 2017, https://www.nytimes.com/inter active/2017/02/28/us/politics/the-highs-and-lows-of-trumps-approval.html.

15. John T. Bennett, "Trump's Winning Pattern with Legislation Might Become a Thing of the Past: CQ Vote Studies," *Roll Call*, February 28, 2019, https://www.roll call.com/2019/02/28/trumps-winning-pattern-with-legislation-might-become-a-thing -of-the-past-cq-vote-studies.

16. Cristina Marcos, "GOP Lawmaker: Donors Are Pushing Me to Get Tax Reform Done," *The Hill*, November 7, 2017, https://thehill.com/homenews/house/359110 -gop-lawmaker-donors-are-pushing-me-to-get-tax-reform-done.

17. Dina Smeltz, "United in Goals, Divided on Means: Opinion Leaders Survey Results and Partisan Breakdowns from the 2014 Chicago Council Survey of American Opinion on US Foreign Policy," Chicago Council on Global Affairs, 2015, https:// web.archive.org/web/20201119185742/https://www.thechicagocouncil.org/sites/ default/files/2014%20Chicago%20Council%20Opinion%20Leaders%20Survey%20 Report_FINAL.pdf.

18. Frank Bruni, "Crying Wolf, Then Confronting Trump," *New York Times*, September 1, 2016, https://www.nytimes.com/2016/09/01/opinion/campaign-stops/ crying-wolf-then-confronting-trump.html.

19. Donald J. Trump, Twitter post, August 23, 2017, https://twitter.com/real DonaldTrump/status/900346953120141312?s=20.

20. Adam Edelman, "Jeff Flake Admits He Couldn't Win Primary as Trump Hails GOP 'Love Fest,'" NBC News, October 25, 2017, https://www.nbcnews.com/politics/ politics-news/flake-admits-i-couldn-t-win-gop-primary-be-proud-n814111.

21. Donald J. Trump, Twitter post, August 25, 2017, https://twitter.com/real DonaldTrump/status/901057864516734978?s=20.

22. Mark Sanford, "Mark Sanford: I Support You, Donald Trump. Now Release Your Tax Returns," *New York Times*, August 14, 2016, https://www.nytimes .com/2016/08/15/opinion/i-support-you-donald-trump-now-release-your-tax-returns .html.

23. Tim Alberta, "'I'm a Dead Man Walking,'" *Politico*, February 17, 2017, https://www.politico.com/magazine/story/2017/02/mark-sanford-profile-214791.

24. Donald J. Trump, Twitter post, June 12, 2018, https://twitter.com/real DonaldTrump/status/1006630395067039744?s=20.

25. http://www.epicjourney2008.com/2018/11/the-d-trip-analyzes-california.html.

26. Donald J. Trump, Twitter post, September 3, 2018, https://twitter.com/real DonaldTrump/status/1036681588573130752?s=20.

27. Sean Trende, "So, Was It a Wave?" RealClearPolitics, November 16, 2018, https://www.realclearpolitics.com/articles/2018/11/16/so_was_it_a_wave_138677 .html.

28. Jay Cost, "Republicans Remain in a Strong Position in State Legislatures," *National Review*, November 12, 2018, https://www.nationalreview.com/2018/11/ midterm-elections-republicans-strong-position-state-legislatures/.

29. United States Elections Project, "National General Election VEP Turnout Rates, 1789–Present," http://www.electproject.org/national-1789-present.

30. Nonprofit VOTE, "America Goes to the Polls: Voter Turnout and Election Policy in the 50 States," March 2019, https://www.nonprofitvote.org/documents/2019/03/america-goes-polls-2018.pdf.

31. Jordan Misra, "Voter Turnout Rates Among All Voting Age and Major Racial and Ethnic Groups Were Higher Than in 2014," U.S. Census Bureau, April 23, 2019, https://www.census.gov/library/stories/2019/04/behind-2018-united-states-midterm -election-turnout.html.

32. Donald J. Trump, Twitter post, November 12, 2018, https://twitter.com/real DonaldTrump/status/1061962869376540672?s=20.

33. Center for Responsive Politics, "Total Cost of Election (1998–2020)," https:// www.opensecrets.org/elections-overview/cost-of-election?cycle=2020&display=T& infl=Y.

34. Center for Responsive Politics, "Most Expensive Midterm Ever: Cost of 2018 Election Surpasses $5.7 Billion," February 6, 2019, https://www.opensecrets.org/ news/2019/02/cost-of-2018-election-5pnt7bil/.

35. Lisa Lerer, "ActBlue, the Democrats' Not-So-Secret Weapon," *New York Times*, November 16, 2018, https://www.nytimes.com/2018/11/16/us/politics/on -politics-actblue-democrats.html.

36. John Bresnahan and Rachel Bade, "McCarthy: 'I Had the Votes the First Day' to Be House Minority Leader,'" *Politico*, November 9, 2018, https://www.politico .com/story/2018/11/09/mccarthy-house-minority-leader-980534.

37. Alex Isenstadt, "Money Troubles: The GOP's Problem with Cash," *Politico*, November 12, 2018, https://www.politico.com/story/2018/11/12/republicans-fund raising-donations-2020-983243.

38. Elise Viebeck and Felicia Sonmez, "'Crisis Level': Republican Women Sound Warning After Election Losses," *Washington Post*, December 16, 2018, https://www .washingtonpost.com/powerpost/crisis-level-republican-women-sound-warning -after-election-losses/2018/12/16/e8c99eba-ffb4-11e8-83c0-b06139e540e5_story .html.

39. Kayla Webley Adler, "Elise Stefanik Wants the Unthinkable: More Women in the GOP," City and State New York, November 17, 2019, https://www.cityand- stateny.com/articles/personality/interviews-profiles/elise-stefanik-wants-the-unthink- able-more-women-in-the-gop.html.

40. Andrew E. Busch, *Horses in Midstream: U.S. Midterm Elections and Their Consequences* (Pittsburgh: University of Pittsburgh Press, 1999), 38.

41. Nicol C. Rae and John J. Pitney, "Class Connections: Congressional Classes and the Republicans of 1994," *The Forum* 12 (2014): 519–40.

42. Remarks by President Trump in Press Conference After Midterm Elec- tions, November 7, 2018, https://www.whitehouse.gov/briefings-statements/remarks -president-trump-press-conference-midterm-elections.

43. Remarks by President Trump in Meeting with Senate Minority Leader Chuck Schumer and House Speaker-Designate Nancy Pelosi, December 11, 2018, https:// www.whitehouse.gov/briefings-statements/remarks-president-trump-meeting-senate -minority-leader-chuck-schumer-house-speaker-designate-nancy-pelosi.

44. U.S. Department of Justice, Special Counsel's Office, *Report on the Investigation tnto Russian Interference in the 2016 Presidential Election*, March 2019, Volume vol. 1, p. 7, https://www.justice.gov/storage/report.pdf.

45. John Bresnahan and Heather Caygle, "Pelosi Wins Breathing Room on Impeachment After Mueller Findings," *Politico*, March 25, 2019, https://www.politico.com/story/2019/03/25/mueller-report-impeachment-pelosi-1234093.

46. Donald J. Trump, Twitter posts, July 27, 2019, https://twitter.com/realDonaldTrump/status/1155073965880172544?s=20.

47. Donald J. Trump, Twitter posts, July 14, 2019, https://twitter.com/realDonaldTrump/status/1150381395078000643?s=20.

48. Benjamin Weinthal, "Ilhan Omar, Rashida Tlaib, Jeremy Corbyn Top List of Worst Antisemites," *Jerusalem Post*, December 20, 2019, https://www.jpost.com/diaspora/wiesenthal-releases-ten-worst-outbreaks-of-antisemiticanti-israel-cases-611310.

49. Donald J. Trump, Twitter post, July 15, 2019, https://twitter.com/realDonaldTrump/status/1150879404593205249?s=20.

50. Amelia Thomson-DeVeaux and Laura Bronner, "Impeachment Didn't Change Minds—It Eroded Trust," FiveThirtyEight, February 18, 2020, https://fivethirtyeight.com/features/impeachment-didnt-change-minds-it-eroded-trust.

51. Domenico Montanaro, "Poll: Americans Overwhelmingly Say Impeachment Hearings Won't Change Their Minds," National Public Radio, November 19, 2019, https://www.npr.org/2019/11/19/780540637/poll-americans-overwhelmingly-say-impeachment-hearings-wont-change-their-minds.

52. David Wasserman, "36 Facts About the 2020 Elections," Cook Political Report, December 22, 2020, https://cookpolitical.com/analysis/national/national-politics/36-facts-about-2020-elections.

53. Wasserman, "36 Facts."

54. Busch, *Horses in Midstream*, 32–35.

55. Sarah Ewall-Wice, "Democrats Tout Fundraising Advantage in 2020 Congressional Elections," CBS News, January 17, 2020, https://www.cbsnews.com/news/dccc-democrats-tout-fundraising-advantage-in-2020-congressional-elections.

56. Jacob F. H. Smith offers a superb, detailed explanation of the frustrations of minority status in *Minority Party Misery: Political Powerlessness and Electoral Disengagement* (Ann Arbor: University of Michigan Press, 2021).

57. U.S. House Press Gallery, Casualty List: 116th Congress, October 26, 2020, https://pressgallery.house.gov/member-data/casualty-list. The GOP figure includes Tom Graves of Georgia, who resigned shortly before the election.

58. Ricardo Alonso-Zaldivar and Hannah Fingerhut, "AP-NORC Poll: Democrats Are Trusted More on Health Care," Associated Press, April 26, 2019, https://apnews.com/article/8e1a8ceef5224cb0b21a8c6aca9277fa.

59. Carroll Doherty et al., "Amid Campaign Turmoil, Biden Holds Wide Leads on Coronavirus, Unifying the Country," Pew Research Center, October 9, 2020, https://www.pewresearch.org/politics/wp-content/uploads/sites/4/2020/10/PP_2020.10.08_Election-and-Voter-Attitudes_FINAL.pdf.

60. William A. Galston, "Why Did House Democrats Underperform Compared to Joe Biden?" Brookings Institution, December 21, 2020, https://www.brookings .edu/blog/fixgov/2020/12/21/why-did-house-democrats-underperform-compared-to -joe-biden.

61. Donald P. Green and Alan S. Gerber, *Get Out the Vote: How to Increase Voter Turnout* (Washington, DC: Brookings Institution Press, 2019), 17.

62. Kate Irby, "California Democrat Said He Was Preparing for a Recount, but He Just Conceded House Race," *Fresno Bee*, December 4, 2020.

63. Sarah Ferris, Heather Caygle, and Ally Mutnick, "Inside the House Demo- crats' Post-Election Reckoning," *Politico*, November 13, 2020, https://www.politico .com/news/2020/11/13/house-democrats-post-election-reckoning-436335.

64. Adam Nagourney, "A Stinging Setback in California Is a Warning for Democrats in 2022," *New York Times*, December 26, 2020, https://www.nytimes .com/2020/12/26/us/california-republicans.html.

65. Rachael Bade and Erica Werner, "Centrist House Democrats Lash Out at Liberal Colleagues, Blame Far-Left Views for Costing the Party Seats," *Washington Post*, November 5, 2020, https://www.washingtonpost.com/politics/house-democrats -pelosi-election/2020/11/05/1ddae5ca-1f6e-11eb-90dd-abd0f7086a91_story.html.

66. Ben Jacobs, "Why 'Socialism' Killed Democrats in Florida," *New York*, November 17, 2020, https://nymag.com/intelligencer/2020/11/republican-socialism -attacks-haunt-democrats-in-florida.html.

67. Jacobs, "Why 'Socialism' Killed Democrats."

68. Author's calculation from data at https://www.opensecrets.org/parties/index .php?cmte=&cycle=2020.

69. Center for Responsive Politics, "Elections Overview," https://www.open secrets.org/elections-overview?cycle=2020&display=A&type=G.

70. Bridget Bowman, "House Recruiter to GOP: 'Do a Better Job of Looking like America,'" *Roll Call*, April 10, 2019, https://www.rollcall.com/2019/04/10/house -recruiter-to-gop-do-a-better-job-of-looking-like-america.

71. Susan Brooks, "Winning with Women," *Ripon Forum*, February 2020, https:// riponsociety.org/article/winning-with-women.

72. Donald J. Trump, Twitter post, April 14, 2020, https://twitter.com/real DonaldTrump/status/1250067500190089217?s=20.

73. Tobias Hoonhout, "Why California Republicans Stopped Complaining about Ballot Harvesting and Embraced the Process," *National Review*, November 22, 2020, https://www.nationalreview.com/news/why-california-republicans-stopped -complaining-about-ballot-harvesting-and-embraced-the-process.

74. Donald J. Trump, Twitter post, December 22, 2020, https://twitter.com/real DonaldTrump/status/1341547750710800385?s=20.

75. "Maine Senate: Collins vs. Gideon," RealClearPolitics, https://www.realclear politics.com/epolls/2020/senate/me/maine_senate_collins_vs_gideon-6928.html.

76. Eliana Miller, "Nine of the 10 Most Expensive Senate Races of All Time Happened in 2020," *Open Secrets*, December 9, 2020, https://www.opensecrets.org/ news/2020/12/most-expensive-races-of-all-time-senate2020.

77. Center for Responsive Politics, "Elections Overview," https://www.opensecrets.org/elections-overview.

78. Stephanie Saul, Kate Kelly and Michael LaForgia, "2,596 Trades in One Term: Inside Senator Perdue's Stock Portfolio," *New York Times*, December 2, 2020, https://www.nytimes.com/2020/12/02/us/politics/david-perdue-stock-trades.html.

79. Paul Kane, "Blacklist, 'Swamp Creature' and 'Potomac Panic Polka': Republicans Turn On Each Other in U.S. Senate Race in Georgia," *Washington Post*, February 15, 2020, https://www.washingtonpost.com/powerpost/blacklist-swamp-creature-and-potomac-panic-polka-republicans-turn-on-each-other-in-us-senate-race-in-georgia/2020/02/15/53282614-4f5f-11ea-9b5c-eac5b16dafaa_story.html.

80. Karl Evers-Hillstrom, "Georgia Senate Races Shatter Spending Records," *Open Secrets*, January 4, 2021, https://www.opensecrets.org/news/2021/01/georgia-senate-races-shatter-records.

81. Donald Judd and Ryan Nobles, "Georgia Republican Senator Willfully Mispronounces Kamala Harris' Name at Trump Rally," CNN, October 17, 2020, https://www.cnn.com/2020/10/16/politics/david-perdue-kamala-harris/index.html.

82. Luis Noe-Bustamante and Abby Budiman, "Black, Latino and Asian Americans Have Been Key to Georgia's Registered Voter Growth Since 2016," December 21, 2020, Pew Research Center, https://www.pewresearch.org/fact-tank/2020/12/21/black-latino-and-asian-americans-have-been-key-to-georgias-registered-voter-growth-since-2016.

83. James Arkin and Andrew Desiderio, "How Warnock and Ossoff Painted Georgia Blue and Flipped the Senate," *Politico*, January 7, 2021, https://www.politico.com/news/2021/01/07/warnock-ossoff-flipped-senate-georgia-456310.

84. Donald J. Trump Twitter post, January 1, 2021, https://twitter.com/realDonaldTrump/status/1345111621430091777?ref_src=twsrc%5Etfw.

85. Amy Gardner, "'I Just Want to Find 11,780 Votes': In Extraordinary Hour-Long Call, Trump Pressures Georgia Secretary of State to Recalculate the Vote in His Favor," *Washington Post*, January 3, 2021, https://www.washingtonpost.com/politics/trump-raffensperger-call-georgia-vote/2021/01/03/d45acb92-4dc4-11eb-bda4-615aaefd0555_story.html.

86. Drew DeSilver, "Split U.S. Senate Delegations Have Become Less Common in Recent Years," Pew Research Center, January 4, 2018, https://www.pewresearch.org/fact-tank/2018/01/04/split-u-s-senate-delegations-have-become-less-common-in-recent-years/.

87. Ben Winslow, "Spencer Cox, Chris Peterson Unite to Plead for Civility, a Peaceful Transition of Power," KSTU-TV, October 20, 2020, https://www.fox13now.com/news/election-2020/spencer-cox-chris-peterson-unite-to-plead-for-civility-a-peaceful-transition-of-power.

88. Nathaniel Rakich and Elena Mejía, "Republicans Won Almost Every Election Where Redistricting Was at Stake," FiveThirtyEight, November 18, 2020, https://fivethirtyeight.com/features/republicans-won-almost-every-election-where-redistricting-was-at-stake/.

89. Trip Gabriel, "How Democrats Suffered Crushing Down-Ballot Losses Across America," *New York Times*, November 28, 2020, https://www.nytimes.com/2020/11/28/us/politics/democrats-republicans-state-legislatures.html.

90. Russell Berman, "The Failure That Could Haunt Democrats for a Decade," *The Atlantic*, November 10, 2020, https://www.theatlantic.com/politics/archive/2020/11/democrats-2020-elections-state-legislatures/617047/.

91. Amanda Zoch, "Voters Pass Majority of 2020 Ballot Measure Issues," *State Legislatures*, November 9, 2020, https://www.ncsl.org/research/elections-and-campaigns/voters-pass-majority-of-2020-ballot-measure-issues-magazine20201.aspx.

92. Megan Brenan, "Support for Legal Marijuana Inches Up to New High of 68%," Gallup, November 9, 2020, https://news.gallup.com/poll/323582/support-legal-marijuana-inches-new-high.aspx.

93. Thomas Peele and Daniel J. Willis, "Yes on Prop. 16 Has Big Fundraising Lead in Effort to Restore Affirmative Action in California," EdSource, October 30, 2020, https://edsource.org/2020/yes-on-prop-16-has-big-fundraising-lead-in-effort-to-restore-affirmative-action-in-california/642647.

94. Mikhail Zinshteyn, "Affirmative Action Has Tons of Endorsements—So Why Is Prop. 16 Trailing?" CalMatters, November 9, 2020, https://calmatters.org/education/2020/10/prop-16-affirmative-action-trailing.

95. California Secretary of State, Official California Voter Information Guide, General Election, November 3, 2020, https://voterguide.sos.ca.gov/propositions/16.

96. Mark DiCamillo, "Close Elections Forecast for Proposition 15 (Split Roll Property Taxes) and Proposition 22 (App-based Drivers) Prop. 16 (Diversity) and Prop. 21 (Rent Control) Trail," Institute of Government Studies, October 26, 2020, https://escholarship.org/uc/item/2pr670k8.

97. Eric Ting, "'They Lost Partly Because of That Ad': How No on Prop. 16 Organizers Knew the Measure Would Fail," *San Francisco Chronicle*, December 2, 2020, https://www.sfgate.com/politics/article/Proposition-16-California-affirmative-action-why-15763791.php.

98. Nikki Graf, "Most Americans Say Colleges Should Not Consider Race or Ethnicity in Admissions," Pew Research Center, February 25, 2019, https://www.pewresearch.org/fact-tank/2019/02/25/most-americans-say-colleges-should-not-consider-race-or-ethnicity-in-admissions/.

Chapter Six

A Republic, If You Can Keep It
Election Aftermath and the Future

If many Americans were concerned about the future of American democracy before the vote, their concerns first grew, and then exploded, in the post-election period. President Trump pressed his claims of fraud, his critics accused him of undermining democracy, and Americans grew even less trusting of their institutions and one another. Then, in early January, long after electoral drama has usually drained away, events cascaded to a crescendo of mob action in Washington. Once the election was (finally) settled, big questions remained about where American politics were headed after January 20, 2021. What will happen to the parties' coalitions? What course would former president Donald Trump take, and to what effect? Would Americans try to settle their differences over explosive issues of ballot access and ballot security? What other institutional questions will occupy the country? And could Joe Biden unify the country as he had promised?

THE POST-ELECTION STRUGGLE: "STOP THE STEAL" VERSUS "PROTECT DEMOCRACY"

The close results in pivotal states led, as many had feared, to an extended post-election controversy that exposed and expanded national divisions even more than the events of 2020 had already done. Unlike Florida in 2000, where everything hinged on a few hundred votes in a single state, the Trump campaign pursued allegations of irregularities that had to reverse tens of thousands of votes in multiple states in order to change the ultimate outcome. Consequently, from the very beginning, Trump's claims were both more extensive and less likely to succeed than anything Al Gore pressed in Florida twenty years before.

On one side, in the early morning hours of the day after the election—long before any solid evidence could have been compiled on such a scale—Trump made the sweeping claim that fraud had denied him reelection. The claim had been telegraphed in the summer and again days before the election, and it came so quickly that many suspected that it was driven less by facts on the ground than by a predetermined strategy for dealing with an unfavorable outcome—perhaps abetted by the president's inability to come to terms with his own loss.[1] His strongest critics immediately saw evidence of authoritarianism and an assault on democracy in the legal battles he subsequently waged.

On the other side, the Biden camp—a group which, it is fair to say, included most of the major media—insisted that fraud on any significant scale does not happen in the United States. Where Trump decided that there was fraud first and then went about trying to find it, others made an a priori assumption that there could not possibly be massive fraud and then summarily dismissed the charges without serious examination. Trump's supporters saw in this attitude a partisan whitewash of what they quickly began to call "the Steal." They noted that there is actually a long list of instances of fraud in contemporary elections,[2] starting with a North Carolina U.S. House race in 2018 where there was sufficient fraud to cause the election to be vacated and run again.[3] About a thousand individuals voted twice—once by mail and once in person—in the 2020 Georgia primary, though prosecutors ultimately declined to charge them.[4] And in 2016, courts stopped Michigan's presidential recount when it was found that 37 percent of Detroit precincts recorded more votes than workers tallied in the poll books.[5]

In reality, the post-election struggle was complex and long did not fit neatly into either narrative. It actually involved a wide variety of different kinds of allegations, some of which were unproven or flatly proven false, some of which were supported by circumstantial evidence only, and some of which were true or probably true but rendered irrelevant by courts for one or more reasons. Ultimately, Trump made legal challenges in Arizona, Georgia, Michigan, Nevada, Pennsylvania, and Wisconsin.[6] Elements of the fight included the following.

Recounts

Wisconsin and Georgia, two states that Biden led by less than one percent, held recounts, Wisconsin in two counties and Georgia statewide. The Wisconsin recount confirmed Biden as the victor,[7] though the Trump camp enjoyed a brief moment of hope in Georgia when two Republican-leaning counties discovered that they had originally reported incomplete results. Updated results narrowed Biden's lead by about a thousand votes but did not change the winner.[8] A second Georgia recount again confirmed Biden as the winner.[9]

Conditions for Fraud

The Trump campaign argued in several states that either laxity or deliberate malfeasance had created conditions making widespread fraud possible. To support this, it produced sworn affidavits by multiple election observers in Pennsylvania and Michigan contending that they had been prevented from effectively observing vote counting in Philadelphia and Detroit.[10] In Philadelphia, Republican observers had to get a court order allowing them to observe from six feet away, and even then there were delays in conforming to the order. Local election officials countered that observers from both parties had been present, though one in Philadelphia had been ejected for violating protocols prohibiting filming.[11] Republicans also noted that Pennsylvania, Georgia, and some other states had discontinued rigorous signature checks or the requirement of a witness signature on mail-in ballots, and that some had allowed unsupervised ballot drop-boxes and/or "ballot harvesting," a practice wherein a private individual or group can collect and deposit a large number of ballots from voters. A strong piece of circumstantial evidence, Trump supporters argued, was that heavily Democratic jurisdictions in the key states had stopped vote counting in the early morning with Trump ahead. Nevertheless, creating the conditions for fraud is not itself proof that fraud occurred.

Voting by Ineligible Voters

The Trump campaign and outside groups claimed that they had evidence in Georgia, Nevada, Michigan, and elsewhere that a non-trivial number of ineligible voters cast ballots. A detailed breakdown was offered in Georgia, where pro-Trump analysts Matt Braynard and Bryan Geels contended that more than 20,000 non-residents, over 66,000 who were too young to legally register, and 10,315 dead people had voted, along with a significant number of ineligible felons and people illegally reporting a PO box as an address. By their count, the total number of ineligible voters who cast ballots far exceeded the 11,000-vote margin separating Joe Biden and Donald Trump. State election officials and competing experts contended the Braynard/Geels analysis was "riddled with errors" resulting from use of unreliable databases and failure to account for complications in the law, and a review found only two "dead" voters.[12] In other states such as Pennsylvania and Michigan, some postal workers testified that they had been instructed by supervisors to backdate ballots; though there was reason to question such claims.[13] In Wisconsin, Trump alleged that election officials "were directed to fill in missing information on ballot envelopes, issued absentee ballots without receiving applications and allowed people to improperly claim a 'confined' absentee voting status."[14] Trump also claimed in Arizona that "many thousands" of ballots had been improperly assessed or been mishandled.[15]

Trump's supporters pointed out, as circumstantial evidence, that several key states had much lower rejected-ballot rates than usual, implying (though not proving) that a significant number of improper ballots that would have been disallowed in past years were counted in 2020. There were other possible explanations, though: state laws were changed to reduce the grounds for rejection and major public information efforts better educated voters about how to avoid ballot rejection.[16] Courts uniformly proved unwilling to halt the election certification process on the basis of these allegations. The evidence was frequently deficient, witnesses sometimes recanted, and the remedy—invalidation of the election results—was too draconian.[17] And in Georgia, a detailed signature audit of a sample of 15,000 Cobb County absentee ballots showed nothing amiss.[18]

Industrial-Scale Election Fraud

Except in extremely close states such as Georgia, votes by ineligible individuals could not have been sufficient to change the result. But the Trump campaign and outside attorneys also made charges that big-city Democrats were guilty of industrial-scale election fraud—that is, the systematic manufacturing and widespread addition or subtraction of votes. In Detroit, Philadelphia, Los Vegas, and Atlanta, eyewitnesses or video evidence was presented alleging that large bundles of pre-marked ballots were dropped into the system or that certain vote-counting supervisors ran the same ballots through vote counting multiple times. Security footage from State Farm Arena in Fulton County, Georgia, caused a stir when it appeared that election supervisors dismissed observers and then proceeded to illegally count a large number of ballots stored under a table. Election officials held that the observers had voluntarily walked away and had never been told that counting was done for the night, but Republican observers said they had been told to leave and news accounts from the time indicated that election officials had declared to the media that counting was suspended for the evening.[19] An investigation by the secretary of state's office, buttressed by a frame-by-frame analysis of the video, concluded that there was no wrongdoing and no mystery ballots had been brought into the building, though it did not fully explain the departure of observers.[20]

The most extreme claim, advanced by both the Trump campaign and outside attorneys Sidney Powell and Lin Wood, was that a widely used vote-counting software (Dominion) had been altered to switch Trump's and Biden's votes in Georgia, Michigan, and (perhaps) elsewhere. Powell went so far as to claim, in a blockbuster press conference with Rudy Giuliani, that communist China, Cuba, and Venezuela might be behind the Dominion troubles. Some Democrats, including senators Elizabeth Warren, Bernie Sanders, and Ron Wyden, had previously expressed concerns about Dominion voting systems,[21] but Powell provided no evidence for her claims. The negative reaction, even among many Republican officeholders and conservative commentators such as *National Review* editor Rich Lowry and talk radio personality Rush Limbaugh, was so strong that team Trump dropped its affiliation with Powell a few days later. Lowry called it "the most outlandish press conference ever held by a team of lawyers representing the President of the United States."[22] The Dominion theory grew out of the experience of one small county in Michigan—Antrim County—that had used Dominion and, on Election Day, reported reversed results to the Michigan secretary of state's office. Nevertheless, officials indicated the problem was not with vote counting, but rather with vote reporting, and that no other county seemed to have such a problem. An unofficial vote audit of Antrim County by a private group called Allied Security Operations Group claimed to find evidence of systematic error benefiting Biden, but its findings were debunked by a hand recount of every ballot cast in the county, which verified the original results.[23] Under threat of legal action, the conservative website American Thinker retracted claims of misconduct, apologizing to Dominion for making false statements and to its readers for abandoning journalistic principles.[24]

A number of circumstantial arguments were made by Trump's supporters for industrial-scale fraud. Most were not well grounded. They asked, for example, how Biden could win the presidency when Republican congressional candidates were doing so well down-ballot. In actuality, George H. W. Bush in 1988, Bill Clinton in 1992, George W. Bush in 2000, and Donald Trump in 2016 all won the presidency while losing House seats. Some argued that no candidate in a hundred years had lost the presidency while winning both Florida and Ohio (actually, Nixon did in 1960, though allegations of fraud in that year cloud the case), but at some point bellwether states stop being bellwethers. Prior to 1936, Maine was widely considered a bellwether; before Alf Landon won the state in the midst of Franklin Roosevelt's reelection landslide, it was said that "As Maine goes, so goes the nation." From 1904 through 2004, only one candidate won the White House without prevailing in Missouri (in 1956, Eisenhower lost Missouri to Stevenson 50.1–49.9 percent). Then Barack Obama did it in 2008, and the state has voted for the presidential loser two more times since then. In any event, political scientists had long ago dismissed the whole idea of bellwethers.[25]

Other circumstantial arguments were based on alleged statistical anomalies. For example, economist Charles J. Ciccetti argued there was less than a one in quadrillion chance that Biden could overcome Trump's election night lead in key states based on how Biden underperformed Hillary Clinton in 50 other urban areas and on random samples of voters. Pennsylvania Attorney General Josh Shapiro called the claim "utter nonsense" and pointed out that the outstanding ballots were long expected to have a pro-Biden tilt, not mirror a representative sampling of voters.[26] Trump supporters on social media also argued that Benford's law, a test having to do with the distribution of numbers in a set, demonstrated the probability of fraud. However, numerous authorities held that Benford's law, which is used by financial regulators to detect the possibility of cooked books, was not a reliable test for the very different phenomenon of vote fraud.[27]

Other analyses assessed the votes that came in after the early-morning halt, which seemed in some places to have produced an unnaturally large margin for Biden, even taking into account that most were mail ballots. In Pennsylvania, purported analyst Phil Waldron calculated that Biden won 99.4 percent of some 575,000 votes that were reported in unusually large batches or "spikes." Similar spikes were allegedly recorded in Wisconsin, Michigan, and Georgia.[28] A Reuters News analysis came up with conflicting numbers that seemed more realistic, and a close study of the Georgia "spike" showed no such thing.[29] By comparing absentee votes from adjacent precincts in different counties, University of Chicago economist John Lott concluded that there may have been as many as 55,000 fraudulent votes in Fulton County, Georgia, and Allegheny County, Pennsylvania.[30] However, others pointed out that Fulton County most likely employed more widespread use of ballot collection boxes and were not easily comparable to their neighbors.[31]

Overall, such circumstantial evidence ran headlong into a different form of circumstantial evidence pointing in the opposite direction. If there had been

Table 6.1. Biden Vote Percentage in Exit Polls vs. Certified Results in Key States

	Exit Polls	Certified Results
Arizona	48.8%	49.2%
Georgia	49.8%	49.5%
Michigan	50.9%	50.6%
Nevada	50.0%	50.1%
Pennsylvania	50.0%	49.9%
Wisconsin	50.1%	49.5%

Sources: CNN 2020 Presidential Election Exit Polls, calculations by author based on reported vote by party; certified results from Dave Leip's Election Atlas, www.uselectionatlas.org

widespread fraud favoring Biden, one would expect that his certified vote totals would be notably higher than his exit poll results in that state. However, in key states where large-scale fraud was alleged, there was no significant disparity between Biden's support in exit polls and his certified vote totals. (Trump supporters would answer that the exit polls may have exaggerated Biden's actual vote much as the pre-election polls did.)

Treatment of "Ballot Curing"

There were also two broad legal or constitutional arguments made by the Trump camp. In these instances, the facts were not in dispute. Rather, the debate was over the proper interpretation of state law or the U.S. Constitution. The narrower of these had to do with the practice of "ballot curing"—that is, allowing mail voters to fix errors (of, for example, address) after having submitted their ballot. State law in Pennsylvania gave county election officials the choice of whether to allow ballot curing; Democratic-leaning counties tended to do so, Republican-leaning counties tended not to. The Trump campaign brought suit on equal protection grounds, insofar as voters in some counties were treated differently from voters in other counties. The courts dismissed the case on the grounds that all counties equally had the option to engage in ballot curing. In any case, relatively few ballots were involved.[32]

Inadmissable Changes in Election Law

In election law, as in all law, state law is inferior to the state constitution, and both state law and state constitution are inferior to the federal constitution. The federal constitution makes clear that state legislatures shall determine the manner in which presidential electors are chosen.

On the basis of this foundation, the Trump campaign challenged Pennsylvania law in two respects. First, it noted that the Pennsylvania state supreme court had essentially rewritten Pennsylvania election law to eliminate signature verification for mail ballots and accept ballots up to three days after Election Day. In October, this dispute had actually gone to the U.S. Supreme Court, which had deadlocked 4–4 over whether to accept the case at that point.[33] Now Trump wanted to bring it back into the court system. But experts estimated that fewer than 10,000 ballots had arrived in the state supreme court's three-day window, not nearly enough to make up Trump's 80,000 vote deficit in the state. Both state and federal court dismissed the suit.[34]

A more serious challenge followed, one that could actually have flipped the state to Trump. The law allowing broad mail-ballot voting in Pennsylvania had been passed in 2019 by the state legislature, but upon examination it seemed to conflict with the state constitution, which established that absentee voting could only be permitted for very limited purposes such as illness or absence from the state. The Trump lawyers argued in state court that the law violated the state constitution, rendering most mail ballots in Pennsylvania problematic, and with them the state's election certification. The state supreme court rejected the argument, not on the basis that it was legally wrong but on the basis that a challenge to the law should have been made before the election, when it was still possible to remedy the mistake painlessly. Relying on the doctrine of *laches*, it was, the court said, too late.[35]

In early December, just when it seemed this line of argument had reached a dead end, the attorney general of Texas, Ken Paxton, filed suit with the U.S. Supreme Court contending that Pennsylvania and three other states had violated the U.S. Constitution when their courts and/or executive officials had changed voting rules without consent of their legislatures. Claiming that its citizens were harmed by the way the named defendants damaged the constitutional integrity of the presidential election process, Texas held that the Supreme Court should hear the case under its original jurisdiction to decide controversies between states. Within days, another eighteen Republican state attorneys general signed on to the suit. The Court declined to take the case, on the grounds that the State of Texas did not have standing to challenge election laws of other states. Only Justices Alito and Thomas supported even hearing the case, and they indicated that they would not actually have supported a remedy.[36] Though it angered Trump supporters, the ruling was widely praised by both liberal and conservative legal scholars, who contended that a nearly boundless field for mischief might have opened if the Supreme Court had allowed a state to claim harm on the basis of another state's voting rules.[37] At the same time, the Court's refusal did not address the merits of the argument.

These six weeks of legal wrangling ended in total failure for Trump. In no state was the election reversed or decertified, though the reasons varied. Often there was simply not enough (or any) credible direct evidence; sometimes the number of ballots involved was insufficient to make a real difference; sometimes the issue was a legal doctrine regarding timing or standing. In more than a few cases, the Trump lawyers themselves scaled back their claims.[38] Almost always, hanging over the proceedings was the question of remedy. If hundreds, or thousands, or even tens of thousands, of faulty ballots were mingled among millions, do we really invalidate the millions?[39] Moreover, no single state alone would make a difference in the end result, so the safe judicial play was always to stand aside and let the certification process play out without interference. Some legal analysts also perceived confusion among Republicans, who lacked a coherent national legal strategy and a well-prepared legal team.[40]

What can one say about Trump's charges? Overall, it seemed clear that Trump had already decided in the early hours of November 4 that he was the victim of a fraudulent election, and his character allowed no subsequent deviation from that conclusion. When the Department of Homeland Security chief of cybersecurity Chris Krebs declared the election had been the most secure ever from a cybersecurity standpoint, Trump fired him.[41] When Attorney General William Barr reported that Department of Justice investigators had not yet uncovered evidence of sufficient fraud to have tilted the election, the president responded with an angry tweetstorm, and Barr resigned not long after.[42] (Barr reportedly told the president privately that claims of massive fraud were "bulls—t."[43]) Shortly before Christmas, presidential advisor Peter Navarro released a thirty-seven-page report summarizing the Trump campaign's claims, and it was a mixed bag of the plausible, the implausible, and the fantastical.[44] Trump's insistence that he had won a landslide was not consistent with reality. That there were actual irregularities, however, including some number of ineligible votes cast and some legally dubious procedures adopted by state and local election officials that padded Biden's vote totals, seems probable. Some statistical anomalies remained. Some continued raising questions about the State Farm Arena video. And the contention that several states violated the constitutional requirement that selection of electors be legislatively defined has some support among legal scholars. While Trump focused on fraud that his legal team could not prove, his bigger problem was the change in voting regulations in many jurisdictions, changes that could have been challenged but were not, or were not effectively, when it would have mattered.

As the legal challenges spun out one by one, the president's side took a more radical turn. Suggestions were floated by Trump supporters, including Donald Trump Jr., that in disputed states with Republican legislatures, the legislature could declare the popular election irremediably contaminated and could instead appoint an alternative set of (pro-Trump) electors.[45] This stratagem had been predicted by the Transition Integrity Project over the summer, having been used by both Republicans and Democrats when they had lost simulations. Leaving aside the legal difficulties with such an approach—state legislatures can undoubtedly decide how their state's electors are selected, but it is far from clear that they can do so retroactively—the political backlash would have been enormous. The maneuver could also have triggered a real constitutional crisis, including refusal by the House of Representatives to affirm the electoral vote that would result. Some Republican legislators were receptive to the idea, especially after a round of hearings featuring witnesses to alleged fraud in Pennsylvania, Michigan, Georgia, and Arizona, but most were not, including necessary legislative leaders.[46] For example, Michigan's House Speaker Lee Chatfield, who had been invited to the White House to hear Trump's case, said, "I can't fathom risking our norms, traditions and institutions to pass a resolution retroactively changing the electors for Trump, simply because some think there may have been enough widespread fraud to give him the win. I fear we'd lose our country forever. This truly would bring mutually assured destruction for every future election in regards to the Electoral College. And I can't stand for that. I won't."[47] In Michigan, some Republican electors showed up anyway on December 14 but were denied entry to the State Capitol.[48] In Georgia, the legislature was not in session and Republican Governor Brian Kemp declined to call it together to consider such a proposal.[49] On December 14, the duly certified electors met in their state capitals and cast 306 votes for Biden and 232 for Trump, as predicted.

From there, responses to Trump's electoral plight radicalized further among some on the right. Shortly after the Supreme Court torpedoed the Texas suit, Texas Republican chair Allen West argued that it might make sense for "law-abiding states" to form a new union, a declaration that sounded to many like support for secession, though West denied that was what he meant.[50] Then, in a television interview, former National Security advisor Michael Flynn endorsed a call by a conservative group called the "We the People Convention" that Trump should consider implementing "limited martial law" to seize voting machines and, in states with electoral controversies, "rerun" the election.[51] The *New York Times* reported that the issue was raised in a White House meeting and that his senior advisors vigorously opposed it. Trump called the report "fake news," but Army leaders felt compelled to issue a statement saying, "There is no role for the U.S. military in determining the outcome of an American election."[52] As with the idea of alternate electors, but much more so, Flynn's suggestion received little support from Trump's side of the aisle.[53] For his part, Senate majority leader Mitch McConnell congratulated Joe Biden on his victory shortly after the Electoral College voted, and voices on the right increasingly urged Trump to abandon the fight. On December 27, the *New York Post*, long a supporter of Trump, ran an editorial urging the president to "Stop the Insanity," as the front-page headline blared.[54]

Led by Representative Mo Brooks (R-AL), some House Republicans declared that they would object to the electors from a number of disputed states when Congress convened to officially count the electoral votes on January 6. After some period when no Republican senators publicly stated their intention to do the same, Josh Hawley of Missouri announced that he, too, would object. Not to be outdone, Texas Senator Ted Cruz led a group of eleven GOP senators who said they would object unless a commission were created to do an "emergency audit" of election results in contested states. Each objection would trigger a two-hour debate in each house of Congress, after which a vote would be taken on whether to accept the official count. Hawley explained his decision by saying, "At the very least, Congress should investigate allegations of voter fraud and adopt measures to secure the integrity of our elections. But Congress has so far failed to act."[55] Hawley also noted that one or more congressional Democrats had objected to the electoral vote counts in 2000, 2004, and 2016, though Barbara Boxer, an objecting senator from California in 2004, contended that the circumstances were "not comparable" because Democratic nominee John Kerry had already conceded.[56] In a sense, Hawley and Cruz were playing both sides, declining to claim that the election was "stolen" but refusing to simply accept the results.[57]

Understanding that even such a debate and congressional vote would not result in a Trump victory, with the House in Democratic hands and most Republican senators refusing to go along, some of the president's supporters employed a last, desperate stratagem. The vice president is officially responsible for announcing electoral vote results, and the Electoral Count Act of 1887 declares that he is essentially bound by the results obtained through the process of certification by states and approval by Congress. Representative Louis Gohmert (R-TX) launched a last-minute lawsuit against Vice President Mike Pence, claiming that it was unconstitutional to require the vice president to recognize the approved results. Rather, Gohmert argued, he should have a free hand to accept or reject electoral votes submitted by the states. However, both Pence and the House of Representatives asked the federal courts to dismiss the suit, which in fact occurred in short order. That such a suit was even entertained was a sign of the degree to which American politics has become a blood sport in which many see defeat not as a temporary setback to be overcome at the next election but as a potentially irremediable turn in an existential struggle. Consequently, consideration of long-term institutional consequences has, in some quarters on left and right, been completely subordinated to short-term tactical imperatives. Of course, Gohmert's approach would have allowed Vice President Al Gore to simply declare himself the winner in 2000. Even after the suit was dismissed, Trump continued advancing the theory that Pence could unilaterally refuse to accept contested electors, though the underlying premise of the suit itself was that under current law he could not.

It was obvious why Democrats would give no quarter in the post-election contest, but why did so many Republicans continue supporting, or at least not opposing, Trump's campaign to stay in office long after it should have become clear that he could not prevail? Some believed sincerely that massive fraud had indeed occurred. They may have thought back to the early months of the Trump presidency when Trump had drawn ridicule by wildly alleging without evidence that Barack Obama had spied on his campaign. It had turned out to be true, at least in a manner of speaking. As journalist Byron York noted, many Republicans had also convinced themselves that Trump was headed for a landslide victory, so how else to explain the result except fraud?[58] Others may have continued the fight in order to discourage fraud by Democrats in future elections. For some, the accuracy of the charge may have been secondary, as long as it was at least plausible; Democrats, in their view, had earned the delegitimization of their winner after spending four years delegitimizing Trump on unproven charges of Russian collusion.

Not least, Trump continued to wield powerful sway over large swaths of the Republican primary electorate. In early December, a Fox News poll indicated that two-thirds of Republicans agreed that the election was "stolen from Trump." Only a quarter of Independents and 10 percent of Democrats agreed.[59] More than a few Republicans did not want to get in the way of the angry Trump steamroller or hoped to capitalize on it to raise funds or position themselves for future office. Former House speaker Newt Gingrich undoubtedly summed up the views of many Republicans when he wrote to explain why he would not accept Biden's victory: "As I thought about it, I realized my anger and fear were not narrowly focused on votes. My unwillingness to relax and accept that [*sic*] the election grew out of a level of outrage and alienation unlike anything I had experienced in more than 60 years involvement in public affairs." That outrage, Gingrich said, was based on Russiagate, four years of unrelenting "resistance" to Trump by Democrats, and consistent media and social media unfairness and censorship. The election itself was "simply the final stroke of a four-year establishment-media power grab."[60]

For the first month of the post-election scrum, Trump relied on conventional legal contests. Though unsuccessful, they were not outside the bounds of normal electoral disputes. For the next month, his strategy devolved into a series of maneuvers that were peaceful but outside the spirit, and arguably the letter, of the law. After the turn of the year, even many of the president's erstwhile supporters concluded that defeat had strained him beyond the breaking point. On the weekend before the congressional session met to formally count electoral votes, the *Washington Post* published a story based on a recorded phone call made by President Trump to Georgia Secretary of State Brad Raffensperger. In the call, the president implored Raffensperger to "recalculate": "I just want to find another 11,780 votes." Raffensperger, who had no legal means to do what Trump asked even if he had wanted to, dismissed the entreaties from the White House.[61] Raffensperger recorded the call for self-protection. Trump "is a man who has a history of reinventing history as it occurs," an aide told *Politico*. "So if he's going to try to dispute anything on the call, it's nice to have something like this, hard evidence, to dispute whatever he's claiming about the secretary."[62] After Trump falsely claimed in a tweet that Raffensperger had been "unwilling, or unable, to answer" questions about fraud, he decided to leak the audio. A few days later, he released a point-by-point refutation of the president's fraud claims as they related to Georgia.[63]

Then, in the days and hours before the January 5 Georgia runoff election, Trump both held a rally urging Republicans to vote and simultaneously escalated his war against the state's Republican leaders, declaring the upcoming Senate elections "illegal and invalid."[64] Many Republicans blamed his antics for their loss of both Georgia Senate seats and hence their Senate majority (see chapter 5). The same day as the runoff election, over 100 Republican state legislators, most from Arizona, Georgia, Michigan, Pennsylvania, and Wisconsin, released letters to Vice President Pence asking him to delay counting the electoral votes to give state legislatures more time to investigate irregularities and consider whether to decertify their electors.[65]

The breaking point came on January 6, the day appointed for the official counting of the electoral votes by Congress. To put pressure on Republican members of Congress, Trump had scheduled a "Stop the Steal" rally at the Ellipse in Washington, DC, for earlier in the day. There will be entire books written about the rally and its aftermath, which was immediately destined to go down as one of the more traumatic moments in peacetime American history; we will confine ourselves to a spare summary.

The rally, with a permit allowing as many as 20,0000 in attendance, featured, among others, the president's son, Donald Trump Jr., presidential attorney Rudy Giuliani, and, of course, the president himself. Each man left his rhetorical mark to contribute to what came next. Don Jr. promised opponents of the scheme to object to electoral votes in contested states that "we're coming for you, and we're going to have a good time doing it." Giuliani suggested the dispute could be settled through "trial by combat." Trump, who had earlier promised supporters a "wild" time in Washington on January 6, complete with a march on the Capitol, laid down the gauntlet himself:

> We do not want to see our election victory stolen by radical left Democrats, that's what they're doing, and stolen by the fake news media, that's what they've done and what they're doing. . . .
>
> If Mike Pence does the right thing, we win the election. . . . All Pence has to do is send it back to the states . . . and we become president, and you are the happiest people.
>
> We will never give up and never concede. We will stop the steal.

After this, we're going to walk down—I'll be with you—we're going to walk down to the Capitol and we're going to cheer on our brave senators and congressmen and women and we're probably not going to be cheering so much for some of them, because you'll never take back our country with weakness. You have to show strength and you have to be strong . . . peacefully and patriotically make your voices heard.

Following the rally, a large contingent—at least several hundred, possibly more than a thousand—marched to the Capitol building. The contingent did not include Trump, who returned to the White House. They arrived shortly after Mike Pence released a letter indicating that he would fulfill the vice president's traditional ceremonial role and would not attempt to assert the right to unilaterally invalidate electors. Debate had begun on the objection to Arizona's electors and Senate majority leader Mitch McConnell had just spoken, calling on senators of both parties to do their duty and accept the legally certified electors without objection. Trump supporters stormed the Capitol, forcing the suspension of the electoral counting process as representatives and senators were forced to evacuate their chambers. The Senate chamber was occupied by rioters, as was Nancy Pelosi's office, and rioters pulled some American flags down from flagpoles, replacing them with "Trump 2020" flags. Helping lead the assault on the Capitol were the Proud Boys, apparently having heeded Trump's call in the first debate to "stand by."[66] The Capitol Police were overwhelmed and required assistance from local, Virginia state, and federal agencies. Fourteen law enforcement personnel were injured, one fatally; another Capitol Police officer who was on the scene committed suicide days later. One rioter was fatally shot, and three other participants died from "medical emergencies."

Hours later, the Capitol was finally cleared, members of Congress returned to their chambers, and the counting process resumed. In the Senate, half of the original Republican objectors withdrew their objections, leaving Cruz, Hawley, and a handful of others. By a 93–7 vote, the electors from Arizona were accepted, and no further objections were raised. In the House, a bit more than half of the Republicans continued supporting at least one objection to the certified electors, but the overall votes were lopsided rejections of the objections. At 3:32 a.m. Eastern time on January 7, the electoral vote making Joe Biden the next president was finally, formally approved.

Through the ordeal, people looked for some word from Donald Trump. There was a tweet attacking Mike Pence for his betrayal, then another calling for his supporters to be peaceful (but not to go home). Finally, there was a short video statement in which Trump repeated his claim that the election was "stolen." Then another tweet, in which he rationalized the mob action by saying, "These are the things and events that happen when a sacred landslide election victory is so unceremoniously & viciously stripped away from great patriots who have been badly & unfairly treated for so long. . . . Remember this day forever."[67]

The reaction across the political spectrum was immediate and fiercely negative. By evening on June 6, before Congress had even concluded its work, a number of close Republican allies of Trump (such as Lindsey Graham and Tom Cotton) had denounced the riot and the president, numerous Democrats had called for Trump's removal, and several conservative commentators had repeated those calls.

The following days were characterized by resignations from cabinet secretaries and White House staff protesting Trump's role in the melee, and by belated and contradictory attempts by Trump to extricate himself from the deepening hole. On January 7, in a morning tweet and an evening address, Trump condemned the riot and committed for the first time to an orderly transfer of power; he also revoked his nomination of Chad Wolf as secretary of Homeland Security after Wolf had appealed to Trump to "strongly condemn" the disorder.[68] Then the president went mostly silent.

One week after the Capitol riot, the House of Representatives impeached Donald Trump for the second time, this time for "incitement to insurrection." The backlash extended to Twitter, which permanently banned Trump; Amazon, which booted Twitter's competitor, Parler; and private employers who fired employees who had participated in the riot. The repercussions were sure to continue beyond Trump's departure from office.

Two weeks after the Capitol riot, Joe Biden was sworn in as president of the United States.

QUESTIONS FOR THE FUTURE

The historical significance of the election or its aftermath will not be clear for many years. It has exposed challenges for both parties, as well as divisions within them. For Democrats, the "fundamental transformation" of America promised by Barack Obama is still far from electorally secure. For their part, Republicans have not found a way to appeal to a majority of American voters; even if they had squeezed out a win in the Electoral College, the wildest claims of fraud would not have come close to erasing Joe Biden's seven million vote lead in the nationally aggregated popular vote.

Political institutions are closely divided. The presidency and the Senate have reverted to Democrats, who also hold the House. But Biden's margin in the states that gave him the Electoral College and the division of parties in both houses is so close that no one can take anything for granted. Joe

Manchin, Susan Collins, and Lisa Murkowski are destined to become the most pivotal members of the Senate. State governments remain predominantly in Republican hands, and the federal courts are (for the time being) infused with conservatives. There is no consensus in the country, and our institutions reflect this.

In 2020, the nation narrowly missed a genuine constitutional crisis at least three times over. Such a crisis could have been occasioned if Trump's gambit to appoint alternate electors in key states had succeeded, or if Mike Pence had succumbed to Trump's insistent entreaties that the vice president usurp powers he clearly did not possess, or perhaps even by an alternate outcome in which Trump won an extra 43,000 votes in three key states and then was reelected by the House despite trailing in the Electoral College, a scenario that might have triggered extraconstitutional Democratic resistance. Next time, we might not be so lucky.

Question: What Will Happen to the Party Coalitions?

In certain respects, we have four parties, not two, and this is likely to remain true for some time. The battle between establishment Democrats and progressives is just beginning. Before Joe Biden was even sworn in, tensions between wings of the Democratic Party over control of the administration were growing. Alexandria Ocasio-Cortez's post-election observation that her party's congressional leadership was tired and past its prime was answered when she was shut out of her preferred Energy and Commerce Committee assignment.[69] More moderate Democrats, such as Representative Abigail Spanberger, expressed open anger that the radicals had cost Democrats House seats.[70] Progressives fired back, with AOC tweeting that "the whole 'progressivism is bad' argument just doesn't have any compelling evidence that I've seen." Instead, she blamed ineffective digital campaigns by House Democrats.[71] House Speaker Nancy Pelosi had to endure a painfully close vote reelecting her as speaker—and she only pulled ahead when several progressives who had held out, including AOC, voted for her at the last minute.

On the other side of the aisle, the struggle between traditional Republicans and Trumpists, largely subsumed for most of Trump's presidency, was inflamed by the post-election disputes over vote fraud. Trump's increasingly aggressive attacks on Republicans who did not fall in line—going so far as to demand the resignations of Georgia's Republican governor and secretary of state—were extraordinary and unlikely to end with his presidency. As Jim VandeHei and Mike Allen argued during Trump's early January meltdown, "President Trump is torching his own party and its leaders on his way out of power. . . . Trump is demanding Republicans fully and unequivocally embrace him—or face his wrath."[72] To the extent that Trump's most vehement supporters' anger over 2020 is directed against Republican "betrayal," the GOP will have its own serious division to manage. For their part, traditional Republicans were furious at Trump and his acolytes in the wake of the loss of the Senate and, much more, the January 6 Capitol riot.

One focus of both parties will be increased competition over racial minorities that Democrats had long taken for granted as an essential part of their coalition. In 2020, to the surprise of many, Democrats gained among white voters while Republicans made modest inroads among minorities. In particular, Trump scored gains in immigrant communities from Cubans in Miami to Mexicans in the Rio Grande Valley to Vietnamese in California.[73] These developments may have been driven by Trump, or they may be longer-term trends. Post-election news reports indicated that Democratic strategists were worried that their demographic coalition was in danger. The *Washington Post* reported that "Party strategists now speak privately with a sense of gloom and publicly with a tone of concern as the election results become clearer. They worry about the potential emergence of a mostly male and increasingly interracial working-class coalition for Republicans that will cut into the demographic advantages Democrats had long counted on."[74] One analyst similarly argued in RealClearPolitics that "A new coalition is taking shape. It's multiethnic, multiracial—and it's conservative. It rejects the regimentation of identity politics, and even rejects the attendant language (just 3% of Hispanics use the term 'Latinx,' for example). It's working class and it's growing."[75] Republicans might learn a lesson from Trump that they can openly oppose "wokeness" and still grow their support among nonwhites by aggressively campaigning for their votes. The most woke people in America, after all, are affluent white people, not Blacks, Latinos, or Asians.

At the moment, however, Democrats still hold the high ground electorally. They can afford to see their minority vote slip as long as they continue compensating by increasing their share of the affluent white vote. In 2020, Biden won sixteen of the twenty-five most affluent counties in America and gained 57 percent of the vote in the one hundred counties with the highest 2019 median incomes.[76] Moreover, affluent whites can offer them more than votes, such as organizational skill, long-term control over education and communications, and the fundraising edge Democrats have enjoyed since 2012. In 2020, Biden developed a huge financial advantage in America's wealthiest ZIP codes, an advantage that also allowed Democrats to spend (and, in several cases, squander) hundreds of millions of dollars on long-shot Senate races.[77] The Democratic edge among the young also gives them a strong base for the future, if they can lock it in. Joe Biden might not seem the best bet to do that, but Ronald Reagan and Bernie Sanders also did quite well among younger voters despite their advanced age. If Republicans want to be competitive over the long term, they will have to win a generation soon.

At the heart of each party's dilemma lay a seemingly simple but bedeviling question: What do we stand for? Retired Republican congressman Trey Gowdy said after the Capitol riot, "That's my challenge for the party, is, if you wanted to stump me with a question, ask me what the modern Republican Party believes, with consistency, cycle after cycle, and then ask me who those defining voices are."[78] Democrats face similar questions.

Question: Whither Trump?

To assess where Republicans might go, it is necessary to assess where Trump might go. Donald Trump, being Donald Trump, will want to remain in the game. He spoke for many Americans who felt betrayed and left behind, and he gave Republicans a new fighting cast that many in the party craved. In the immediate aftermath of the 2020 election, Trump made noises about running again in 2024, and polls showed that he would carry into such an attempt a hard core of ongoing support. One survey published in *Politico* in late November 2020 showed Trump with the support of 53 percent of Republican voters if he chose to run again in 2024, far ahead of vice president Mike Pence and other potential rivals.[79] Candidate or not, it is almost inconceivable that Trump will fall silent once out of the White House, though Twitter was doing its best to achieve just that. Some have suggested he might launch a Trump TV network or build an organization outside of the Republican Party.

On the flip side, it is also possible that Trump will become ensnared in one or more legal disputes of a civil or even criminal character which will occupy his time and energy.[80] An even greater danger to his fortunes will be the lingering memories of his final weeks in office, when the defects of character and temperament long ascribed to him by his critics seemed to burst forth in full bloom. From November 1, 2020, to January 6, 2021, Trump's average approval rating recorded by RealClearPolitics went from 46.0 percent to 43.9 percent. By Inauguration Day, it had fallen to 41.1 percent and was a full fifteen percentage points underwater.[81]

Regardless of the role he sees for himself, Trump never succeeded in making himself acceptable to a majority, or even a plurality, of Americans. The cold fact remains that he has now been outvoted by three million votes by the most disliked Democratic nominee since polling began and seven million votes by an unexceptional career politician who barely campaigned and who entered office older than Ronald Reagan was when he left office. There is no reason to believe Trump has the potential to expand his appeal enough to produce a different result in the future. And that was before factoring in the bad taste he left in many Americans' mouths as a result of his response to defeat, which began as a defensible appeal to the courts and ended up, in the view of many, as a demagogic power grab.

The foremost question for Republicans is whether they will be able to salvage what worked for Trump while learning how to appeal to a broader electorate. This task will require that they disaggregate the varying components of Trumpism, successfully separating the wheat from the chaff among the take-no-prisoners approach to politics, the cult of personality, the attention to legitimate issues such as trade and immigration that appealed to millions of Americans who felt left out, the inattention to other legitimate issues such as fiscal solvency, the resistance to wokeness and the cancel culture, and the appeal to adherents of unsavory conspiracy theories. The congressional elections of 2020 might be evidence that they had already started to construct such an amalgam and that voters were receptive to it. The next question is whether Donald Trump will get out of the way and let them proceed or instead suck the oxygen out of the room, leaving a strong bench—Nikki Haley, Tim Scott, Marco Rubio, Tom Cotton, and perhaps Ted Cruz, to name a few—gasping for air. Though few Republican officeholders would say so openly, Trump's ego and post-election meltdown pose a bigger threat to a Republican recovery than Joe Biden does. At the same time, Senator Rand Paul estimated that one-third of Republican voters would have left the party if Republican senators had voted to convict Trump in the second impeachment trial.[82]

Question: What about American Institutions?

Several major questions face American political institutions. Two of them have reemerged frequently in recent elections. Others are newer.

Since 2000, the Electoral College has been the object of close scrutiny. Twice in that time, candidates have become president through its mechanisms without having won a plurality of the aggregated votes of Americans across the country. In 2020, the nation was 43,000 votes in three states away from experiencing another instance of the phenomenon. Defenders of the Electoral College argue that it accomplished its purpose—that is, to require winning candidates to build a broad geographical coalition. It is not, and in this view should not be, enough to pile up huge margins in a few populous states. We are a federal republic, and the Electoral College recognizes and respects that reality and forces candidates to do the same if they want to win.

At the same time, critics of the Electoral College have been increasingly energized. The system is not consistent with American democracy, they charge, and they point to the growing imbalances in the electoral vote. In

2000, Al Gore outpolled George W. Bush by 500,000 votes nationally (half a percent of the total) and barely lost the electoral vote; in 2016, Hillary Clinton led Donald Trump by three million votes (about two percentage points) and lost decisively in the electoral vote; in 2020, Joe Biden outpolled Trump by seven million votes (over four percentage points) and nearly lost in the Electoral College anyway. Republicans say that Democrats should do what American parties typically do: change their approach to become more acceptable in more places. Democrats reply that they should not have to change their approach, which has outvoted the Republican approach at the presidential level in seven of the last eight elections. In 2020, Democrats doubled down on their coastal progressivism when Biden named Kamala Harris rather than, say, Amy Klobuchar, as his running mate, simply hoping that Trump's unpopularity would carry Biden over the line in the states Clinton had almost won in 2016. It worked with little room to spare, but a growing chorus on the left has made it clear they would rather change the rules than compromise their policy or ideological commitments. The conflict over electoral votes in 2020 gave critics additional ammunition.[83] The critics also point to surveys showing that a majority of Americans want to replace the Electoral College with a direct popular vote.[84]

Given the difficulty of amending the Constitution, opponents of the Electoral College have fixed on an extraconstitutional means of eviscerating it: the National Popular Vote Interstate Compact.[85] The idea is that states will form a compact, or interstate agreement, in which they pledge their electors to vote for the "winner" of the nationally aggregated popular vote regardless of the preference expressed by the voters of their state. The Compact is supposed to begin operating once states with at least 270 electoral votes have joined. As of December 2020, fifteen states and the District of Columbia, totaling 196 electoral votes, had joined the compact. In 2020, Colorado voters narrowly rejected a ballot initiative that would have rescinded the state's participation in the Compact.[86]

Aside from the obvious obstacle that many states with at least 74 electoral votes have to be persuaded to join, there are a number of possible complications to the plan. One is that it may require congressional approval to go into force. Another is that there is no actual national popular vote "winner," because there is no official national popular vote. Votes are taken state-by-state and are administered by state and local governments. For the same reason, it is not clear what would happen if the nationally aggregated popular vote were extremely close. Determining a winner would require a recount in every state, but there is no mechanism that can force states to conduct a recount if the vote is not close in that state. Finally, although the Supreme Court has recently indicated that states can compel their electors to vote in accordance with the pledges, there is still an open question regarding whether it would uphold the Compact, which can be seen as a means of amending the Constitution without going through the amendment process.

Another perennial question, brought back in 2020 with a vengeance, has been how to balance concerns about accessible voting with concerns about secure voting. Much of the post-election anger of Republicans was built around their perception that Democrats had taken advantage of the pandemic to promiscuously expand accessibility at the expense of security by massively expanding mail ballot voting while insisting on reduced safeguards such as rigorous signature verification. Whatever one thinks of the relative value of accessibility and security, it is clear that Americans face a conundrum. Few would argue in the abstract against the proposition that both values are important and that together (properly understood) they reinforce each other. But the parties are now so wedded to one of the values that they can hardly admit the importance, or even the validity, of the other. Until they can overcome this dynamic, there will almost inevitably be an odor of illegitimacy hanging over every close victory, at least in the nostrils of those who come up short. When legislatures or courts push accessibility, losers such as Donald Trump will cry "fraud." When they push ballot security, losers such as Stacey Abrams in 2018 will shout "vote suppression."

One can imagine melding several components together, if anyone is actually interested in a good-faith compromise. On one side would be making Election Day a national holiday, developing a system of automatic (but regularly updated) voter registration, and significant expansion of in-person early voting. On the other would be insisting on voter identification, prohibiting "ballot harvesting," and returning mail-ballot voting to its more modest origins—limited to absentee votes for limited and specified reasons. The odds for such a compromise are not great, and our federal system means that most components would have to be adopted state by state, though the federal government could provide financial incentives, as it did in the Helping Americans Vote Act in 2002.

In addition to familiar questions about the Electoral College and the access/security voting tradeoff, the fate of the Supreme Court is unclear. After the Kavanaugh nomination, and even more so after the Barrett nomination, voices on the left were raised to suggest (or demand) that the size of the Supreme Court be increased under the next Democratic president so the impact of the Trump nominations could be negated. This reprise of Franklin Roosevelt's 1937 "court-packing" plan was not popular among Americans in general, but it was probable that with control of the presidency and both houses of Congress, Democrats' more radical wing would push for action on this front. For his part, during the campaign Joe Biden disclaimed support for abolishing the Electoral College but was unwilling to commit himself either way on the issue of expanding the size of the Supreme Court.[87]

After four years of the Disrupter-in-Chief, the nature of the presidency itself is at question. Will Trump's trespasses on the norms of the office become the new norm? Or will Trump prove an aberration? Have we endangered republican government by making the presidency too powerful, too much of a prize? A key element of this question depends on whether one sees Trump as an entirely unique departure or just an extreme extension of prior trends (and perhaps a reflection of society, which critics say is increasingly dismissive of tradition and values of self-control). Biden alone will not be able to answer that question. In twenty years, we will know more. After all, Warren Harding and Calvin Coolidge seemed to have restored normalcy after the disruption of Woodrow Wilson—until Franklin Roosevelt took Wilson's model, hypercharged it, and cemented it as the new norm.

Wilson not only challenged the norms of the presidency, arguing that the institution should play a more central role in American life, use rhetoric more aggressively, and beat down the restraints of separation of powers, but also was crucial in the evolution of presidential selection. Generally unconcerned about the potential of demagogues to threaten order and liberty, Wilson's goal—achieved by reformers in stages over more than a century—was to remove powerful parties as intermediaries and put the people directly in command of presidential nominations. The result is our current system, based overwhelmingly on primary elections that are determined directly by voters.[88] Donald Trump was the ultimate product of this system, a complete outsider with virtually no support among Republican officeholders who received the Republican nomination in 2016 anyway. The democratic and plebiscitary ethos of the modern system is so thoroughly entrenched that it is difficult to imagine unwinding any significant portion of it, but it needs to be part of the discussion.

Perhaps the most critical question facing the country's institutions was the nebulous one of institutional legitimacy. A subset of Democrats has a long history of regarding any defeat as the result of foul play. Nixon's forty-nine-state sweep in 1972 was later explained by Watergate; Reagan's 1980 win was retroactively blamed on Gary Sick's debunked claim that the Reagan team conspired with the Ayatollah Khomeini to delay release of the hostages in Iran; George H. W. Bush, in this view, won in 1988 thanks to a racist campaign focused on Willie Horton; his son won in 2000 through illegitimate interference by the Supreme Court and in 2004 by winning Ohio through rigged Diebold voting machines; and Trump in 2016 colluded with Russia and took the White House through the anti-democratic Electoral College. As noted above, every time a Republican has won the presidency since

2000, Democratic members of Congress have objected to the Electoral College count. Driven largely by Donald Trump, some Republicans have now picked up the same approach. Trump himself spent years pushing conspiracy theories that Barack Obama was not a natural-born citizen before asserting that Biden won in 2020 due to a rigged election. The deeper problem driving this phenomenon is that many Americans do not accept the legitimacy of their partisan adversaries. The rise in "negative partisanship"—or partisanship defined largely by dislike of the other party—has been well documented by political scientists and means that more and more Americans are willing (indeed, anxious) to believe the worst about their foes.[89]

Hovering over or alongside the question of electoral legitimacy are a pair of concepts that cast doubt on the legitimacy of the American system writ large. On the left is an increasingly entrenched conviction that America is beset by "systemic racism" that taints every institution. It is a concept not susceptible to falsifiability, as doubts or presentation of contrary evidence are simply dismissed as evidence of the doubter's own racial insensitivity. On the right is a concern that America no longer operates on the basis of the consent of the governed, which has been submerged under the power of unaccountable bureaucracies, unaccountable judges, and, in one version, the "deep state" of secretive intelligence and law enforcement agencies. As "systemic racism" and the "deep state" grow as explanatory frameworks for more Americans, the challenge to maintaining popular support for the American system grows as well.

Question: Can Joe Biden Unify the Country?

With polarization approaching a boiling point, Biden was the choice of three-fourths of those saying that capacity to unify the country was the most important candidate quality. Early indications were not promising.[90] For one thing, the divide in the country is quite deep, probably beyond the salving of any single political figure. Within weeks of the election, Republicans like Allen West had seemingly suggested secession while a number of prominent progressives had suggested that Trump supporters face "truth and reconciliation commissions" to be called to account for their "crimes," a demand for revenge and the silencing of opponents that only grew in intensity after January 6.[91]

Then there was the case of Biden himself. On one hand, he had a long history of working with senators across party and ideological lines. On the other hand, he also had a long history of divisiveness ranging from his treatment of Robert Bork as chair of the Senate Judiciary Committee in 1987 to his remarks on the campaign trail in 2012 that Republicans wanted to put

Black Americans back in chains to calling Trump supporters "chumps" at a New Hampshire campaign event the weekend before Election Day. After the members of the Electoral College met in each state and confirmed Biden's win on December 14, Biden gave an address that was billed as a call for unity. "The integrity of our elections remains intact," said Biden. "Now it is time to turn the page, to unite, to heal." After that appeal, however, Biden also moved to criticize the Texas lawsuit as "a position that refused to respect the rule of the people, refused to respect the rule of law and refused to honor our Constitution."[92] The Capitol riot elicited another schizophrenic reaction from Biden. His initial comments were widely praised as mature and calming, but many conservatives took exception when he suggested that BLM protestors would have been treated more harshly, a theme quickly picked up by Kamala Harris and Barack Obama.

The response by Republicans to the December unity offensive was not favorable. In their view, Democrats who had spent four years chanting "not my president," peddling Russian conspiracy stories, impeaching Trump, and calling the president illegitimate had no business calling for unity or expecting Republicans to embrace it.[93] For their part, progressive activists and journalists urged Biden to forget about reaching accommodations across the aisle and dismissed Republican calls for unity during the January 13 debate over impeachment.[94]

For Biden to contribute to healing the national breach, he will have to deliberately forego pushing his advantages, which grew considerably in January 2021, to the fullest limit. He will not have a Republican Senate to help moderate his agenda, but his fiftieth vote is still centrist Democrat Joe Manchin. Biden would be well advised to read political scientist Stephen F. Knott's 2019 book *The Lost Soul of the American Presidency*, in which the author posits that much of our national distemper is a consequence of the presidency moving away from its origins as a constitutional (rather than popular) office grounded in the role of head of state.[95] That role is suited for Biden's more relaxed approach, described by journalist Gabriela Debenedetti as "lowest drama possible."[96] Writing for *Politico*, John F. Harris likewise argued that Biden's "boring" approach was more likely than soaring rhetoric to unify the country, especially if he concentrates on concrete accomplishments such as infrastructure and vaccine distribution.[97] Focusing on the role of head of state is also suited for the most sensible interpretation of the election, as a referendum against Trump and a "mandate for centrist policies" rather than a "mandate for progressive policies," as a post-election survey by Democratic pollster Douglas Schoen found.[98] It is at odds, however, with the transformative policy aims of the Democratic Party's progressive wing, many of which Biden has endorsed. Of course, transformative progressive policy aims are a significant driver behind national disunity, since at least half the country has no desire to see America fundamentally transformed. In any event Biden, too, is wrapped up in a history of advocating executive overreach, and may not be prepared to reel it in. Biden will have to make choices he has thus far eschewed. Is this a dilemma he can navigate? And does he even want to try?

Failure to lower the national temperature could have dramatic national consequences. Allen West was not the only Republican to talk of secession in the aftermath of the election, and some Democrats had seemed prepared to broach the subject if they had lost. Antifa and right-wing militias are openly seditious, and BLM remains a radical force. They are not going away. Indeed, they might be emboldened if they see Biden as weak. During the long transition period, violence on both the left and the right flared from Portland and Seattle to Washington, DC, peaking in the Capitol riot of January 6 but continuing through Inauguration Day.[99]

The return of the partisan press has clearly exacerbated this division.[100] As numerous commentators have noted, Americans seem increasingly to be inhabiting two different worlds—Red America and Blue America—offering not only different interpretations but also different sets of facts (one post-election analyst argued there were three Americas: Red, Blue, and Trump[101]). "Cocooning" has been a matter of consumer choice, not easily solved by any political or governmental device. Attempts by social media giants to impose a monolithic view through private censorship were unlikely to draw the nation closer. Indeed, the war against Trump and Parler waged by the tech giants fed fears by conservatives that their opponents intended to drive them from public discourse *en masse*.[102]

In the wake of the election, some big thinkers addressed the parlous state of national unity. One, writing under the pseudonym "Rebecca," called for a "Great Separation"—not a formal division, but rather radical decentralization that leaves all questions but national defense, trade, and great questions of national finance in the hands of state and local governments.[103] Christopher Caldwell, writing in *The New Republic*, argued that America was headed for a subjugation of Red (conservative) America by Blue (progressive) America, in the same way that "less dynamic" portions of Germany and Italy were subjugated by the "more dynamic" in the nineteenth century.[104] Michael Anton responded on the website The American Mind that Blue America needs Red America at least as much as (if not more than) the reverse; tradition, in his view, serves as a necessary ballast for dynamism.[105] The conversation made clear that national division had escalated to a level unprecedented in the modern era. Trump had undoubtedly contributed, having proven more adept at burning bridges than building them. But there could be little doubt that he was also a symptom of a division that had been percolating and deepening for half a century. Social historian Peter Turchin provided a foreboding of ongoing trouble. Turchin predicted in 2010 that the following decade would feature increasing instability, due largely to what he calls "elite overproduction"—in practical terms, too many lawyers and PhDs to be gainfully employed. In November 2020, having correctly predicted the tumultuous decade, Turchin declared that the next ten years could be worse.[106]

During the Trump years, many issues served as flashpoints for tumult, from immigration policy to Nike shoe designs. In the election year of 2020 and its immediate aftermath, those divisions were exacerbated. Americans were deeply divided over whether state and local lockdowns were a necessary and responsible step to contain COVID or a dangerous overreach by officials abusing their power and infringing on fundamental rights (and perhaps deliberately undermining Trump's reelection prospects). They were deeply divided over whether the summer protests were a long-overdue reach for social justice or a spasm of violence and disorder that threatened the American constitutional order and a common understanding of our history. They were divided over whether the election results represented a vindication of democracy or a steal. And America's authoritarian adversaries abroad watched and bided their time.

As James Madison noted in his famed Federalist 10 essay, "faction is sown into the nature of man." Varying interests and different convictions concerning religion and politics are to be expected in every free society. We cannot expect, and should not want, a rigid homogeneity that would erase all division. The United States Constitution was designed to both reflect and contain division, not eliminate it. In 2020, division exploded and the Constitution remained standing; pandemic raged and the country remained standing. But underneath the division, there must be a foundation, something at the core of politics held in common, or, at some point, what stands may fall. The great challenge of American politics will be to find and nurture—or perhaps, what is harder, to reforge—what is held in common before it is too late.

NOTES

1. Jonathan Swan and Zachary Basu, "Episode 1: A Premeditated Lie Lit the Fire," Axios, January 16, 2021, https://www.axios.com/trump-election-premeditated-lie-ebaf4a1f-46bf-4c37-ba0d-3ed5536ef537.html.

2. "A Sampling of Recent Election Fraud Cases from Across the United States," https://www.heritage.org/voterfraud; John Fund, *Stealing Elections: How Voter Fraud Threatens Our Democracy* (New York: Encounter Books, 2008).

3. David A. Graham, "There's No Such Thing as a Do-Over Election," *The At-lantic*, September 5, 2019, https://www.theatlantic.com/ideas/archive/2019/09/north -carolina-ninth-district-fraud-mccready-bishop/597412/.

4. Mark Niesse, "Inquiry shows 1,000 Georgians may have voted twice, but no conspiracy," *Atlanta Journal-Constitution*, September 30, 2020, https://www.ajc.com/ politics/inquiry-finds-1000-georgians-may-have-voted-twice-but-no-conspiracy/ RGS3UI7JRJE5XP4OAL3T3BYDDI/.

5. Joel Kurth and Jonathan Oosting, "Records: Too Many Votes in 37% of De-troit's Precincts," *Detroit News*, December 13, 2016, http://detroitnews.com/story/ news/politics/2016/12/12/records-too-many-votes-detroits-precincts/95363314/.

6. For a detailed overview of this action, see "A Running Compendium of Chal-lenges to Election 2020," RealClearInvestigations, December 7, 2020 (subsequently updated), https://www.realclearinvestigations.com/articles/2020/12/07/a_running_ compendium_of_fraud_charges_in_election_2020_126261.html.

7. Scott Bauer, "Wisconsin certifies Joe Biden as winner following recount," AP, November 30, 2020, https://apnews.com/article/election-2020-joe-biden-donald -trump-wisconsin-lawsuits-2e9cf60550f519537d31b6b71aa32c3c.

8. "Another Georgia county has uncovered 2,700 missing votes, Secretary of State's office says," WSB-TV, November 17, 2020, https://www.wsbtv.com/news/ politics/another-georgia-county-has-uncovered-2700-missing-votes-secretary-states -office-says/5W734FA755CK3NCR4P7A27DXVM/.

9. Chandelis Duster, "Georgia reaffirms Biden's victory for 3rd time after recount, dealing major blow to Trump's attempt to overturn the results," CNN, December 7, 2020, https://www.cnn.com/2020/12/07/politics/georgia-recount-recertification-biden/ index.html.

10. See, for example, https://www.chicagotribune.com/election-2020/ct-2020 -election-fraud-explainer-20201111-iemnh3kuhbh4tepuaeupdhkoji-story.html.

11. Bill McCarthy, "Ted Cruz falsely claims Philadelphia is counting votes in 'shroud of darkness,'" *Politifact*, November 6, 2020, https://www.politifact.com/fact checks/2020/nov/06/ted-cruz/ted-cruz-falsely-claims-philadelphia-counting-vote/.

12. David Wickert, "Georgia rips Trump's voter fraud claims in court," *At-lanta Journal-Constitution*, December 18, 2020, https://www.ajc.com/politics/election/ georgia-rips-trumps-voter-fraud-claims-in-court/P6TI4J3CKVDQZMNVG66Q2G BQCE/; Hope Yen, Jeff Amy, and Michael Balsamo, "AP FACT CHECK: Trump's made -up claims of fake Georgia votes," January 3, 2021, https://apnews.com/article/ap-fact -check-donald-trump-georgia-elections-atlanta-c23d10e5299e14daee6109885f7dafa9.

13. Saranac Hale Spencer, "Pennsylvania Postal Worker Waffles on Election Fraud Claim," FactCheck.org, November 12, 2020, https://www.factcheck.org/ 2020/11/pennsylvania-postal-worker-waffles-on-election-fraud-claim/; Bill McCar-thy, "Allegations of USPS election fraud in Michigan don't hold up," *PolitiFact*, November 5, 2020, https://www.politifact.com/article/2020/nov/05/allegations-usps -election-fraud-michigan-dont-hold/.

14. Makini Brice and Tom Halls, "Trump campaign challenges election results in Wisconsin Supreme Court," Reuters, December 1, 2020, https://www.reuters

.com/article/us-usa-election-wisconsin/trump-campaign-challenges-election-results-in-wisconsin-supreme-court-idUSKBN28B5KA.

15. https://www.chicagotribune.com/election-2020/ct-2020-election-fraud-explainer-20201111-iemnh3kuhbh4tepuaeupdhkoji-story.html; Jacques Billeaud, "Arizona Supreme Court Rejects GOP Bid to Undo Biden Victory," *U.S. News & World Report*, December 8, 2020, https://www.usnews.com/news/best-states/arizona/articles/2020-12-08/judge-peppers-lawyer-with-questions-on-arizona-election-suit.

16. Pat Beall et al., "Fewer rejected ballots seemed to be a win for voter access. Trump and others disagree," *USA Today*, December 28, 2020, https://www.usatoday.com/story/news/investigations/2020/12/28/trump-and-others-not-happy-lower-2020-rejected-ballot-numbers/3964007001/.

17. For a point by point examination of charges related to Detroit, see Craig Mauger, "Why 8 claims from Rudy Giuliani's Michigan witnesses don't add up," *Detroit News*, December 4, 2020, https://www.detroitnews.com/story/news/politics/2020/12/04/why-8-claims-rudy-giulianis-michigan-witnesses-dont-add-up/3824210001/.

18. Associated Press, "Audit of Georgia county's 15,000 absentee-ballot signatures turns up zero fraud," *Market Watch*, December 30, 2020, https://www.marketwatch.com/story/audit-of-georgia-countys-15-000-absentee-ballot-signatures-turns-up-zero-fraud-01609368663.

19. Bill McCarthy, "No, Georgia election workers didn't kick out observers and illegally count 'suitcases' of ballots," *Politifact*, December 4, 2020, https://www.politifact.com/factchecks/2020/dec/04/facebook-posts/no-georgia-election-workers-didnt-kick-out-observe/; Mollie Hemingway, "No, The Georgia Vote-Counting Video Was Not 'Debunked.' Not Even Close," The Federalist, December 7, 2020, https://thefederalist.com/2020/12/07/no-the-georgia-vote-counting-video-was-not-debunked-not-even-close/.

20. Ronn Blitzer, "No 'mystery ballots' hidden under table in Fulton County, Georgia investigator swears in affidavit," Fox News, December 7, 2020, https://www.foxnews.com/politics/fulton-county-georgia-no-mystery-ballots-under-table-investigator-affidavit; Justin Gray, "Georgia Election Officials Show Frame-By-Frame What Happened in Fulton Surveillance Video," WSB-TV, December 4, 2020, https://www.wsbtv.com/news/politics/georgia-election-officials-show-frame-by-frame-what-really-happened-fulton-surveillance-video/T5M3PYIBYFHFFOD3CIB2ULDVDE/.

21. Claes G. Ryn, "Memorandum: How the 2020 Election Could Have Been Stolen," *The American Conservative*, January 5, 2020, https://www.theamericanconservative.com/articles/the-2020-election-what-happened-a-political-scientists-memorandum/.

22. Ben Mathis-Lilley, "Reality Forecloses on the Trump Presidency," *Slate*, November 23, 2020, https://slate.com/news-and-politics/2020/11/trump-campaign-disavows-sidney-powell-as-too-ridiculous-even-for-rudy-giuliani.html; Ted Johnson, "Rudy Giuliani's 'Hair Dye' Press Conference: Fox News Carries Live, CNN and MSNBC Skip It," *Deadline*, November 19, 2020, https://deadline.com/2020/11/rudy-giuliani-hair-dye-press-conference-1234618943/; Joseph A. Wulfson, "Rush Limbaugh knocks Trump's legal team: They promised 'bombshells' at press confer-

ence and 'nothing happened,'" Fox News, November 23, 2020, https://www.foxnews.com/media/rush-limbaugh-knocks-trumps-legal-team-they-promised-blockbuster-stuff-and-then-nothing-happened.

23. "Hand audit of all Presidential Election votes in Antrim County confirms previously certified results, voting machines were accurate," State of Michigan, December 17, 2020, https://www.michigan.gov/som/0,4669,7-192-47796-547883--,00.html. Out of almost 16,000 votes cast, the recount showed Trump gaining eleven votes and Biden losing one for a net Trump gain of twelve, fully in line with normal expectations in a hand recount.

24. Thomas Lifson, "Statement," *American Thinker*, January 15, 2021, https://www.americanthinker.com/blog/2021/01/statement.html.

25. Edward R. Tufte and Richard A. Sun, "Are There Bellwether Electoral Districts?" *Public Opinion Quarterly* 39 (Spring 1975): 1–18, https://www.jstor.org/stable/2748067?seq=1.

26. Erik Larson and Greg Stohr, "Texas Stands by Claim That Biden Win Statistically Impossible," *Bloomberg News*, December 11, 2020, https://www.bloomberg.com/news/articles/2020-12-11/texas-stands-by-claim-that-biden-win-statistically-impossible.

27. "Fact check: Deviation from Benford's Law does not prove election fraud," Reuters, November 10, 2020, https://www.reuters.com/article/uk-factcheck-benford/fact-check-deviation-from-benfords-law-does-not-prove-election-fraud-idUSKBN27Q3AI.

28. Paul Kengor, "Pennsylvania Bombshell: Biden 99.4% v. Trump 0.6%," *American Spectator*, November 28, 2020, https://spectator.org/pennsylvania-bombshell-biden-99-4-vs-trump-0-6/.

29. "Fact check: Vote spikes in Wisconsin, Michigan and Pennsylvania do not prove election fraud," Reuters, November 10, 2020, https://www.reuters.com/article/uk-factcheck-wi-pa-mi-vote-spikes/fact-check-vote-spikes-in-wisconsin-michigan-and-pennsylvania-do-not-prove-election-fraud-idUSKBN27Q307; Scott Johnson, "After the Lights went Out," Powerlineblog.com, January 17, 2021, https://www.powerlineblog.com/archives/2021/01/after-the-lights-went-out.php.

30. John R. Lott Jr., "A Simple Test for the Extent of Vote Fraud with Absentee Ballots in the 2020 Presidential Election: Georgia and Pennsylvania data," December 21, 2020, https://ssm.com/abstract=3756988.

31. John Hinderaker, "HOW MUCH VOTER FRAUD WAS THERE?" Powerlineblog.com, January 1, 2021, https://www.powerlineblog.com/archives/2021/01/how-much-voter-fraud-was-there-2.php.

32. Jack Tomczuk, "Trump suit challenging PA votes dismissed," *Philly Metro*, November 22, 2020, https://philly.metro.us/trump-suit-challenging-pa-votes-dismissed/.

33. Mark Sherman, "Democrats: Justices' 4–4 tie in election case ominous sign," AP, October 22, 2020, https://apnews.com/article/virus-outbreak-state-courts-voting-pennsylvania-amy-coney-barrett-c13e057a7fd30c57fbf23c1e98a4be9c.

34. Zach Montellaro, "Pennsylvania's top election officer says just 10,000 ballots were received after Nov. 3," *Politico*, November 10, 2020, https://www.politico.com/news/2020/11/10/pennsylvanias-top-election-officer-says-just-10-000-ballots-were-received-after-nov-3-435972.

35. Matthew Santoni, "Bid to Toss Mail-In Votes Is Two Elections Too Late, Pa. Says," Law 360, November 24, 2020, https://www.law360.com/articles/1332028/bid-to-toss-mail-in-votes-is-two-elections-too-late-pa-says.

36. Lisa Hagen, "Supreme Court Tosses Texas Lawsuit in Fatal Blow to Trump's Hope of Upending Election," *U.S. News & World Report*, December 11, 2020, https://www.usnews.com/news/elections/articles/2020-12-11/supreme-court-tosses-texas-lawsuit-in-fatal-blow-to-trumps-hope-of-upending-election.

37. The opposition of liberal legal scholars was to be expected. For conservatives, see, for example, John Yoo, "Texas Lost, and Conservatives Won," *National Review*, December 15, 2020, https://www.nationalreview.com/2020/12/texas-lost-and-conservatives-won/.

38. See, for example, Andrew C. McCarthy's analysis of the Wisconsin Supreme Court decision against Trump, "A Stunning Passage from the Latest Court Rejection of Team Trump," *National Review*, December 13, 2020, https://www.nationalreview.com/2020/12/a-stunning-passage-from-the-latest-court-rejection-of-team-trump/.

39. William A. Jacobson, "Where things stand at this hour," *Legal Insurrection*, December 14, 2020, https://legalinsurrection.com/2020/12/where-things-stand-at-this-hour/.

40. Jacobson, "Where things stand at this minute"; John Hinderaker, "Trump Has Gone Nuts," Powerlineblog.com, January 5, 2021, https://www.powerlineblog.com/archives/2021/01/trump-has-gone-nuts.php.

41. Gopal Ratnam, "Cybersecurity chief who oversaw 'most secure election' fired by Trump," *Roll Call*, November 17, 2020, https://www.rollcall.com/2020/11/17/cybersecurity-chief-who-oversaw-most-secure-election-fired-by-trump/.

42. Kevin Johnson, "Attorney General Barr: Justice Dept. finds no evidence of fraud to alter election outcome," *USA Today*, December 1, 2020, https://www.usatoday.com/story/news/politics/elections/2020/12/01/attorney-general-barr-no-evidence-widespread-election-fraud/3783305001/.

43. Jesse Byrnes, "Barr told Trump that theories about stolen election were 'bulls—': Report," *The Hill*, January 18, 2021, https://thehill.com/homenews/administration/534672-barr-told-trump-that-theories-about-stolen-election-were-bulls-report.

44. "Peter Navarro: 'The Immaculate Deception' Report News Conference Transcript," *Rev*, December 17, 2020, https://www.rev.com/blog/transcripts/peter-navarro-the-immaculate-deception-report-news-conference-transcript.

45. Tim Murphy, "Donald Trump Jr. Just Promoted a Brazen Plan to Steal the Election," *Mother Jones*, November 5, 2020, https://www.motherjones.com/politics/2020/11/donald-trump-jr-just-promoted-a-brazen-plan-to-steal-the-election/.

46. See, for instance, Melissa Nann Burke, "Michigan state GOP leaders won't interfere with electors, overturn vote," *Detroit News*, December 14, 2020, https://www.detroitnews.com/story/news/politics/2020/12/14/michigan-state-gop-leaders-wont-interfere-electors-overturn-vote/6541560002/.

47. Burke, "Michigan state GOP leaders."

48. Daniel Villareal, "Michigan Republicans Tried to Submit Fake Electoral Votes to Capitol," *Newsweek*, December 15, 2020, https://www.newsweek.com/michigan-republicans-tried-submit-fake-electoral-votes-capitol-1555028.

49. Zach Budryk, "Georgia governor warns state lawmakers they cannot choose Trump electors," *The Hill*, December 8, 2020, https://thehill.com/homenews/state-watch/529185-georgia-governor-warns-state-lawmakers-they-cannot-choose-trump-electors.

50. Jeremy Wallace, "Texas GOP Chair Denies He Meant to Advocate for State to Secede," *Houston Chronicle*, December 14, 2020, https://www.houstonchronicle.com/politics/texas/article/Texas-GOP-chair-denies-that-he-advocated-for-15800598.php.

51. "Michael Flynn to Newsmax TV: Trump Has Options to Secure Integrity of 2020 Election," *Newsmax*, December 17, 2020, https://www.newsmax.com/politics/trump-election-flynn-martiallaw/2020/12/17/id/1002139/.

52. Zach Budryk, "Trump pushes back on reported talk of martial law: 'Fake News,'" *The Hill*, December 20, 2020, https://thehill.com/homenews/administration/531032-trump-pushes-back-on-martial-law-reports-fake-news.

53. See Byron York, "Byron York's Daily Memo: SPECIAL EDITION: Dangerous talk about the election and the military," *Washington Examiner*, December 20, 2020, https://www.washingtonexaminer.com/opinion/byron-yorks-daily-memo-special-edition-dangerous-talk-about-the-election-and-the-military; Bonchie, "Michael Flynn Calls for 'Limited' Martial Law to Force a New Election," RedState, https://redstate.com/bonchie/2020/12/03/michael-flynn-calls-for-limited-martial-law-and-a-new-election-n288705; Jonathan Turley, "'How Scared Should We Be?' CNN's Jake Tapper Leads Show with 'Conspiracy in the Oval Office' on Possible Declaration of Martial Law," December 20, 2020, https://jonathanturley.org/2020/12/20/how-scared-should-we-be-cnns-jake-tapper-leads-show-with-conspiracy-in-the-oval-office-on-possible-declaration-of-martial-law/.

54. "The Post says: Give it up, Mr. President—for your sake and the nation's," *New York Post*, December 27, 2020, https://nypost.com/2020/12/27/give-it-up-mr-president-for-your-sake-and-the-nations/.

55. Brittany Bernstein, "Hawley Says He Will Object to Electoral College Certification," Yahoo News, December 30, 2020, https://news.yahoo.com/hawley-says-object-electoral-college-161312128.html.

56. David Mark, "Trump allies' Electoral College certification challenge follows in Democrats' footsteps," NBC News Think, January 5, 2021, https://www.nbcnews.com/think/opinion/trump-allies-electoral-college-certification-challenge-follows-democrats-footsteps-ncna1252873.

57. Their strategy was reminiscent of the hair-splitting utilized by John Kerry when he voted to authorize George W. Bush to use force against Saddam Hussein but later argued that he wasn't for the war, just for the president's right to start it on his own judgment.

58. Byron York, "Byron York's Daily Memo: Electoral College Day," *Washington Examiner*, December 14, 2020, https://www.washingtonexaminer.com/opinion/byron-yorks-daily-memo-electoral-college-day.

59. Dana Blanton, "Fox News Poll: Most Republicans say President Trump was robbed," Fox News, December 11, 2020, https://www.foxnews.com/politics/republicans-president-trump-robbed-poll.

60. Newt Gingrich, "Why I will not accept Joe Biden as president," *Washington Times*, December 21, 2020, https://www.washingtontimes.com/news/2020/dec/21/why-i-will-not-accept-joe-biden-as-president/.

61. "'I just want to find 11,780 votes'—In extraordinary hour-long call, Trump pressures Georgia secretary of state to recalculate votes in his favor," *Washington Post*, December 3, 2020, https://www.washingtonpost.com/politics/trump-raffensperger-call-georgia-vote/2021/01/03/d45acb92-4dc4-11eb-bda4-615aaefd0555_story.html.

62. Marc Caputo, "POLITICO Playbook: The Backstory of Trump's Georgia Call," *Politico*, January 4, 2021, https://www.politico.com/newsletters/playbook/2021/01/04/the-backstory-of-trumps-georgia-call-491268.

63. Max Greenwood, "Georgia elections chief refutes election claims in letter to Congress," *The Hill*, January 7, 2021, https://thehill.com/homenews/campaign/533135-georgia-elections-chief-refutes-election-claims-in-letter-to-congress.

64. Celine Castronuovo, "Trump calls Georgia Senate runoffs 'both illegal and invalid' in New Year's tweets," *The Hill*, January 1, 2021, https://thehill.com/homenews/campaign/532348-trump-claims-georgia-senate-runoff-is-both-illegal-and-invalid-in-new-years.

65. "State lawmakers ask Pence for more time to address election results," AP Newswire, January 5, 2021, https://apnews.com/press-release/pr-newswire/legislature-constitutions-state-elections-phill-kline-elections-ca6900e718670f42ad2ef5332bcc69cd.

66. Georgia Wells, Rebecca Ballhouse, and Keach Hagey, "Proud Boys, Seizing Trump's Call to Washington, Helped Lead Capitol Attack," *Wall Street Journal*, January 17, 2021, https://www.wsj.com/articles/proud-boys-seizing-trumps-call-to-washington-helped-lead-capitol-attack-11610911596.

67. For a chronology of Trump's responses to the riot, see Heather Mac Donald, "Trump's Exit," *City Journal*, January 8, 2021, https://www.city-journal.org/trumps-exit.

68. Morgan Chalfant, "White House announces Wolf nomination withdrawn after he says Trump should 'strongly condemn' Capitol violence," *The Hill*, January 7, 2021, https://thehill.com/homenews/administration/533105-acting-dhs-secretary-says-trump-should-strongly-condemn-violence-at.

69. Quint Forgey, "Ocasio-Cortez takes direct shot at Pelosi and Schumer," *Politico*, December 16, 2020, https://www.politico.com/news/2020/12/16/ocasio-cortez-new-leaders-pelosi-schumer-4462472020; Dartunorro Clark, "Ocasio-Cortez passed over for Kathleen Rice on Energy and Commerce Committee," NBC News, December 17, 2020, https://www.nbcnews.com/politics/congress/kathleen-rice-picked-over-ocasio-cortez-spot-house-energy-commerce-n1251640.

70. Chris Cillizla, "This Democratic congresswoman just spoke some hard truth to her party," CNN, November 6, 2020, https://www.cnn.com/2020/11/06/politics/abigail-spanberger-house-democrats-2020-election/index.html.

71. Christina Marcos, "Ocasio-Cortez defends progressives from blame for Democratic 'underperformance,'" *The Hill*, November 6, 2020, https://thehill.com/homenews/campaign/524805-ocasio-cortez-defends-progressives-from-charges-of-democratic.

72. Jim VandeHei and Mike Allen, "Trump, the GOP arsonist," Axios News, January 2, 2020, https://www.axios.com/trump-republicans-georgia-runoffs-tweets-7997c1d8-9f1b-47ae-8353-94864426eaea.html.

73. Michael Barone, "Immigrant support for Trump a significant election factor," *Omaha World-Herald*, December 31, 2020, https://omaha.com/opinion/columnists/michael-barone-immigrant-support-for-trump-a-significant-election-factor/article_bae6b8d6-488f-11eb-9d5e-bf5bbcf37ad4.html.

74. https://www.washingtonpost.com/politics/biden-election-democrats-losses/2020/12/20/b5b2cec4-3ff5-11eb-8db8-395dedaaa036_story.html.

75. Kevin Roberts, "New Conservative Coalition Is a Foundational Shift," RealClearPolitics, https://www.realclearpolitics.com/articles/2020/11/28/new_conservative_coalition_is_a_foundational_shift_144741.html.

76. "America's Wealthiest Counties Became Bluer in the 2020 Election," Social Explorer, November 11, 2020, https://www.socialexplorer.com/blog/post/americas-wealthiest-counties-became-bluer-in-the-2020-election-11047; Steven Hayward, "The Geek in Pictures (2)," PowerlineBlog.com, December 2, 2020, https://www.powerlineblog.com/archives/2020/12/the-geek-in-pictures-2.php.

77. Shane Goldmacher, Ella Koeze, Rachel Shorey and Lazaro Gamio, "The Two Americas Financing the Trump and Biden Campaigns," *New York Times*, October 25, 2020, https://www.nytimes.com/interactive/2020/10/25/us/politics/trump-biden-campaign-donations.html.

78. David Rutz, "Trey Gowdy: Republicans must figure out what they truly believe after brutal week for party," Fox News, January 7, 2020, https://www.foxnews.com/politics/trey-gowdy-gop-figure-out-truly-believe.

79. Matthew Choi, "Poll: Majority of Republicans would support Trump in 2024," *Politico*, November 24, 2020, https://www.politico.com/news/2020/11/24/poll-republicans-support-trump-2024-439757.

80. See, for example, Jane Mayer, "Why Trump Can't Afford to Lose," *New Yorker*, November 9, 2020, https://www.newyorker.com/magazine/2020/11/09/why-trump-cant-afford-to-lose; Ryan Lucas, "Once Out of Office, Trump Faces Significant Legal Jeopardy," NPR, November 20, 2020, https://www.npr.org/2020/11/20/937044524/once-out-of-office-trump-faces-significant-legal-peril; Simon Shuster and Vera Bergengruen, "Donald Trump Couldn't Be Prosecuted in Office. What Happens When He Leaves?" *Time*, November 12, 2020, https://time.com/5910879/trump-lawsuits/.

81. "President Trump Job Approval," RCP, https://www.realclearpolitics.com/epolls/other/president_trump_job_approval-6179.html. In the public polls taken on or after January 6 through January 19, Trump was "underwater" by 6, 10, 11, 12, 13, 14, 15, 19 (twice), 22 (twice), 27 (twice), 28 (four times), and 29. In only one poll in this period, Rasmussen conducted January 14–18, Trump was approved by 51 percent and disapproved by 48 percent, a result that was clearly an outlier.

82. Mica Soellner, "Rand Paul: One-third of Republicans will leave party if GOP senators go along with convicting Trump," *Washington Examiner*, January 15, 2021, https://www.washingtonexaminer.com/news/rand-paul-warns-senate-conviction-will-destroy-gop.

83. David Edward Burke, "Yes, Biden Won the Electoral College. But It's Still a Huge Problem," *Washington Monthly*, December 28, 2020, https://washington-monthly.com/2020/12/28/yes-biden-won-the-electoral-college-but-its-still-a-huge-problem/.

84. Megan Brenan, "61% of Americans Support Abolishing Electoral College," Gallup, September 24, 2020, https://news.gallup.com/poll/320744/americans-support-abolishing-electoral-college.aspx.

85. See National Popular Vote, https://www.nationalpopularvote.com/.

86. Sherrie Peif, "National popular vote repeal comes up short; organizers hope other states inspired to fight compact," *Complete Colorado*, November 4, 2020, https://pagetwo.completecolorado.com/2020/11/04/proposition-113-comes-up-short/.

87. "The RS Politics 2020 Democratic Primary Policy Guide," *Rolling Stone*, March 3, 2020, https://www.rollingstone.com/politics/politics-lists/2020-democratic-candidates-issues-policy-positions-820811/. In 2019, Biden opposed court-packing, but in 2020 he repeatedly refused to answer the question clearly, saying at various points that he would not announce his view until after the election, that he was "not a fan" of the idea, and that he wouldn't rule out considering it if a panel of constitutional law experts recommended it.

88. See James W. Ceaser, *Presidential Selection: Theory and Development* (Princeton, NJ: Princeton University Press, 1979).

89. See, for example, Alan I. Abramowitz, *The Great Alignment: Race, Party Transformation, and the Rise of Donald Trump* (New Haven, CT: Yale University Press, 2018).

90. Mark Halperin, "The Unity of Joe Biden," Wide World of News, January 20, 2021, https://markhalperin.substack.com/.

91. See Elie Mystal, "We're Going to Need a Truth and Reconciliation Commission to Recover From Trump," *The Nation*, October 20, 2020, https://www.thenation.com/article/politics/trump-truth-reconciliation/; Omar G. Encarnacion, "Truth After Trump," *Foreign Policy*, November 30, 2020, https://foreignpolicy.com/2020/11/30/truth-commission-trump-corruption-rule-law/; Paul Bedard, "Liberal Media Scream: Calls for 'Truth Commission' to take Trump down," *Washington Examiner*, December 21, 2020, https://www.washingtonexaminer.com/washington-secrets/liberal-media-scream-calls-for-truth-commission-to-take-trump-down.

92. Christina Wilkie, "Biden calls for unity and healing after Electoral College certifies his victory," CNBC, December 14, 2020, https://www.cnbc.com/2020/12/14/biden-calls-for-unity-and-healing-after-electoral-college-cements-his-victory.html.

93. John Hinderaker, "UNITY, DEMOCRAT STYLE," Powerlineblog.com, December 23, 2020, https://www.powerlineblog.com/archives/2020/12/unity-democrat-style.php.

94. Ronald Brownstein, "Does Joe Biden Understand the Modern GOP?" *The Atlantic*, reprinted in RealClearPolitics, December 17, 2020, https://www.realclear politics.com/2020/12/17/does_joe_biden_understand_the_modern_gop_531621.html.

95. Stephen F. Knott, *The Lost Soul of the American Presidency: The Decline into Demagoguery and the Prospects for Renewal* (Lawrence: University Press of Kansas, 2019).

96. Gabriela Debenedetti, "A Biden Style of Government Is Emerging: Lowest Drama Possible," *New York Magazine*, December 20, 2020, https://nymag.com/intel-ligencer/2020/12/joe-biden-cabinet.html.

97. John F. Harris, "Biden's Inaugural Speech Won't Unite the Country. Here's What Could," *Politico*, January 19, 2021, https://www.politico.com/news/magazine/2021/01/19/joe-biden-can-unite-the-country-by-being-boring-460258.

98. The survey found that 62 percent of voters thought the result was a mandate for centrist policies, while only 28 percent thought it was a mandate for progressive policies. Doug Schoen, "Schoen & Cooperman: Election 2020—Biden, Dems hurt by this and here's how they can bounce back," Fox News, November 16, 2020, https://www.foxnews.com/opinion/election-2020-biden-dems-hurt-bounce-back-doug-schoen-carly-cooperman.

99. Louis Casiano and David Aaro, "Portland rioters damage ICE building; police declare 'unlawful assembly,'" Fox News, January 20, 2021, https://www.foxnews.com/us/anti-biden-antifa-portland-police.

100. Matt Taibbi, "We Need a New Media System," RealClearMarkets, January 12, 2021, https://www.realclearmarkets.com/2021/01/12/we_need_a_new_media_system_656154.html.

101. Jim VandeHei, "Our new reality: Three Americas," Axios News, January 10, 2021, https://www.axios.com/capitol-siege-misinformation-trump-d9c9738b-0852-408d-a24f-81c95938b41b.html.

102. Rod Dreher, "The Left's Reichstag Fire," *The American Conservative*, January 8, 2021, https://www.theamericanconservative.com/dreher/left-reichstag-fire-soft-totalitarianism-social-credit-system-live-not-by-lies/.

103. Rebecca, "The Separation," *The American Mind*, November 30, 2020, https://americanmind.org/features/a-house-dividing/the-separation/.

104. Chris Caldwell, "The Biden Popular Front Is Doomed to Unravel," *The New Republic*, November 23, 2020, https://newrepublic.com/article/160338/biden-popular-front-doomed-unravel.

105. Michael Anton, "Blue America Needs Red America," *The American Mind*, December 1, 2020, https://americanmind.org/salvo/blue-america-needs-red-america/.

106. Graeme Wood, "The Next Decade Could Be Even Worse," *The Atlantic*, December 2020, https://www.theatlantic.com/magazine/archive/2020/12/can-history-predict-future/616993/.

Index

Abrams, Stacey, 169, 201
abuse of power, by Trump, D., 19–20
ACA. *See* Affordable Care Act
ActBlue, 155
activism, 83
affirmative action, 84, 173
Affordable Care Act (ACA), 5–6, 9, 38, 40, 151
African American voters, 39, 49, 58, 60, 197; Biden, J., connection with, 59; wooed by Republican Party and, 94–95
age, 35, 130, 198
al-Assad, Bashar, 41
Alberta, Tim, 94
Alcindor, Yamiche, 75
alcoholism, 45
Allen, Mike, 196–97
American Revolution, 93
Antifa, 6–7, 102n83, 136
anti-Semitism, 14
Anton, Michael, 125, 205
AOC. *See* Ocasio-Cortez, Alexandria
Arrington, Katie, 153
arson, 81
Asian Americans, 75
Atwater, Lee, 166
authoritarianism, 182

Avenatti, Michael, 12–13
Azar, Alex, 73

ballot curing, treatment of, 187
ballots, mail, 124, 125, 135
Barr, William, 18, 189
Barrett, Amy Coney, 114, 117, 166
Bass, Karen, 93
Becerra, Xavier, 173
Benford's law, 186
Bennet, Michael, 42
Beshear, Andy, 171
Betts, Connor, 22
Bevin, Matt, 171
Bice, Stephanie, 163
Biden, Beau, 34, 57
Biden, Hunter, 18–19, 20, 115–16, 131
Biden, Joseph Robinette, xi–xii, 19, 83; 2020 elections won by, 129–38; African American voters' connection with, 59; age of, 35; Blake spoken to by, 89; Bloomberg as threat to, 53; as boring, 112; character of, 111; confidence for, 122–23; court-packing opposed by, 214n87; on defunding police, 85; on Electoral College, 201–2; fundraising for, 51, 90, 113; Georgia won by, 182–83;

Harris and, 50, 113; involvement with Biden, H., 115–16; issues reflecting negatively on, 145n92; likeability of, 137–38; McCain, J., friendship with, 94; McConnell congratulating, 190; Obama, B., and, 48–49; political career of, 33; presidency won by, ix; pressure of, to denounce violence, 89; primary campaign of, 48, 52–59; progressive positions of, 39; results for, 125–28; running mate choice for, 91–93; Sanders as running mate for, 92; Sanders beat by, 57; senior moments had by, 70–71; told not to concede, 124; unification by, 203–6; "very important" issues for voters of, *133*; as vice president, 34; vote margin for, 128; vote percentage in exit polls compared to certified results, *186*; vulnerability of, 34; Warren as running mate for, 92

Biden Victory Fund, 90

Bisbee, James, 60

"black bloc" militants, 7

Black Lives Matter movement, 83, 87, 89, 136, 204

Blake, Jacob, 88, 89

Blasey Ford, Christine, 12–13

Blasio, Bill de, 42

Bloomberg, Michael, 34, 47, 60; debate performance by, 55–56; as threat, 53; withdrawal by, 58

"Blue Mirage," 125

Blue Wall, *126*

blue wave, 147, 154, 160

Bobulinski, Tony, 115, 116

Bolton, John, 115

Bonaparte, Napoleon, 111, 137

Booker, Cory, 12, 35, 43–45, 51, 53, 64n42, 83

Border Patrol, 157–58

border wall, 9

Bork, Robert, 203

Bowers v. Hardwick, 61n8

Bowman, Jamaal, 162

Bowser, Muriel, 82, 136

Boxer, Barbara, 191

Braun, Carol Moseley, 43

Brindisi, Anthony, 159

Brooks, Mo, 37, 190

Brooks, Susan, 162–63

Bruni, Frank, 152

Bryner, Sarah, 155

Bullock, Steve, 42, 167, 171

Burisma, 18–19

Bush, Cori, 161–62

Bush, George H. W., xi, 10, 92, 109, 185

Bush, George W., 5, 10, 119, 185, 211n57; 2004 election percentages for, 129; approval ratings for, 24; globalist policies of, 151–52

Bush, Jeb, 2

Buttigieg, Pete, 35, 37, 47–48, 51, 54, 57–58

Cain, Herman, 90

Caldwell, Christopher, 205

California State Assembly, 93

capitalism, views of, 38

Capitol, riots at, ix, 193–95, 197

Capitol Hill Autonomous Zone, Seattle (CHAZ), 84

Capitol Police, ix, 194

CARES. *See* Coronavirus Aid, Relief, and Economic Security Act

Carson, Ben, 83

Carter, Jimmy, 109, 110, 148

Castro, Fidel, 93

Castro, Julian, 38, 42, 63n35

Catholics, 118, 130

caucuses, 54, 67n88

census (2020), 171

Centers for Disease Control and Prevention (CDC), 72–73, 78

Central Intelligence Agency (CIA), 11

Chafee, John, 149

Chambliss, Saxby, 167

Charlottesville, Virginia, protests in, 6–7

Chatfield, Lee, 190
CHAZ. *See* Capitol Hill Autonomous Zone
chemical weapons, Syria using, 16
Cheney, Dick, 19
Cherokee Nation, 46
children, detaining immigrant, 9–10
China: trade war with, 22, 24; travel ban for, 72; Trump, D., disrespecting, 75–76
Chisholm, Shirley, 36
Christians, xii, 37
Christie, Chris, 44
CIA. *See* Central Intelligence Agency
Ciccetti, Charles J., 186
citizenship, of Duckworth, 93
civil disorder, 3, 70, 159
civil rights: legislation for, 39; organizations for, 16; riots during movement for, 78–79; support for, 59–60
Civil War, ix, 21, 89
Cleveland, Grover, 63n34
climate change, 41, 87, 112
Clinton, Bill, xi, 5, 39, 157, 185; approval ratings for, 20, 24; election of, 21; impeachment of, 20–21; reelection of, 40
Clinton, Hillary, 8, 109, 122; in 2016 election, 2–4; as disliked, 111; explosive devices mailed to, 14; and Gabbard, 41; popular vote for, 36; support for, 39, 40
Clyburn, James, 56, 57, 85
Cobb, Rachael, 113
cocooning, 24
Cohen, Michael, 115, 157
Cole, Tom, 43, 155
Collins, Chris, 151, 154
Collins, Doug, 168, 170
Collins, Susan, 117, 166, 196
collusion, 8, 11, 16–17, 116, 192
Comey, James, 8, 17
communism, 37, 56
community types, 130

concentration camps, 10
Congress: 116th, 156–59; composition and party balance in, 156; lame duck session of, 16; members of, wounded in bombing, xiiin3; women in, 36
Congressional Leadership Fund, 150
Connolly, Gerry, 157
Conservative Opportunity Society, 156
conspiracy theories: Russia and, 121; Trump, D., pushing, 203
constancy, elements of, 24–27
contingencies, 111–13, 168
Coolidge, Calvin, 202
Cooper, Roy, 171
Corker, Bob, 152, 153
Coronavirus Aid, Relief, and Economic Security Act (CARES), 76, 85
Cotton, Tom, 199
coup, Trump, D., plotting, 125
court-packing plan, 201, 214n87
COVID-19 virus, x, 70, 93, 138n2; avoiding panic associated with, 115; change in geography of, 77; containing, 206; death rates from, 114; debate about, 118; economic plunge due to, 110; impact of, 70, 76; outbreak of, 53, 60; protests and, 87–88; school closures caused by, 72–73; surge of, 87, 119–20; travel restrictions due to, 72; Trump, D., address about, 74; Trump, D., contracting, 114, 119–21; Trump, D., downplaying, 70; unemployment produced by, 69, 85, 109–10; voters impacted by, 134–35; voting procedures changed due to, 96
COVID relief package, 86
COVID tests, 74, 75
Cox, Spencer, 171
Cox, T. J., 161
crack cocaine, reduced penalties for, 16
crime, 71, 203; homosexuality as, 36; violence and, 80; violent, 34
criminal justice, 34, 95
Crowley, Joseph, 38

Crusius, Patrick, 22
Cruz, Ted, 2, 15, 41, 190–91, 199
Cummings, Elijah, 157–58
Cunningham, Cal, 166
Cuomo, Andrew, 73, 114
cybersecurity, 189

DACA. *See* Deferred Action on
  Childhood Arrivals
Daines, Steve, 13
"dark money," 150
DCCC. *See* Democratic Congressional
  Campaign Committee
debates: cancellation of, 121;
  Democratic primary, 49–54, 55–56,
  58–59; minus in-person audience,
  58–59; presidential, 118–19; vice-
  presidential, 119
decentralization, 205
"deep state," 16, 203
defense spending, increase in, 16
Deferred Action on Childhood Arrivals
  (DACA), 9
Delaney, John, 40
Democratic Congressional Campaign
  Committee (DCCC), 153–54
Democratic convention, 93–94
Democratic National Committee (DNC),
  8, 49–50, 51, 90, 93
Democratic Party, 87, 114; from 1988 to
  2020, 34–39; California popular vote
  relied on by, *127*; fundraising by,
  155; leftward shift of, 14; perceived
  radicalism of, 136; popular vote won
  by, 148; Senate control for, 147;
  state election results for, 171–73
Democratic Senate Majority PAC, 166
Democrats, x, 14; differences
  between Republicans and, xi–xii;
  filibusters abolished and launched
  by, 11; results of elections per, xi;
  skepticism from, 44
Department of Homeland Security, 26,
  85, 121, 189
deportations, 9, 10

Devine, Tad, 50
Dewey, Tom, 137
Dhillon, Harmeet, 164
Diebold voting machines, 202
Dinkins, David, 80
disruption, by Trump, D., 1–27, 174,
  202
DNC. *See* Democratic National
  Committee
Dodd, Chris, 93
Dole, Bob, 34
Dominion software, 185
Donnelly, Joe, 15
Dorsey, Jack, 131
Dow Jones Industrial average, 85–86
Draper, Robert, 150
drone strikes, 23
drugs, liberalization of attitudes toward,
  172
Duckworth, Tammy, 93
Dukakis, Michael, 39
Duran, Gil, 49
Durham, John, 18

Eagleton, Thomas, 91
early voting, 154–55
Eastland, James, 34, 50
economic developments, before 2020
  election, 114
economic policy, of Trump, D., 23–24
economic recovery, 131
economy, xii; COVID causing plunge
  in, 110; crashed, 60; reopening, 86
education, 130, 151
Eisenhower, Dwight D., 148
election fraud, 201; conditions for, 183;
  industrial-scale, 184–87; Trump, D.,
  claiming, 125, 181–95
election law, 187–88
elections, presidential (2016): Clinton,
  H., in, 2–4; margins for Trump, D.,
  127; Trump, D., winning, 2–4; vote
  distribution by groups for, *132*
elections, presidential (2020), xi; Biden,
  J., winning, 129–38; as close, 135–

38; economic developments before, 114; foreign interference in, 121–22; lack of choice in, 137–38; margins for Trump, D., *127*; media events before, 114–16; results of, 125–28; Trump, D., losing, xi, 132–38; vote distribution by groups for, *132*; voter turnout for, 126

elections, state, 171–74

election workers, 113

Electoral College, 3, 128, 190, 195, 196, 199–200, 201–2

elite overproduction, 206

Ellison, Keith, 37

Engel, Eliot, 162

Enten, Harry, xii

Environmental Protection Agency, 26

environmental reform, 15, 87

exit polls, Biden, J., vote percentage in, compared to certified results, *186*

explosive devices, 14

Facebook, 8, 48

"faithless electors," 4, 127

fake news, 26, 190

family separation, 10

fascists, 7

FDA. *See* Food and Drug Administration

Federal Bureau of Investigation (FBI), 11, 17–18

federal courts, infused with conservatives, 196

Federalist Society, 151

Federal Reserve, 86

Feinstein, Dianne, 12, 117

Feldman, Noah, 117

Ferraro, Geraldine, 36, 91

filibusters, 11

firearms, 22, 88

FIRST STEP Act, 16

FISA. *See* Foreign Intelligence Surveillance Act

Fischbach, Michelle, 163

Flake, Jeff, 152, 153

Flores settlement, 10

Floyd, George, 70, 78, 81, 82, 87, 88, 92

Flynn, Michael, 8, 17, 18, 190

Food and Drug Administration (FDA), 78

Ford, Gerald, 93

Foreign Intelligence Surveillance Act (FISA), 17–18

foreign policy, 16, 22–24, 118

fossil fuels, 87, 119, 131

Franken, Al, 42, 43

free trade, 23

Frieden, Thomas R., 73

fundraising, 51, 69; for Biden, J., 51, 90, 113; Democratic Party, 155; ragefunding, 166–67; for Trump, D., 90, 113

Gabbard, Tulsi, 35, 41, 51, 92

Galen, Reed, 91

Galston, William, 161

Garcetti, Eric, 42

Garcia, Mike, 163

Gardner, Cory, 164, 165

Garfield, James A., 40

Garland, Merrick, 11, 117

gender discrimination, 36

Georgia: Biden, J., winning, 182–83; Democratic vote in Senate runoffs, *169*; Senate runoffs in, 149, 164, 167–71; Trump, D., losing, 170

gerrymandering, 160

Gianforte, Greg, 171

Gidon, Sara, 166

Gillibrand, Kristen, 42, 92

Giménez, Carlos, 162, 163

Gingrich, Newt, 156, 192

Ginsburg, Ruth Bader (RBG), 114, 116–18

Giuliani, Rudolph, 47, 80, 185, 193

Gohmert, Louis, 191

Goldwater, Barry, 20, 37

GOP. *See* Republican Party

Gore, Al, 37, 39, 119, 181, 191

Gorman, Matt, 41
Gorsuch, Neil, 11
Gowdy, Trey, 198
Graham, Lindsey, 166
Great Depression, 86, 110
Great Recession, 3, 38, 86, 96
Green New Deal, 71, 87
Green Party, 7
Griffin, Jennifer, 115

Haley, Nikki, 199
Hamill, Mark, 90
Hamilton, 26
Hannity, Sean, 72
Harding, Warren, 111, 202
Harris, John F., 204
Harris, Kamala, 12, 35, 43–44, 60,
    147, 200; background of, 92; Biden,
    J., and, 50, 92–93, 113; campaign
    of, 49; endorsement from, 58;
    fundraising for, 51; issues addressed
    by, 112; mocked, 170; superiority
    demonstrated by, 119
Harrison, Benjamin, xi
Hatfield, Mark O., 84
Hawley, Josh, 190, 191
Hayes, Rutherford B., 124
Hazel, Shane, 168
Health and Human Services, 73
health care, reform for, 5–6
Heitkamp, Heidi, 15
Helping Americans Vote Act, 201
Heritage Foundation, 151
Herrell, Yvette, 163
Hickenlooper, John, 41–42, 164–65,
    167
Hill, Katie, 163
Hispanic voters, 38
Hodgkinson, James T., 7
Holmes, Josh, 155
Homer, 33
homosexuality, as crime, 36
Honig, Dan, 60
Hoover, Herbert, 109, 110
Hoover Institution board, 72

Horton, Willie, 202
House Judiciary Committee, 19
House of Representatives (House), ix,
    15, 159–64, 163, 189–90
Humphrey, Hubert, 48, 61n7
Humphrey, Muriel, 61n7
Hunt, Jesse, 168
Hunter, Duncan, 154
Hussein, Saddam, 211n57
hydroxychloroquine, 78

immigration, 112; lawful, 95; of
    Muslims, 5; radical positions on, 15
Immigration and Customs Enforcement
    (ICE), 10, 85
immigration policy, 9, 10
impeachment, 53, 159; articles of, 19;
    of Clinton, B., 20–21; of Johnson,
    A., 20–21; Pelosi opinion of, 46; of
    Trump, D., x, 17, 19–20, 60, 92, 122,
    195, 204
income, 22, 130
income tax returns, of Trump, D., 25,
    115
Independents, 48, 86, 129
influence peddling, 19, 116
insider trading, 154
Inslee, Jay, 41
insurance claims, rioting resulting in, 84
insurrectionists, ix
Intelligence Committee, 19
interregnum period, 69–96
Iran, 16, 22, 122, 202; nuclear deal, 23
Iraq War, 93
Isakson, Johnny, 168
Islamic radicalism, 8

Jackson, Hallie, 55
Jackson, Jesse, 26, 39, 58
Jefferson, Thomas, 6, 25
job creation, 20
Johnson, Andrew, 20–21
Johnson, Lyndon B., 21–22, 91–92
Jones, Doug, 43, 165
Jordan, Jim, 84–85

Jorgensen, Jo, 127–28, 145n82
Judiciary Committee, 43–44, 50
Justice Department, 17, 80

Kaba, Mariame, 84
Kaine, Tim, 74
Kasich, John, 94
Kassebaum, Nancy, 36
Kavanaugh, Brett, 11, 12–13, 44, 45, 118, 161, 166
Kelly, John, 131
Kelly, Mark, 164
Kemp, Brian, 168, 169, 170, 190
Kendi, Ibram X., 117
Kennedy, Anthony, 11
Kennedy, John F., 33, 91–92, 148
Kent State University, massacre at, 79
Kerry, John, 39, 191, 211n57
Kesler, Charles, 25–26
Keyser, Leland, 12
Khomeini, Ruhollah (ayatollah), 202
Kilimnik, Konstantin, 18
Kim, Young, 163
Kim Jong Un, 22–23
King, Martin Luther, Jr., 79, 169
King, Rodney, 110
KKK. *See* Ku Klux Klan
Klobuchar, Amy, 35, 36, 45, 52, 55, 58, 92, 200
Knott, Stephen, 25, 204
knowledge silos, x–xi
Krebs, Chris, 189
K-shaped recovery, 86, 96
Kudlow, Larry, 72
Ku Klux Klan (KKK), 6–7
Kunin, Madeleine, 36

Landon, Alf, 185
law and order, 78–85, 137
Lawrence et al. v. Texas, 61n8
lawsuits, Democratic, 160
liberalism, 26, 39
Libertarian Party, 127
Lieberman, Joseph, 37
Limbaugh, Rush, 185

Lincoln, Abraham, 74, 136
Lincoln Project, 91, 94
Lipinski, Dan, 162
Locke, Gary, 76
Loeffler, Kelly, 168–69, 170
looting, 81, 136
loss aversion, 6
The Lost Soul of the American Presidency (Knott), 204
Lott, John, 186
Lowry, Rich, 185

Mace, Nancy, 163
Madison, James, 206
Malliotakis, Nicole, 163
Manafort, Paul, 17, 18
Manchin, Joe, 13, 15, 117, 195–96, 204
manufacturing, restoration of, 112
marijuana, legalization of, 172
martial law, 190
masks, x, 73, 77
Mattis, James, 82, 131
McCain, Cindy, 94
McCain, John, 2, 6, 33, 94, 131
McCarthy, Andrew, 20
McCarthy, Kevin, 155
McCaskill, Claire, 15
McCloskey, Patricia, 95
McConnell, Mitch, 44, 64n42, 116–17, 155, 166–67, 171, 190
McGrath, Amy, 166–67
McSally, Martha, 164
Meadows, Mark, 95
media events, before 2020 election, 114–16
media technology, x–xi
Medicare for All, 38, 51, 52
Messam, Wayne, 43
Messonnier, Nancy, 72–73
"Me Too" movement, 12, 48
midterm congressional elections, 14–15, 153–56
Mikulski, Barbara, 36
military aid, to Ukraine, 16, 20
military strikes, against Syria, 16

military veterans, Biden, J., win and, 131

Miller-Meeks, Mariannette, 163

Millennial generation, 48

Miller, Steven, 9

Milley, Mark, 82

Molinari, Susan, 94

monuments, torn down or damaged, 84, 136

Moore, Michael, 2

Moore, Roy, 165

Moran, Jerry, 150

Moulton, Seth, 41

Mucarsel-Powell, Debbie, 162

Mueller, Robert, 8, 157

Mueller report, 16–17, 21, 157

Murkowski, Lisa, 13, 196

Muslims, immigration of, 5

NAFTA. *See* North American Free Trade Agreement

National Popular Vote Interstate Compact, 200–201

National Republican Congressional Committee (NRCC), 43, 150, 162–63

National Republican Senatorial Committee (NRSC), 150

National Security Council, 18–19, 26

NATO. *See* North Atlantic Treaty Organization

Navarro, Peter, 189

negative partisanship, 203

Nelson, Bill, 15

neo-Nazis, 6–7

The New Republic (Caldwell), 205

New York Stock Exchange, 168

Nixon, Richard, 202; forced resignation of, 20–21; unfit for office, 21; Wallace and, 79

Norpoth, Helmut, 109, 138n2

Northam, Ralph, 153

North American Free Trade Agreement (NAFTA), 23–24

North Atlantic Treaty Organization (NATO), 23

North Korea, 22–23

NRCC. *See* National Republican Congressional Committee

NRSC. *See* National Republican Senatorial Committee

nursing homes, 73

oath of office, violation of, ix–x

Obama, Barack, xi, 1, 4, 19, 154, 157; approval ratings for, 24; Biden, J., and, 48–49; explosive devices mailed to, 14; fundamental transformation promised by, 195; health care reform by, 5–6; presidential norms deteriorating under, 25; reelection of, 40; terrorism policies of, 41; Trump, D., accusing, 192

Obama, Michelle, 4

Obamacare. *See* Affordable Care Act

Ocasio-Cortez, Alexandria (AOC), 14–15, 38, 136, 156, 158, 196

Occupy Wall Street, 7

Odyssey (Homer), 33

offshore drilling, 87

oil and gas industry, 19, 110

Ojeda, Richard, 43

Omar, Ilhan, 84, 136, 158

O'Rourke, Robert Francis "Beto," 15, 22, 41, 58

Ossoff, Jon, 147, 168, 169–70

Our Revolution, 46

Owens, Burgess, 163

Page, Carter, 17–18

Palin, Sarah, 91

pardons, by Trump, D., 154

Paris Climate Accords, 23

Parscale, Brad, 90

partisan polarization, 24

party coalitions, 87, 196–98

Paterson, David, 42

Patrick, Deval, 42

Paul, Rand, 199

Paycheck Protection Program (PPP), 85

payroll tax, deferral of, 96

Pelosi, Nancy, 17, 19, 46, 75, 123, 156, 196

Pence, Mike, ix, 26, 119, 191, 194, 196

Perdue, David, 165–66, 167–68, 169–70

Perdue, Sonny, 167

Peters, Gary, 165

Peterson, Chris, 171

Podesta, John, 124

police: Capitol Police, 194; defunding, 84–85, 137, 162; shootings, x, 51, 92

police violence, 34, 78–79; concern about, 80–81; controversial incidents of, 88

political institutions, future of, 199–203

Pompeo, Mike, 95, 150–51

popular vote: for Clinton, H., 36; Democratic Party winning, 148; Democratic reliance on California for, *127*; nationally aggregated, 3, 21; plurality of, in 2016, 40

Powell, Sidney, 184–85

PPP. *See* Paycheck Protection Program

presidential conduct and norms, 25, 71, 134, 202

Pressley, Ayanna, 158

protests, ix–x; anti-shutdown, 87; armed, 88; against COVID restrictions, 87–88; in Charlottesville, 6–7; after Floyd killing, 70, 78, 81–83, 84, 92; history of, 78–79. *See also* riots

Proud Boys, 118, 122, 194

Putin, Vladimir, 8, 121; Trump, D., meeting with, 10–11; on Trump impeachment, 122

Quayle, Dan, 91

race relations, 51, 83, 112, 129

racial discrimination, 80, 83, 84

racism, 7, 50, 203

Raffensperger, Brad, 192–93

Ramirez, Deborah, 12

Ratcliffe, John, 122

RBG. *See* Ginsburg, Ruth Bader

Reagan, Ronald, 10, 21–22, 35, 93, 154, 198; Bush, G. H. W., and, 92; reelection of, 40; tax cutting and, 23; win for, 123

Reconstruction, 124, 167

recounts, 182–83

"Red Mirage," 124

refugees, from Central America, 13–14

Reid, Harry, 11

religion, xii, 37, 57, 130

Republican National Committee (RNC), 14, 94, 113, 120

Republican Party (GOP), 74, 198

Republicans, x, 14; differences between Democrats and, xi–xii; masks and social distancing declined by, 77; as shy voters, 128; wooing African American voters, 94–95

results: of 2020 election, 125–28; Biden, J., vote percentage in exit polls compared to certified, *186*

retirement, mandatory, 35

Rice, Susan, 93

riots: at Capitol, ix, 193–95, 197; civil rights movement, 78–79; insurance claims due to, 84

RNC. *See* Republican National Committee

Roe v. Wade, 44

Romney, Mitt, 5, 8, 15, 20

Roosevelt, Franklin Delano, xi, 25, 70, 74, 185, 201, 202

Roosevelt, Theodore, 33, 47

Rosenstein, Rod, 7, 17

Rouda, Harley, 162

Rubio, Marco, 199

Russia: collusion, Trump campaign and, 16–17, 116; collusion and, 16; conspiracy and, 121; as strategic threat, 8; Trump campaign assisted by, 7

Rust Belt, 3

Ryan, Paul, 3, 8, 23, 118

Ryan, Tim, 41

Salazar, Maria Elvira, 163
SALT. *See* state and local tax deduction
same-sex marriage, 37
sanctuary cities, 9
Sanders, Bernie, 7, 35, 41, 60, 185, 198; Biden, J., beating, 57; as Biden, J., running mate, 92; campaign of, 46–47, 49, 54, 55, 56; Democratic socialism embraced by, 37–38; endorsement by, 59; fundraising for, 51; heart attack, 52; Jackson, J., nomination speech given by, 39
Sanders Institute, 46
Sanford, Mark, 152–53
Sasser, Jim, 149
Sayoc, Ceasar, 14
Scalia, Antonin, 11, 116, 117
Scalise, Steve, 7
school closures, COVID causing, 72–73
Schroeder, Pat, 36
Schumer, Charles, 156, 164–65, 167
Scott, Tim, 199
Secret Service, 81–82
segregationists, 34, 82
self-defense, right to, 22
Senate, ix, 42, 164–67; Democratic Party control of, 147; Democratic vote in Georgia runoffs, *169*; Georgia runoffs for, 149, 164, 167–71; midterm congressional elections for, 15; segregationists in, 34; split, 147
Senate Intelligence Committee, 18
Senate Leadership Fund, 166
Sessions, Jeff, 7, 43, 154, 165
Sestak, Joe, 41
sexual assault, Kavanaugh accused of, 12–13, 45
Shapiro, Josh, 186
Shapp, Milton, 37
shootings: in Dayton, Ohio, 22; in El Paso, Texas, 22; police shootings, x, 51, 92
shutdowns, 70, 86–88; of government, 156–57

Sick, Gary, 202
Sinema, Kyrsten, 164
"small-n problem," 96
Smith, Margaret Chase, 36
social distancing, 70, 73, 77
socialism, 37–38, 47, 158, 162
social media, 8, 48, 90–91, 116, 122
"soft money," 149
Soleimani, Qasem, 23
Soros, George, 14
Spanberger, Abigail, 162, 196
Specter, Arlen, 37
Spencer, Richard, 6
Squadron, Daniel, 172
Stahl, Lesley, 91
state and local tax (SALT) deduction, 8–9, 14
Steel, Michelle Park, 163
Steele Dossier, 18, 116
Stefanik, Elise, 155–56, 163
Stein, Jill, 7
Stepien, Bill, 90
Stevens, Libya J. Christopher, 3
Steyer, Tom, 35, 36, 46, 57
stock market, 20, 74
Stone, Roger, 18
Super Tuesday, 58
Swalwell, Eric, 41
Swetnick, Julie, 13
Syria, 16

Talmadge, Herman, 50
Tapper, Jake, 51
tax cutting, 23
tax reform bill, 8–9
tax revolt (1978), 173
Taylor, Miles, 26
Tea Party movement, 23
Tenney, Claudia, 159, 163
terrorist organizations, xiiin3
Tester, Jon, 15, 167
Thurmond, Strom, 166
Tillis, Thom, 166
Tlaib, Rashida, 158
trade war, with China, 22, 24

Transition Integrity Project, 124
transportation, 87
travel ban: for China, 72; for Muslims, 5
travel restrictions, due to COVID, 72
Truman, Harry, 48, 148
Trump, Donald: 2016 election won
by, 2–4; 2020 election loss by, xi,
132–38; abuse of power by, 19–20;
age of, 35; approval ratings for, 20,
24–25, 71–72, 74, 213n81; attacked
on television/social media, 90–91;
attitude toward politics, 151–52;
bipartisan legislation supported by,
16; campaign of, 89; character of,
111, 189; collusion, Russia and
campaign of, 16–17, 116; conspiracy
theories pushed by, 203; coup plotted
by, 125; COVID address by, 74;
COVID contracted by, 114, 119; and
Cummings, 157–58; deportations
increased by, 9; disruption by, 1–27,
174, 202; downplaying COVID,
70; early years of, 78–79; economic
policy of, 23–24; election fraud
claimed by, 125, 181–95; empathy
of, 94; as favored, 138n10; fear of,
60; fundraising for, 90, 113; Georgia
loss by, 170; government shutdown
and, 156–57; history reinvented
by, 192–93; hydroxychloroquine
advocated for by, 78; impeachment
of, x, 17, 19–20, 60, 92, 122, 195,
204; inauguration of, 4–5; income
tax returns of, 25, 115; issues
reflecting positively on, 145n92;
leaving office, 144n69; margins for,
in 2016 and 2020, *127*; McCain,
J., spats with, 131; next moves for,
198–99; norms disregarded by, 71,
134; oath of office violation by, ix;
Obama, B., accused by, 192; pardons
by, 154; Pelosi relationship with, 75;
performance disapproval, 83; Putin
meeting with, 10–11; as racist, 7,
158; rallies held by, 112; results for,

125–28; riots at Capitol denounced
by, 195; sexual exploits bragged
about by, 2–3; support for, xii;
threats by, 17; unfit for office, 21;
"very important" issues for voters of,
133; views on, 1; violence glorified
by, 81; vote for winning Republican
Senate candidates compared to, *165*
Trump, Donald, Jr., 189, 193
Trump, Ivanka, 82
Trump, Melania, 120
Trump Organization, 80
Tuberville, Tommy, 165
Turchin, Peter, 206
Turner, Bill, 113
Twitter, 22, 25, 48, 116, 133

U.S.-Mexico-Canada agreement
(USMCA), 24
Ukraine, 16, 18–19, 20
unemployment: COVID producing, 69,
85, 109–10; fall in, 20, 114; increase
in, 76; lowering, 131; special
benefits for, 120
United Nations, 10

vaccination, x
Valadao, David, 163
VandeHei, Jim, 196–97
Van Drew, Jeff, 159
Venezuela, 16
Vietnam War, 76, 79
violence: in aftermath of Floyd killing,
88–89; anticipation of, 125; crime
and, 34, 80; Kent State massacre, 79;
planned, 102n83; police violence, 34;
pressure on Biden, J., to denounce,
89; of protests, 70; racial, 7; Trump,
D., glorifying, 81; xenophobic, 22.
See also shootings
voter registration, 154–55
voters: 2020 election turnout of, 126;
African American, 39, 49, 58,
59–60; COVID impacting, 134–35;
first-time, 131; groups of, in 2016

compared to 2020, *132*; Hispanic, 38; mobilization of, 137; primary elections determined by, 202; shy, Republican, 128; survey of, 215n98; "very important" issues for, *133*; voting by ineligible, 183–84
voter suppression, 201
voting procedures, change in, 96

Waldron, Phil, 186
Walker, Herschel, 94–95
Wallace, Chris, 118
Wallace, George, 79
Wallace, Henry, 1
Wall Street, 44
Walz, Tim, 81
Warner, Mark, 153
Warnock, Raphael, 147, 169–70
Warren, Elizabeth, 35, 36, 40, 60, 185; as Biden, J., running mate, 92; campaign of, 46, 47, 49,54; and Bloomberg, 55–56; fall in standings for, 52; fundraising for, 51
Washington, George, 136
Wasserman, David, 159
Watergate, 21, 202
Weeks, Jerome, 73
Weiss, Bari, 26
welfare reform, 10
West, Allen, 190, 203, 205
We the People Convention, 190

white supremacists, 6–7
Whitman, Christine Todd, 94
Whitman, Meg, 94
Whitmer, Gretchen, 88, 93, 125
WikiLeaks, 18
Williamson, Marianne, 43
Willkie, Wendell, 61n5
Wilson, Reid, 150
Wilson, Rick, 162
Wilson, Woodrow, 25, 202
WinRed, 155, 162
wokeness, 197
Wolf, Chad, 195
Wolfson, Howard, 152
Wolverine Watchmen, 125
Wood, Lin, 184–85
Woodward, Bob, 72, 115
World War I, 61n5
World War II, 74, 96, 154
Wray, Christopher, 121–22
Wu, Wenyuan, 173
Wyden, Ron, 185

xenophobia, 22, 72
Xi Jinping, 76

Yang, Andrew, 35, 36
York, Byron, 192

Zelensky, Volodymyr, 18, 19, 20
Zuckerberg, Mark, 113